KERALA ECONOMY

HARSHA V K . KAVEYA P. KRISHNA R

This book is dedicated to Jith George and Zanoobiya, who are best friends who extend their hands of compassion to those who have received loving touches.

Contents

Foreword

This book is an overview of Kerala's economy.This book is meant to be read at an academic level.

By
Abitha, Mphil scholar

Research students will find this book more informative and useful.This book brings forward new experiences of reading.

By
Vishnu,Research scholar

Preface

All the sectors of Kerala's economy have been explained in this book. The Pre-Independence period to Future Economy, it has been explained. It explains about bank economy and new topics like KIIFB, Kerala Bank etc.This book can be effectively used for all the exams conducted in Kerala and under Central Government. KAS,PSC Exam, Assistant Professor, UPSC Exam, IES, PhD Entrance can be used for various competitive exams.This book is helpful for studying undergraduate and postgraduate subjects related to economics conducted by all universities.

Acknowledgements

Looking through this book, you can understand that every moment of this book is made by the blessings of others. I would like to dedicate my thanks to my best friends Jith George and Zanobiya who gave me all kinds of support to write the book. I also thank the publication that gave me the opportunity to write this book. Also thanks to the Researchers venture team,Kaveya P, Krishna R and co-authors.

Notion press publication,Red Cross Rd, Egmore, Chennai, Tamil Nadu 600008

Prologue

Each of its writings is adopted to benefit future generations. Development and development bottlenecks during the advancement of the Kerala economy are tirelessly described.This book is mainly useful for BA,MA Economics students,KAS, Economics Entrance exam,PhD entrance exam,PSC and other competitive exams. This book also cover the pre-post reform and future economy, sectoral performance, growth and development, educated unemployment, underemployment, Old- age economy,Covid-19 in Kerala,Tourism,Lesbian,gay,bisexual,transgender and intersex (LGBTI),Migration,Kerala government schemes,KIFBI,Kerala bank,Lottary,GST etc..

First Author And Editor

Harsha v k

She is pursuing PhD in Economics, University college at Thiruvanathapuram.Proactive researcher courses on under graduation, post graduation, Mphil and PhD in Economics. Authored 2 books on Athmahridhayam and charumanikavithakal. Published over one article in a journal and one chapter in a book. Paper presented over 3 presentations in National and 4 presentations in international level.Won in best paper award international conference and Insc Young researcher award 2021. I have successfull Mentor in Researchers venture.

WhatsApp contact

Second Author And Editor

Kaveya P

She is pursuing PhD in Economics, University college at Thiruvanathapuram. Published over 36 articles in many journals and editor in 7 books. Paper presented over 7 presentations in National and 5 presentations in international level.Won in Intelligence Brilliant Award 2021,Malayala Manorama Merit Scholarship Topper in BA (**Gold Medal Winner**) (2010-2011) ,Gold Medal winner)HSST DISTRICT TOPPER-From Ex governor-ShankaraNarayanan,Editor at IRJMETS,Futuristic Trends of Social Science (IIP),IJADST, The Sustainability Journal Collection, Asia pacific journal of multidisciplinary journal and Insc Young researcher award 2021.

Third Author And Editor

Krishna R

She is pursuing PhD in Economics, University college at Thiruvanathapuram. Published over 6 article in many journals and one chapter in a book. Paper presented over 5 presentations in National level.Won in best paper award international conference and Insc Young researcher award 2022,Dr. A P J Abdul Kalam Educational Excellence Award 2022,GISR Foundation 4th IARE Young Researcher Award 2022,Second and Third Prizes in Hindi elocution in Kerala University Youthfest in 2018&2019 and Best Speaker award in Sree Narayana Centenary Debate Competition 2017.

Coauthors

1)**Shamnad N**,M A Economics,Government college,Attingal,Thiruvanathapuram

2)**Dr Jinu G V**,Assistant professor on contract,S N college,Punalur,MA,Mphil,PhD

3)**Aadithya Prakash**,BA in Social Science,Tata institute of social science,Guwahati off campus

4)**Devi V**,MA Economics,Kariavattom campus,Thiruvanathapuam

5)**Sreethi Krishnan U**,Research scholar,Department of Economics,University college,Thiruvanathapuram

6)**Dr C A Priyesh**,Associate professor,Department of Economics,Government college,Attingal,Thiruvanathapuram

7)**Ashna**,MA Economics,Kariavattom campus,Thiruvanathapuam

8)**Shibin Y**,H.K.M. College of Education,Umayanalloor

9)**Vijitha S Vijayan**,MA Economics,Kariavattom campus,Thiruvanathapuam

10)**Alfiya K S Ahammed**,MA Economics,University of Kerala

11)**Abin Abraham**,Research Scholar,Fatima Mata National College, Kollam,University of Kerala

12)**Muzna Muhammed P**,Research Scholar in Economics,PG and Research Department of Economics,Govt. Arts and Science College, Calicut

13)**Dhanusree Ullas K**,Research Scholar, Research and P.G. Department of Economics, Panampilly Memorial Government College, Chalakudy, Thrissur

14)**Seena V**,Assistant Professor,Department of Economics,T.K. Madhava Memorial College Nangiarkulangara

15)**Shabna S S**,M com,Kariavattom campus,Thiruvanathapuam

16)**Parvathi Renju S**,Research scholar,Department of Economics,University college,Thiruvanathapuram

17)**Muhamed Naseef K**,Research scholar in Economics,Malayalam University,MA,BEd, Mcom, MBA, PGDHM,SET,NET,Kozhikode

18)**Dr Sheela M C**,Associate professor,Department of Economics,University college,Thiruvanathapuram

19)**Fasla Rahman K**, Research Scholar in Economics, PG And Research Department ssof Economics Government Arts and Science College, Calicut

20)**Krishna Priya**,Psychologist,Kerala

CHAPTER ONE

Pre- Post Economy

Kerala Economy in pre – Independence and Post – Independence Period

An Overview

SHAMNAD N

The economy of Kerala is the 9th largest in India, with an annual GSDP of Rs 9.78 lakh crore in 2020–2021. Kerala's high GDP and Productivity figures with higher development figures is often dubbed as the "Kerala phenomenon" or "Kerala Model" of development economists, political scientists and sociologists. Kerala, which accounts for 2.8 percent of India's population and 1.2 percent of its land area, contributes more than 4 percent to the GDP of India. Southern states' GDP is 60 percent higher than India's average. This has fuelled internal migration to Kerala for low – end jobs, even as keralites have emigrated mostly to the Gulf countries – in search of better paying jobs. Kerala's economy was gradually shifting from an agrarian economy into a service – based one during the period between 1960 and 2020. Similar to Indian economy, Kerala economy was also an agrarian economy. The location of the region on the Arabian sea coast permitted trading and cultural relations with outside world in the history. Musiris situated on the coast and the numerous minor ports attracted traders from all around the world. The growth in trade had increased the production of spices and other cash crops which in turn have generated more trade (Ibid). But there was not much growth in manufacturing during this period. 'Kerala could sustain itself as a trading region without a manufacturing base. This might have led to the fact that the Malabar Coast, though acknowledged for long as an important trading region, never developed a manufacturing hinterland like other trading regions of India' (Ibid). In the colonial period the level of agricultural products are lower. During the colonial period, the policies followed by the colonial power on imports and exports and taxation had very unfavourable effect on the generation of economic activities and employment outside agriculture sector. The taxation policy in the colonial period stood as a barrier to expansion of economic activities and employment outside agricultural sector. Colonial administration - imposed taxes on skilled workers such as carpenters, ironsmiths etc and also implements like handloom, oil presses, fishnets etc. We have evidence to show that a very high tax rate was levied on this category of people during the early decades of 19th century. The institution of caste system in Kerala also influenced the consumption pattern and the financial activities of the society. Like all other economies in the world, Kerala economy also adversely affected by the pandemic COVID – 19. Also, Kerala now a days have to face with natural calamities like landslide, floods etc in the years 2018 and 2019 which brings the needfulness of disaster management in the curriculam and in the common behavioural knowledge of the society. This article tries to make an overview on the Kerala economy in both pre independence and post independence period and also the COVID -19 impact.

Keywords : Gross state domestic product (GSDP), Gross domestic product (GDP), Kerala Model, Migration, Internal Migration, Gulf Diaspora, Emigration, Agrarian economy, Service sector, Taxation policy, COVID – 19

The large proportion of Christian and Muslims in the state's population may be partly due to the historic trading and cultural contracts rather than through muslim conquests as in rest of the country. The symbiosis of different religious groups and cultural streams has led to communal harmony and social stability in the state. The historical and cultural contacts with the Arabs helped Malayalees to easily avail of employment opportunities following the oil boom in the Arab world from the 1970s. It is the remittances from emigrants especially those in the Arabian Gulf countries and the Growth of the Service sector which have helped to sustain Kerala economy in recent decades.

Kerala has become a model for social development with limiting improvement in a industrialization sector. Furthermore, Kerala has undermined the broadly accepted idea that the improvement in the standard of living of people can only be achieved after the successful, rapid and steady economic development. Kerala model of development took on the theory that economic growth is the only way to meet basic needs of people in poverty, to raise them above poverty and generate employment. What's more, Kerala model of development improved and extended basic education, introduced better health care and land reforms as well as access to better social security in terms of pensions and employment rights. These achievements come without huge investments in economic growth. The fact is that Kerala is also socially and politically different from the rest of India. While the other states in India refashioning itself in the image of western lifestyle and economy, Kerala remains a communist state with very strong influence of trade unions, and more or less centralize politics. Also, Muslim and Christian minorities co – exist peacefully with Hindus, which make this state outstanding of all India. On the other hand, despite large capacity of natural resources, Kerala suffers from lack of the industrial investment from international and Indian companies, mostly for fear of the state's difficult trade unions, pro – union courts and high minimum wages. As a consequence, Kerala has the highest unemployment rates among India's states. One of the main successful stories of Kerala's development is education. Kerala has been able to reduce the regional and gender gaps in education, literacy and enrolment at all level of education.

Kerala Economy: In Pre – Independence Period

The course of economic development of the state is closely related to its location, climate and topography. In a way, Kerala's unique pattern of development and its population profile are products of its history as much of its geography. The location of the region on the Arabian sea coast permitted trading and cultural relations with outside world. Musiris (present day kodungalloor) situated on the coast and the numerous minor ports attracted traders from all around the world. These ports developed into trade centres between the Arab countries, North Africa and the Roman empire (Kerala Council for Historical Research 2010; Tharakan 2005). Arabs, Jews and Christians first came to Kerala as traders. The overwhelming availability of Arab accounts of the Kerala region known as Malabar do indicate the importance of Arabs in the overseas trade originating from this region. Similarly, there are evidences of Chinese trade relations with Kerala. As a result of such trade, use of money and different types of coins increased in this region, leading to minting of coins here itself. The growth in trade had increased the production of spices and other cash crops which in turn have generated more trade. (Ibid)

Malabar was the first centre for European colonisation in India following the landing of Vasco de Gama in Calicut in 1498 AD. Portuguese conquest of the region was followed by those of the Dutch and the British. However, except Malabar, the other parts of the present - day Kerala Viz, Travancore and Cochin were not directly ruled by the British. Almost all the present differences between Kerala and the rest of the country in social development can be traced at least to the last two centuries. It may be noted that the princely states of Travancore and Cochin had established very clear leads in all indicators of social development over other princely states and British India, much before Independence (Issac and Tharakan 1986; Nair 1989; Saradamoni 1994; Ramachandran VK 2010).

Both in Travancore and Cochin, area under cultivation especially that of cash crops like Coconut, Tea, Coffee, Spices and Rubber was constantly expanding. Many of these important crops were introduced by the Europeans in Kerala from their other colonies in Africa and Latin America. The Europeans initiated cultivation of some of these crops under the plantation system in vast tracts of forest and hilly areas. The local population followed this way of cultivation. As most of the expansion of area under crops, both cash and food crops had taken place in virgin forest land and also in land reclaimed from backwaters, the period also saw increase in agricultural productivity (Panikar et al. 1978). Along with agricultural production, agro – processing industries like coir, cashew also expanded (Issac and Tharakan 1986). In Malabar, Basel Mission, a Swiss Missionary cum trading organization introduced modern factories using the latest available technologies in spinning and weaving and also in manufacturing of roofing tiles (Raghaviah 1990). Large amount of capital invested in modern industries, together with the investment in plantation companies enabled Travancore to overtake other major princely states in total corporate paid – up capital (Mahadevan 1991). This period also witnessed large growth of exports leaving a favourable balance of trade. Both the net barter terms of trade and income terms of trade were favourable to the state during most of the pre independence period.

The growth of the banking business in Travancore and Cochin was well ahead, not only of Malabar, a part of Madras Province of British India, but also of other provinces and other regions. During 1926 – 30, Travancore alone accounted for about one-fifth of the total number of banks then existing in the combined area of erstwhile British India and Travancore. Around 1936, the population served by Joint – stock banks in Travancore was about 1,85,000 against 2,76,000 in undivided India as a whole and 79,000 for USA and 20,000 for France (Muranjan S K 1952 as quoted in Oommen 1976). In the range of area and population served by an office of a commercial bank, Travancore – Cochin had been credited with the highest position at the time of Indian independence. The economic expansion of Travancore state had helped its revenue raising capacity. Unlike today, revenues of the state then included income tax, excise duties and customs duties (Singh 1944). It was the continuous growth in revenue together with the state's expenditure priorities in favour of social services and the lower cast of providing education mostly at the school level and health care mostly at the primary level that brought about the phenomenal social development in pre – independence period (National Council of Applied Economic Research 1967).

Kerala Economy: In Post – Independence Period

Kerala state formed in 1956 November 1, by integrating Thirukochi and Malabar formed a state for people using Malayalam language -which is called Kerala , this integration was under the State reorganisation Act 1956. The economy of Travancore and Thirukochi was in a much better state as it is ruled by kings and Malabar was under the British rule and having a pathetic economic condition. This clearly shows that there is an economic disparity in Kerala in its two parts, during the time of its formation. Travancore rulers have commercialised the agriculture and tenants were given property rights, all this boosted its economy and living standard of the people and also increased productivity and production of agricultural products. Some of the characteristics of the Kerala economy at the time of its formation :

- Backward Agrarian Economy
- No full self – sufficiency in food
- Less Agricultural Production
- Per capita income is low or very less
- Tenancy System
- Unemployment
- Poverty rate is high
- Little Infrastructure
- Poor health and education

Indian Government followed a Market Intervention policy in an excessive manner , Kerala's import has been blocked due to this policy of India Government. Kerala economy has only low foreign exchange because of this restrictive attitude of centre as well as state government . Kerala economy overly depend on Public funding and all the planning and development were decided by the planning commission. Infrastructure sectors like power, Water supply, irrigation, communication, roads were put under the state ownership and Monopoly. Policies totally prohibited all private efforts to develop infrastructure items. Industrial policies of the state were aimed at starting Public Sector units, Industrial co-operatives, reviving sick units etc. Modernisation and Mechanisation were prohibited . Kerala economy focused only on education and health sectors. Education policies of the state aimed only to promote Public Education institutions through public spending and prohibited private investment in higher education sector. A number of big bureaucratic institutions, Construction of big irrigation projects, creation of credit agencies etc were started for agricultural development. From 1956 onwards the economic growth rate of Kerala was low i.e, less than 5 percentage because of low private investment, Imports were blocked, over influence of trade unions. In 1960s Backward industries with dominance of traditional and labour intensive industries like Coir, Cashew, Handloom etc . There was massive poverty and high rate of unemployment . According to one estimate the percentage of poor people in Kerala was 90.75 Percentage in 1960 – 61 (Dandekar and Rath). From 1960 onwards Kerala economy shows a mild increasing trend on the economic growth rate of 5 percentage .

In 1970, there was huge gulf diaspora , huge folks of Keralites migrated to the Gulf countries in search of jobs. The backward economy began to witness rapid changes, mainly after 1970s with the large scale migration of Keralite workers to the Gulf countries . The large scale migration and flows of remittances have resulted in unprecedented economic changes in Kerala. The total stock of Keralite emigrants in Gulf increased from 2.5 lakh in 1979 to 6.7 lakh in 1990 and In the year 2020, it is estimated to be 3.5 million. The Remittances received from the Keralite emigrant workers increased from about Rs 824 crore in 1980 to Rs 1310 crore in 1990, in 2018 these remittances were estimated to be 85000 crores. With the Gulf Diaspora, wide spread changes had taken place in the labour Market, Consumption, Savings, Investment, Poverty, Income distribution and regional development. In 1980, The Tourism sector has started its growth and become one of the major revenue - creating venture for the Kerala economy. Within a short span of time all the tourist spots of Kerala has become popular and Kerala has been permanently depicted in the tourist map of the World with the tag "God's Own Country" and stated to provide both revenue and employment opportunities for the Kerala economy.

In 1990, The New Economic Policy was announced i.e, Liberalization, Privatization and Globalization (LPG), At first Kerala Government opposed LPG and later Kerala also joined in the New Economic Policy. With the NEP created a favourable condition for private investment and there was rapid increase in private investment. There was also increase in emigration and flow of remittances from places other than Gulf countries, some of the major destinations are USA, UK, Canada and Australia. Higher rate of investment and technical progress is happening in the Kerala Economy. NEP helped Kerala to attain rapid reduction in poverty and unemployment, the state moved to a higher level of economic growth, technological change and speedy transformation of economy and generation of more employment. In this period along with Kerala model of Development the state also followed Gujarat Model of Development i.e, starting investing more in infrastructure along with health and education. Along with these positive impacts of LPG policy Kerala economy has to face some negative impacts . Kerala was more focused on cash crops and price of food crops get reduced as demand lowered, so the farmers has to face huge loss. All agriculture and allied activities get marginalised. Kerala cannot attract more private – public partnership as compared to other states. Because of all these negative effects of LPG Policy unemployment get lowered comparatively to the 1956 level. This is why Kerala still has large rate of unemployment. Some of the weaknesses of Kerala economy are Chronic Unemployment, External Dependency i.e, extreme dependence on outside the state and outside the country both for employment and for remittances, second generation problems arise due to the success of Kerala economy which is similar to the case of all developed countries unlike these countries the state does not have the financial ability to solve or to tackle them all by itself. Another problem is the large graying population or ageing of the state , this has several implications in relation to health needs, service pension requirements of the government and social security system. The changing Demographic profile is also likely to increase the demand for expenditure on health services. Changing profile of Employment seekers is another problem, Higher levels of education have changed the character of unemployment in Kerala to that of educated unemployed as seen earlier. Degradation of the Environment is another problem.

Since 2020, the state implemented lockdown and other restrictions since March 2020 to contain the pandemic. Available evidences indicate that the COVID – 19 pandemic has created unprecedented recession in the state. There was huge fall in production of goods and services (GSDP) and loss of jobs in all sectors of the state's economy during 2020 – 21 . In 2022 , There was high uncertainty prevails about the containment of the pandemic and resumption of economic activities to pre COVID – 19 level. Also the Kerala economy started showing positive economic growth after two years of negative growth (in 2019 – 20 there was only a growth rate of 0.9 percent, which is only a meagre growth rate).

B. A. Prakash in his work " Sixty years of Kerala's Economy: Economic Policies, Development Strategy and Development" classified the development of Kerala economy into four phases : (1956 – 1975), (1976 – 1990), (1991 – 2020), (since 2020).

The below table shows the GSDP growth of Kerala economy at constant price :

Table 1.1:-KERALA GSDP AT CONSTANT PRICES (1960 – 2020) (in crores of rupees)

Year	GSDP	Primary Sector	Secondary Sector	Tertiary Sector	Per Capita Income
1960 - 61	462	241 (52.16%)	68 (14.72%)	153 (33.12%)	276
1970 - 71	1255	653 (52.03%)	163 (12.99%)	439 (34.98%)	594
1980 - 81	3823	1682 (44.00%)	841 (22.00%)	1300 (34.00%)	1508
1990 - 91	12195	4756 (39.00%)	3171 (26.00%)	4268 (35.00%)	4207
2000 - 01	63715	14017 (22.00%)	14017 (22.00%)	35680 (56.00%)	19951
2009 - 10	180812	15966 (8.83%)	38249 (21.15%)	126597 (70.02%)	47360
2015 - 16	467243	49206 (11.58%)	111177 (26.17%)	264408 (62.25%)	136811
2017 - 18	516190	47619 (10.34%)	129866 (28.18%)	283269 (61.48%)	149650
2018 - 19	549673	46004 (9.40%)	138034 (28.21%)	305304 (62.39%)	158564
2019 - 20	568636	42374 (8.44%)	141806 (28.25%)	317781 (36.31%)	163216

SOURCE: Economic Review, Kerala (2016 and 2020)

NITAQAT and the Kerala Economy

The NITAQAT (classification) law being implemented by the Kingdom of Saudi Arabia makes it mandatory for Saudi Companies to reserve 10 percent of jobs foe Saudi nationals. Saudi Arabia has very strong socio – economic reasons to justify such a policy. Unlike other gulf countries Saudi Arabia itself has large number of unemployed citizens. In 2012, there were 3,40,000 firms in the Kingdom that did not employ any Saudi. Of late there is a growing feeling of resentment among the citizens of Saudi Arabia resulting from the labour market competition they face from expatriate workforce. The NITAQAT law is aimed at eliminating unemployment and localising jobs in the Kingdom. NITAQAT seeks to replace the 1994 scheme of Saudization which required 30 percent of the jobs to be reserved for Saudi citizens. This scheme failed in 1994 because of inherent loopholes in the system. The new law divides the Saudi labour market into 41 activities and each activity into 5 sizes (Giant, Large, Medium, Small and Very Small) to have in total 205 categories. NITAQAT classifies establishments into ranges (Excellent, Green, Yellow and Red) based on the ratio of the citizens working in the establishments. The Excellent and Green range, which are the ranges with the highest localisation ratios, will be rewarded with incentives. The new law proposes to deal firmly with the Red range, the range characterised by the lowest localisation ratio. More time is given to the Yellow range to improve their positions, it being the medium range.

The NITAQAT law states that an expatriate worker should work only under his sponsor and the worker is not mean to perform any job other than the one mentioned on his job card , this has raised much panic among the expatriate workers. More over the Saudi government has increased the fee for renewing labour cards (iqamas) to SAR 2,500 to SAR 100 (Saudi Arabian Riyal). The strict implementation of the NITAQAT law has raised much concern in Kerala. Majority of the Indian Migrant labour in Saudi Arabia are from Kerala. In 2011, some 5,70,000 Keralites were working in Saudi Arabia. Though the impact was only on less than 3 percent of the migrant population , remittances by them were consistently contributing to the economy of the state especially to the northern districts of Malappuram, Kozhikode, Kannur and Kasargode. The inflow of remittance payments from Saudi Arabia has considerably raised living standards in these districts. Saudi Arabia continues to be the most desired destination among the low and semi – skilled Keralites. The strict adherence to the NITAQAT regulations has resulted in immediate job losses and reduced the job opportunities. Many small - scale shops and establishments in Saudi Arabia were run by Keralites under licenses in the name of Saudi nationals. Under the new law , all these shops and establishments must have 10 percent of their employees from among Saudi nationals who should be paid at least 3 times more salary than their expatriate counterparts, it is almost impossible to run companies on the licenses given to Saudi nationals. Strict actions are being taking against benami businesses. Most shops run by Keralites were closed. The impact of the crackdown on illegal foreign workers in Saudi Arabia has serious consequence on Kerala Economy. The sudden exodus of the unemployed has trigger off economic crisis and social unrest in the state. The sudden fall in remittances from Saudi Arabia has led to a ripple effect on interlinked sectors like real estate, Construction, Transport etc.

GST and the Kerala Economy

As the catchword of GST ads in India reveals GST is materializing what could be rightly called "One Market, One Nation, and One Tax". Indeed, GST is an internationally proven revenue productive and growth accelerating indirect tax system that prevails in 160 countries in the world. GST, simply put, is a comprehensive tax regime replacing the existing indirect tax system. GST heralds not only the dawn of a new era in the tax realm of the country but also it ushers in a 'behavioural change' in the transactions that happen in the economy. Different from the current indirect tax system, GST is collected at the time of consumption of goods and services, and hence it is recognised as a destination-based tax. GST does not attempt to make a division between goods and services and, in this sense, it attempts to dismantle a dichotomized tax system where goods and services are differently treated. GST replaces indirect taxes like Value Added Tax (VAT), service tax, Entry Tax, Luxury Tax, Advertisement Tax and custom. India being a federal country both the Centre and States must be financially empowered to discharge different economic functions. Hence, we need to allow both the Centre and the States to levy and collect indirect taxes. Taking this into account, three types of GSTs have been devised. These three types of GSTs have been designed based on the 'Place of Supply' of goods and services ("Place of Supply" in GST decides whether the transaction needs to be reckoned as intra-state or inter-state). For intra-state movement of goods and services, there are two types of taxes: Central GST (CGST); and State GST (SGST), and for inter-state movement, we have one tax, called Integrated GST (IGST). In other words, the GST levied by the Centre on intra-State supply of goods is called CGST and the GST levied by the State on intra-State movement of good is called SGST. Taxes levied by the Centre on the inter-state movement of goods and services and imports is called IGST. IGST goes to the hands of the Central Government. GST is a path-breaking event in the history of post-independent India. Many countries have embraced GST as an efficient and profitable indirect tax system. GST bestows many benefits on the nations in the form increasing indirect tax proceeds and enhancing the efficiency in economic activities' duty. On the positive side, GST will bring forth more revenue for the State as well as Central governments. This happens because of two reasons: first increase in tax compliance, and second, the widening tax base as more commodities and services which are hitherto untaxed will come under the ambit of taxation. For the economy as a whole, GST benefit occurs in the form of enhancing market efficiency. As one tax begins to rule the entire transactions in the country, this will usher in vibrancy and dynamism in the market, thereby increasing competitive spirit, leading to slash in prices which ultimately benefit the consumers at large. It is expected that GST will make tax filing easier, ensuring transparency and speed in tax filing. This would be a fillip to the ease of doing business in India, leading to an increase in investment and investor confidence. Economists believe that in the long run GST would push down the prices of most of the commodities and services as multiple indirect taxes which now exist will be replaced by GST. But the success regarding this aspect depends on the fixation of prices by the manufacturers.

Now, let us think of the impacts that GST may spawn on Kerala Economy. Brushing aside all ideological differences, the Finance Minister of Kerala, Dr. Thomas Isaac has always been supportive to the GST only because of the reason that this would be financially advantageous for a consumer state like Kerala. As under GST, the tax is imposed at the time of consumption rather than at the time of production, Kerala being a consumer state, GST would fetch more tax revenue for the State. Only 2.75 percent of India's population lives in Kerala but they account for 15 percent of the market for durable commodities in the country. It needs to be reiterated here that the producer states like Tamil Nadu and Maharashtra would experience a shortfall in their tax receipts for which definitely compensation will have to be given by the Central government. It may sarcastically be pointed out that GST benefit that Kerala accrues in future would be a reward for not being a producer-centric State. Not only being a consumer state does become a boon for Kerala as far as GST is concerned, but the structure of the State as reflected in the sector-wise contribution to SGDP also mirrors how GST would benefit the State enormously. Today, the share of Service sector in State's SGDP has increased to the level as large as more than 70 percent whereas the goods sectors like the agriculture and the industrial sectors roughly share the rest 30 percent. Banking, finance, tourism, IT, hotels, communication, health care and education etc. have become the major contributors of State's SGDP. As these service sectors would be taxed under GST on par with the goods (remember GST does not make any discrimination between goods and services), Kerala is likely to get more tax receipts in its kitty, which will cushion the budget position of the State government. Currently, on a rough estimate, State's total expenditure grows at a rate of 15 percent per annum while the total revenue lags behind with nearly 11 percent per annum. With GST adding more revenue in the form of IGST from the Centre, besides SGST collected by the State government, surely the total revenue receipts of the State at least will catch up with the total expenditure, narrowing the deficit figures to a comfortable position. Moreover, this would help Kerala to fulfil the FRBM provisions on the expected lines. Being a consumer state, price levels are important for us as any untoward upward revisions in general price level would unbalance the household budget in the State. As claimed by the supporters of GST, GST will have prices brought down to the extent to which multiple taxes have been replaced by a single tax called GST. A decline in the prices of essentials would help households fetch more balances and enhance the household financial savings. But, the immediate post-GST developments in the State, unfortunately, do not share a hope of getting prices slashed in the case of many commodities. The reports of inflating hotel bills and the increase in the prices of boiler chickens stand testimony to this fact. Reports show that in the name of GST even the prices of goods for which GST does not apply have been artificially revised up by small traders to fish in the troubled water. This has already started casting shadows over the price front outcomes of the implementation of GST in the State. IGST is a big boon for Kerala. As we know Kerala has been witnessing a construction boom in recent times. The increasing demand for housing especially flats in urban and suburban areas, the growing presence of shopping malls even in small towns, the demand for healthcare, educational institutions, and space for IT companies have all sustained the demand for construction activities in Kerala. High-value construction materials including marbles and tiles are purchased from other states. Now, with GST, Kerala is eligible to get the IGST on all these materials transported to Kerala wherever they are bought from. This will enormously add to the revenue receipts of the State government. E-way bills that the transporters carry play an important role in this respect. Now the GST revenue collection shows an increasing trend as compared to the previous year, in October 2022 it has an increase of 29 percent.

Kerala Economy and the Natural Calamities

In the month of August and September in 2018 and 2019, there was heavy downpouring in Kerala due to climate change and change of Monsoon wind pattern. This heavy rainfall severely affected the regions of Idukki, Ernakulam, Kollam, Kottayam, Pathanamthitta, Malappuram and Wayanad districts of Kerala. The Monsoon induced flood has had severe impact on state GDP. Heavy downpouring in Kerala during August and September in 2018 and 2019 has a wide spread effects in socio – economic livelihood of the people in Kerala. The Key sectors of the Kerala economy are Tourism and agro – based industries which suffered huge losses due to flood and other natural calamities. The agro – based industries and Plantation industries have suffered a loss estimated around 1000 crores. In total around 2.2 percent of the state GDP has been diminished due to the flood and flood related natural calamities which lead to a fiscal deficit of 5.4 percent. Employment opportunity of a large number of people has affected, agricultural household and other workers are in distress as they lost their livelihood income earning. Around 10 lakh people were rehabilitated during the month of August and September which may caused an over burden to the government leads to a further set back in the financial position of the state. The state has been facing a high revenue deficit over the past years as it cannot maintain fiscal deficit within 3 percent of SGDP and also it carries a high debt burden of 31 percent of SGDP. The revenue expenditure of the state account about 80 percent of state's total expenditure in the period of 2018 – 19 which constraints the state government to undertake capital creation activities for future development. Post flood activities like flood relief, rehabilitation and reconstructionhas widen the revenue deficit and fiscal deficit of the state. This traumatic period, increase the demand for some sections of the workforce especially like electricians, Construction workers, maintenance workers, health care workers etc.

The production of food crops especially rice shown a deep decline as the paddy fields were floated with water and the flooded water dumped waste material and soil which create hardship to the farmers. Around 57000 hectres of cropped area has affected by the heavy rainfall of August which has caused a loss of around 1356.5 crores. Paddy and banana were the worst affected agricultural products which risen the financial burden of the farmers. Landslides were another problem that the economy faced during those days which resulted many causalities and homeless peoples on the one hand and deterioration of soil and soil fertility on the other. This has adversely affected the debt repayment capacity of farmers. As per the estimate tea and rubber industry together witnessed severe loss. Apart of rubber and tea industries other cash crops like ginger, banana, cardamom etc also faced a negative impact in the production leads to a disruption in supply for these products. Foreign remittances are the backbone of Kerala economy, over 10 percent of the state's population is living abroad and they contribute about more than 35 percent of state 's GDP every year. It will affect every aspect of Kerala economy directly or indirectly. Kerala Model of Development success story can be credited to Kerala migrant labour force and their remittances even though the state has been witnessing a steady decline in foreign remittance during the past years due to economic slowdown and nationalization policy of gulf nations, the flows of remittances had increased in support of Kerala people during the flooded time of 2018 as well as 2019 for rehabilitation and reconstruction of the economy. Okhi in 2017 also affected the Kerala economy in a similar way but its impact was comparatively less to the flood in 2018 and 2019.

Kerala Economy and the COVID – 19 Pandemic

The first COVID – 19 case in India was reported in the Thrissur district of Kerala. The factors responsible for the low growth rate of infection and death (comparatively) in Kerala during an early phase is because the lockdown implemented by the Kerala government for 68 days to prevent the spread of the pandemic (March 25 to May 31, 2020). Also Kerala had the experience in containing the outbreak of Nipah virus during May and June 2018. Another factor prevent the further spread of pandemic is the effective public health system of Kerala which consists of hospitals in panchayat, Taluk and district levels. District wise data of COVID – 19 cases as on September 9, 2020 is given in the below table:

Table 1.2 Number of COVID – 19 cases in Kerala (District wise)

No	District	Confirmed cases	Active cases	Death
1	Thiruvananthapuram	19,260	4,590	29
2	Malappuram	11,327	2,192	26
3	Ernakulam	8,087	2,572	43
4	Kozhikode	7,421	1,827	38
5	Alappuzha	7,041	1,734	15
6	Kasargode	6,677	2,123	36
7	Thrissur	5,935	1,734	19
8	Kollam	5,903	1,712	26
9	Palakkad	5,588	932	4
10	Kottayam	5,394	1,838	3
11	Kannur	5,093	1,532	35
12	Pathanamthitta	4,368	1,092	3
13	Idukki	2,014	345	3
14	Wayanad	1,810	327	5
	TOTAL	**95,918**	**24,550**	**385**

Source: https://www.COVID-19india.org/

More relaxations were announced in the lockdown from May 4, 2020 by the central government. More freedom was given to people for travel, use of motor vehicles, opening up of trading establishments and economic sectors. The Keralites in other states and foreign countries were given permission to return to Kerala. Due to this large number of Keralites from other states and especially from gulf countries returned to Kerala and contributed to a substantial increase in the number of COVID – 19 patients since July 2020. The number of tests conducted in the state is meagre compared to the requirement. To prevent the spread of the pandemic, strict restrictions were introduced to restrict travel of people from their residence to outside world. Also, social distancing and quarantine were also introduced. In order to overcome this crisis, producers, traders, hotels, educational institutions etc introduced new way of doing business like shifting of activities from work place to homes. Government and private establishments, IT industrial units etc began to provide their employees work from home facility, Schools, colleges and other educational institutions changed to Online teaching Mode. Shops, Hotels etc began to deliver the items to the residences of the consumers. So, there is an unprecedented change in the way of living of the people in the Post – COVID – 19 and the availability of electricity, water, internet and TV connection became a pre – condition for life ahead.

The lockdown of 69 days is classified by B. A. Prakash in his paper "The Impact of COVID – 19 on Kerala's Economy: A Preliminary Assessment" into three phases based on the restrictions imposed. The first phase of 27 days (March 24 to April 19) a lockdown similar to a curfew was implemented in the state. All mode of transport were stopped, all educational institutions, places of worships, functions and gatherings were stopped. Except a few essential services like shops dealing with food, groceries, fruits, ration shops, banks and ATMs, Telecom services, delivery for food and medicines, Petrol pumps, LPG distribution, Power supply etc. The police enforced the lockdown strictly throughout the state similar to a curfew by inspecting movements of people and motor vehicles on the roads. In the second phase of lockdown of 14 days (April 20 to May 3) a few relaxations and in the third phase of 28 days (May 4 to May 31) more relaxation had allowed. In an estimate the total loss of GSDP was 82 percent in the first phase, 72 percent in the second phase and 61 percent in the third phase. The secondary sector consists of industries, electricity, gas, water supply and construction suffered a huge loss due to the lockdown. The loss in construction was 100 percent in first phase, 95 percent in second phase and 85 percent in third phase. The estimate of total loss of GSDP for 69 days is Rs 105431 crores. This loss will be equivalent to 13.5 percent of the GSDP for a year. The lockdown implemented in all sectors of the economy. Due to prolonged lockdown, quarantine, physical distancing and other isolation measures to supress transmission of COVID – 19, the state's economy is heading towards a recession. Non – essential services and production were directly affected by the lockdown, which led to the reduction in working hours and to job losses. The lockdown has resulted in huge loss of employment of all categories like Self - employed, regular and casual labourers. In tertiary sector, more than 50 percent of employment loss were in trade, repair of motor vehicles, transport and storage, accommodation and food services, financial and insurance, education, entertainment and recreation and other services. The return of migrant workers to their native states has created only a temporary unemployment in the state. These migrant workers from West Bengal, Assam, Bihar etc has came back to the state after the restrictions were taken away. And this migration has given an opportunity to a good portion of unskilled and semi-skilled workers returned from the Gulf countries and other states to take up the jobs done by those migrant workers So, there will be no unemployment in the long run. There was no real labour shortage but the return of Keralites from Gulf countries has created a fall in remittances which had some serious consequences in the Kerala Economy. In the Post – COVID – 19 period, almost all the Keralites who has returned from Gulf countries and other states have returned to their working destinations. All things became once again normal and optimistic. The pandemic gave new ventures for self-employment like Vloging, Content creating, craft making etc in a more commercialised way which can provide a stern income.

Kerala Economy and the Migration of Young Population

In the older times the migration especially to the GCC countries, particularly towards UAE was the Distress migration. But now the aim and objectives of migration for younger population has changed to Skill development and Higher education, other than migrating for a livelihood. The migration of Young Keralites migrate to countries like UK, Canada, Australia etc which provide jobs and citizenship for them, in short the younger Keralites has a good taste in Permanent Migration other than Temporary Migration towards Gulf countries which provide remittances to the Kerala Economy. Students from India spend an estimated amount of 690.9 million dollar as education expenses. According to the data of 2021, this is 30.24 percent of the outward remittances. This migration can create many serious problems in the long run. Unlike other countries, India does not have in- migration proportional to out-migration which creates a balanced migration situation which benefits many countries with low or negative population growth. This migration can be stopped with increasing the quality and rankings of Higher Education, Kerala is also passing through the same situation, the percent of Keralites passed the entrance of reputed universities demanding more focus on the higher education and its modification according to the time demands. Financial problems due to the non – remittances of the NRIs are not only the problems that will affect Kerala in future. If Kerala's next generation continues to migrate to other countries by mortgaging their properties and getting loans, Kerala will become a land of old aged people. The brain drain of a talented generation will cause many social impacts. The number of vacant houses is increasing in Kerala. According to the 2011 census report, there are 12 lakh vacant houses in Kerala. This is 11 percent of the vacant houses in India and 60 percent of these are belong to non – resident Keralites settled in European countries. And these are 11– year- old figures. To control this brain drain, it is imperative that the state and central governments came out with effective plans to stop the growing trend.

CONCLUSION

Kerala, in the pre independence period includes three regions Travancore, Malabar and Kochi. Among these regions Malabar was under british rule and the other two regions were ruled by kings. The disparity in the economic growth and development in these regions, i.e, the pathetic state of Malabar and the progressive growth of Travancore. In the ancient time onwards Kerala region has a significant position in the trade map of the World. In 1956 November 1 Kerala organised as state under the State Reorganisation Act of 1956 by the recommendations of Fazal Ali Commission. With the Gulf Boom in 1970, there was large scale migration towards Gulf region, and these expatriates has provided remittances which has increased the living standard of Kerala in a holistic way. With the introduction of New Economic Policy in 1991, Kerala has some positive impacts but it cannot reap as much private investment as other states or countries can. In 2008 there was a Financial crisis hit all over the world, the over issuing and trading of mortgage backed securities, but this crisis has only minimal effect in Indian economy and Kerala economy. 2017, 2018 and 2019 were the years of hardships for Kerala economy. In 2017 , Okhi affected Kerala badly and both in 2018 and 2019 two floods which shake the pillars of Kerala Economy. In 2020, the COVID – 19 pandemic cause devastating effect in the Kerala Economy. Kerala has tremendous potential in high value added crops such as fruits, Plantation crops, Organic products and medicinal plants. Kerala's agriculture sector faces several challenges like predominance of small land holders, the declining area under cultivation, falling productivity etc. To fully explore this potential the state needs to adopt modern farming practices such as contract farming, electronic trading and farmer producer companies need to be promoted. The state's current agricultural development strategy relies heavily on government support. The state's potential can be explored better if the private sector is provided adequate opportunity to develop the agriculture sector. The services sector has been a major source of growth for Kerala. Kerala's economy has undergone a significant structural transformation over time, with the growing dominance of the services sector. However, one major area of concern is that the services sector growth in Kerala is fuelled by low value adding and non- exportable services such as real estate, public administration and communication. Despite being a lender in education and health attainment, Kerala is yet to become an IT software powerhouse like her neighbours. Therefore, the state needs to create an eco- system conducive to the growth of high value adding services such as IT software, financial services and Luxury tourism. Kerala's tourism potential remains underutilised. Within IT software Kerala should strive to move up the value chain and become a leader in high value- added services such as engineering and research and development of software products. With its high human development index and quality of life, Kerala is in a better state to attract the best brains to pursue this ambitious goal, which can also prevent the permanent migration of Young Keralites. Kerala's industrial backwardness has been attributed to structural factors such as heavy labour unionisation, Investment unfriendly image and hostile attitude of civil society towards private investment, the fact remains that promoting industrialization through a large factory set up is not feasible in Kerala due to non – availability of a vast tract of land and concerns regarding environmental degradation. Therefore, the promotion of Micro, Small and Medium Enterprises seems to be the best option for Kerala to industrialize. An analysis of CMIE data on investment projects reveals that during the 10 years from 2011 to 2021, Kerala received only 0.63 percent of private investment projects completed in India, which is much lower than the top performing states – Gujarat (13.39 percent) and Maharashtra (11.99 percent).

Goblin or ghosts :are tulu brahmins a unique specimen?an economic approach

JINU G V

Tulunadu represents an ecologically sensitive and economic zone of agglutinative practices and theoretical performances of legacies to the Indian culture and civilization in general and Karnataka in particular. Tulunadu is the undivided district of Kasargode district of Kerala state. With its serenic beauty and landscape, Tulunadu is charismatic surmounted by mountains and rivers. Coconut (cocus nucifera) palms and arecanut gardens add to the greatness of the land. Tulunadu is richly adorned with various cultural affiliations and assimilations. The cultural realm of Tulunadu is fashioned by folk literature, folk songs, Paadanas, Goblin culture or demonolatry worship to have a paramount place in Tulunadu. A micro -level analysis of Tulu Nadu is mentioned by eminent thinkers like B.A Saletore, K.V Ramesh, Gururaja Bhat, H.A Stuart, J. Sturrock etc. The Tuluva history and culture is detailed in their eminent scholarship writings. The socio-cultural aspect of Tuluva society and Tuluva Brahmins are articulated in the theatre of Bhutaradhana. Tradition has a vital role in Tuluva culture.

Tulunadu, the land of Parasurama stretches from Gokarna payaswani to the coastal belt of Sahyadri. Tulunadu is a conglommeration of different religions, languages, cultures and those who were expert in Vedas. From Sangam age onwards, Tulu Nadu presents an independent state from Christian era. The inhabitants of Tulu Nadu lived for three thousand years. Alupas, Bangas, Ayilas,Chouttas,Tholawar were the Tulu Kingdoms who reigned Tulu Nadu. Among them Alupas reigned a greater part of administration from 6 AD to 13 AD. Tulu Nadu was under Vijayanagar Empire till 14th and 17th centuries onwards. In due course of its downfall, Gowda Saraswathy, Konkani etc came into forefront. The Jains also rapidly spread in Tulu Nadu. Their legacy lies in Karkkala and Venur's Bahubali statue.

Christians also migrated from Goa to Tulu Nadu from sixteenth century. They established many educational institutions and factories in Tulu Nadu. The eighteenth century witnessed the attack of Haider Ali on Tulu Nadu. Tulu Nadu was incorporated into Madras Presidency by drubbing Tipu Sultan by the British. Later these places were known as North Canara, South Canara etc. Till 1956 it was under Madras Presidency. By the linguistic reorganization of States it came under the presidency of Karnataka and Kasargode came under the aegis of Kerala. Geographically, Tulunadu is changing continuously and remarkably. Climatic variation played a paramount role in moulding the history of Tulunadu. Tulunadu has a particular geography cultural, political, and linguistic from time immemorial. It is located between 12°4'15" and 13°58'38" north latitude and 74°44'26" and 75°44'31" east longitude. Aminidis Islands are linked to the land and Arabian sea lies on the West of Tulunadu, precipitins cliffs surrounded the area formed the sanctorum of the land. The Western Ghats moulded the culture of Tulunadu. The district is benedicted with rivers streams and the volume of the water is high. Nethravadi, Gangothri, Payaswani, Chandragiri, Swatna and Sitanadi were the rivers.

The history of Tuluva is traced to Paleolithic period by G. Bhatt and or Tulunadu is bound up with the history of Karnataka and Kasargode. It is the representative of the history of the political, economic and social life of the people of Tulunadu through the ages. It is settled by elements of ethnic tribal, jati, linguistics, religious socio cultural identities that had been contributed in various contexts of time and space. The political history of Tuluva till the annexation of the District by the British in 1789 A.D falls into the following divisions.

a. The Alupa's sway which extended over a thousand years from the second till the fourteenth century AD.
b. The Suzerabati of the Vijayanagar monarch which lasted from the fourteenth century AD till the end of the sixteemth century.
c. Hegemony of the Kannada Kings of Ikkeri (also known as Bednore or Keladi) for nearly a century.
d. The rule of Hyder Ali and Tippu Sultan of Mysore from whom the British wrested the district.

The Alupas were a family of great antiquity by the epigraph of the later half of the seventh century AD and reigned over Tulunad till the fourteenth century in the present Udupi taluk. The Vijayanagar rule forms an epoch in the history of Tuluva. Tuluva was ruled by the efficient centralized Government. The indecisive interference of Venkatappa Nayak succeeded the ruler of Keladi in the affairs of Tuluva have placed the systematic acquisitions of the district under the late Keladi rulers. Shivappa Nayak ascended the throne in succession who is known as the builder of a series of strong forts. To five maganes of the southern taluk the present Hosdurg Taluk formed part of Malabar till recent period till 1737. The present Hosdurg Taluk comprised of the five maganes like Alavathanad, Paduvannad, Kavanad, Nileshwar and Thayakat. After 1760, Hyder Ali and Tipu become the sole authorities of the whole of South Canara district including Kasargod Taluk. After the fall of Tippu, South Kanara was included in the Madras presidency. Vijayanagar by 1514 established their supremacy on the extreme south of Tuluva. The Kumbla Rajas territory lays to the north of the Chandragiri or ancient perumpula river demarcates the traditional boundary line between Tuluva and Malabar. The Raja of Kumbla whose ancestors reined the southern part of Tuluva and who receives a political pension even this day. The bifurcation of Tulunadu into pre-historical and historical and the pioneers of the pre-historical Tulunadu were R. Rajendran, Vasanta Shetty, P.N Narasimha Moorthy and A Sundara. A graphic picture of antiquity of Tulunadu was got from Maurya's reign.

The customs and manners appertaining to the Malayali people are quite different from the customs and manners of their people of Tulunadu. The Brahmins in Tulunadu follow the Mitakshara Law and impartiability is unknown among them. The Shivalli Brahmins speak Tulu at home.

The origin of the Aliyasanthana system of Law is followed by Sudra classes is attributed to Bhootala Pandya of Tulunadu which is different from the Marumakkathayam system in several respects. The peculiar system followed by the Namboodiri Brahmins of the South is unknown among the Tulu Brahmins and every male member in the family marries within the caste.

The Brahmins intruded into Kerala preoccupied with their settlements in Tulunadu. Tulu Brahmins dwelled in Opamus. The Tuluva speaking people has linguistic affiniations with Malayalam, Telugu, Tamil and Kodagu language.

The Tuluva land's distinct identity makes up of ethnographic groups of Jain, Brahmins, Christians and Muslims . It has contributed scholars in literature, social sciences including medicine, social work and entrepreneurship etc. The Tuluva speaking people has one of the higher rates of literacy among men and women. The sex ratio is in favour of women. Tulu is spoken by about, 1158,419 of people through out India. Tulu is one of the ancient and richest languages and was one of the five major Dravidian langauges, the other four being Tamil, Malayalam, Kannada and Telugu. Tuluism confined to a small region of India and possess a very rich vocabulary. Grammar, oral literature has a proto- Dravidian feature. It is difficult for the people of Tulu to come in close contact with each other in olden days because Tulu spoken region comprises many forests, hills, and other geographical barriers. Tulu can speak Kannada language fluently whereas in Kerala state most of the Tulu people can easily converse in Malayalam. Tulu is spoken in a smaller geographical area by a smaller group of people. The Tuluvas have their own culture infused into the larger social frame work of Kerala. The historical existence of a host of minor ruling families was another highlight of Tuluva culture. During the colonial regime there was an affirmation and resettlement for the people of Tuluvas. A cultural evolution by the synthesis and amalgamation of various faiths can be seen in Tuluva culture.

The centre of 'focus' here is the Sivalli Tulu . They belonged to the 'main stem' of Brahmin dialect. They were highly influenced by the Sanskrit languages. They developed their own 'lingua franca with differing modes of ecclesiastical affairs and educational overtones. Caste was the impediency among the Brahmins which isolated their dialects with other communities. It is a difficult task to pursue Brahmin dialect. Retroflex and non-retroflex sounds of indigenous group ie, Dravidian stock of languages were frequently used. This dialect of Tulu displays remarkable variations between aspirated and unaspirated sounds. The dialect lingered in the southern part of Tulu country employed in all the ancient classical works. Linguists consider Tulu has a rich vocabulary although it was spoken by fewer communities in South India. Moreover, Tulu Nadu is encompassed by rich flora and fauna, hills, rivers and a place of serenic beauty. There was regional differences in speech habits as the process of accessibility was lacking in traditional times. The regions comprised of the following:- they are-

1. South West- The South West comprised of Tulunadu comprising the Kasargode Taluk of Kerala state.
2. South West- The South east part of Tulunadu comprised up to Kodagu (Coorg).
3. South Central-This area includes Puttur, Belthangady and Bautical.
4. North west-This areas includes Mangalore and Udupi taluks.
5. North East-includes the Karkala Taluk.
6. Jain Dialect- The root of this dialect can be traced in the northern part of Tulu Nadu. There was a close similarity of Jaina religion in the Tulu speaking areas. Thus a remarkable status of adorning Tulu with Jain aspect can be seen here.
7. Common Dialect-

Mogaveera dialect, Billava dialect, Gowda dialect, Kumbara dialect were common among them. There is close similarity among these dialects. So these were regarded as common dialects. Thus the etymology, 'common Tulu' or common Dialect for Tulu came into existence. It is used in speeches, mass media, public meetings etc. Paadana, the oral poetry has a rich stock of this dialect. Moreover, fiction, plays, poems, novels were written in this dialect. Thus the well-known Tulu is reflected in Tulu dialect. Thus by assimilating words esp, borrowed, the dialect differ from the Brahmin dialect.

(d) Harijan and Tribal Dialect

The Tulu language is spoken by tribal, communities and the forgotten lot, 'Koragas' of Kasargode form another group of Tulu dialects.

Tulu has sentences of no 'copula' and with no article. The picture shows the distribution of South Dravidian stock of languagesl3.

Malayalam language trace its genesis, growth, and development in Kannada and Tulu language. The affinity between these two linguistic traits are intertwined and interlinked. *Lilatilakam* gives ample reference about Tulu linguistic traits. One can draw an inference about the political, social, cultural isolation from Tulu speaking regions and adjoining places of Kerala. Phonologically, these two languages occupies an unique position. The enlightened scenario, Brahmins brought about this type of alteration. The outputs of Brahmin colonization paved the way for the peculiaristic traits of Tulu and Kannada language. The post-phase of Sangam age are replete in references about this. A 'network of settlements (say,64) were put forward by them. Out of which 32 were in South Canara including Tulu speaking areas. Thus dual cultures came into limelight. These authorities paved the way for the 'depositories and repositories' of Tulu characteristic lineage and affiliation. 'The migrational aspect of Brahmins from Tulu land brought about matriarchical system in the congenial soil of Kerala. The coinage of two terminology, 'aliyasantanam' and 'marumakkathayam' came into vogue.

Tulu was the debute language isolated from proto-south Central Dravidian subgroup[1]. Thus Tulu is a south -Dravidian language and F.W Ellis considered Tulu as a distinct dialect of Malayalam. Specimens of Malayalam character were present in Tulu[2]. The dialect complexities of Tulu were not undertaken properly to bring into attention. Dialectologically, this study will immensely help in nurturing the systematic nature of Tulu linguistics. Caldwell says that it differs far more widely from Malayalam than Malayalam does from Tamil[3]. One can identify lexical, phonological, morphological parallelism from among Tulu, Kannada and Malayalam. Thus there was intermingling and intermixing of racial cultures and elements.

The Tulu language is one of the most highly developed languages of the Dravidian family[4] and it is spoken in the northern fringer of Kasargod district of Kerala as well. The legacy of this community was commendable with respect to socio, cultural, ecclesiastical, artistic traditions and theatrical form. Thus an amalgamation of cultural synthesis took its root form. It has got the peculiarities, customs and norms of the Dravidian tongue. *A Comparative Study of Dravidian Languages* can be brought to lime light by the analytical study of Tulu. Tulu dialects on new sources is political necessary for the synchronic multiplicities and in socio-political linguistics[5]. It is an ample evidence to language use in mass media and educational preparation of lexicons, technical courage names, standardization of language etc.

Tulu speakers are mainly concentrated in South Canara of Mysore and the contiguous areas of North Kerala. Beyond Kalyanapura river in the North upto Baraken a few families of native speakers as found.Though the Tulu speakers are originally found in these areas, they are distributed all over India including Amomi, Maldiwis, Andaman and Nicobar Islands. According to the Census Report of 1971, the number of Tulu speaking people throughout India is1,158,414. In Mysore there are 1,042,865 people and in Kerala 78,637. Remaining 36,917 native speakers of Tulu are found distributed in other States of India. Among the other state, in Maharashtra alone there are 31,917 speakers. Next is Tamil Nadu with 3,837 speakers. In addition to this there are Tulu native speakers in foreign countries especially in Gulf countries. Among the Tulu native speakers settled outside the Tulu country, the majority are Tulu Brahmins. They are mainly the owners of Udupi hotels, priests in temples etc. There are very few people from non Brahmin communities who stay outside the Tulu desa except Bombay. In Bombay there are good number of Tulu native speakers who went there for job seeking.

Caldwell is of the opinion that Tulu, being one of the five major languages of the Dravidian stock, has been characterized as one of the most highly developed language of that family (Caldwell, 1956 Edn.) But Tulu does not have any written literature up to modern age, except some references about Tulu, tracing the origin and periodical development of Tulu would be difficult. However, from a close study of the spoken Tulu one can notice that it presents own linguistic peculiarities.

Tulu shares a number of features with Kannada as Kannada is the dominant language in the Tulu speaking area. But it also shares its features with the others major languages like Tamil, Malayalam and Telugu. It also shows striking similarities with the Kodagu language. Interestingly, Tulu shares common features not only with South Dravidian languages but also with the Central Dravidian Languages, as a few existences would show.

South Kanara including Kasargod Taluk is an interesting area where four or five languages are in contact. Kannada is the dominant language in the schools, colleges other educational institutions, all offices and in their main folk dance, Yakshagana. But the language of the bazaar is Tulu. In addition to these two languages, there are also people who speak Malayalam, Konkani, Marathi and Urudu in these areas, Hevyalia and a few other communities speak Kannada dialect. All these non. Tulu speakers used to communicate to Tulu speakers in Tulu only. Thus almost all the people in that area know the Tulu language. The influence of other languages mentioned above over Tulu will be very few because the speakers of other language will not usually speak in their languages to a Tulu speaker. Whenever they went to speak they well speak in Tulu, although Muslim sometimes talk to a Tulu speaker in their dialect of Malayalam. But the servants, both male and female, whose mother tongue is Tulu go to landlords who speak a language other than Tulu, for daily wages will be able to pick up their language by observation and talking to the children there most of the people of that area are competent atleast in two language. But some people are capable to handle three or four languages or even five languages. But the Girijano (Koragas) are not biling nats. They speak only Tulu even though they go to the houses of other language speaking people for selling their baskets.

Agrarian Economy under Tuluvas

About 75% of the population rely on cultivation for their mode of subsistence The groups which lived here were the Brahmins, Bunts, Jains and Christians. They were the Jenmis. Rice was the staple crop. There were tenants and sub-tenants working in cultivation Bullocks and buffaloes were used for cultivation. Specialization in rice cultivation was a feature of this period Besides rice, sugarcane cultivation was also done. Buffaloes were used in Kambala race or were known as Kambalada or kodnagalu. Manures, fertilizers, irrigation modes were all used for the purpose.. The transplantation of seedlings was also done. The items for trades were coffee, rice and paddy, sand, wood, oils, cardamoms tobacco etc. Barter system was in vogue Money-system was also in practice.

Marriage System

Caste played a pivotal rule in marriage system. So intercaste marriage was avoided by them. But we can see social and economic cooperation among these communities. The matriarchical system revolved among the Tuluvas. Temples play a great role in marriage as well as in cultural practices. Brahmins offer prayers to Gods during marriage. There will be a sacrificial priest or poojari to conduct the ceremony.

Religion among Tuluvas

Christianity in Tulunadu existed which contributed to the culture of the region. Madhva sect exerted influence here. Jainism was in vogue. Mohemmadeans had their role in Tuluva land. Religious toleration existed among them Mutual reverence of sects prevailed among them. Jainism was in vogue. Barakuru is the place where earliest Jainrelic was found currently. Two pontifical seats of Jainism were established at Mudabidune. The well-known centres of the Jain faith were Mudabidure, Karkala, Keravase, Vananga, Enuru, Barakuru and Hattiyangadi. The monastic orders of the Jaina church were. Mula-Sangha and kranurgana Kalorgana Kranurgana Kalorgana, Belat kara- gena, Designna, kunda- Kundanveya, Panasokvelisvera Srimet Maladhri Lalilakirti Bhattaraka deva, Mula sangha, Kanurgana, Desigana, Nishidhi, Desigana parasaravalisvarali and Nandi Sangha,Balat Kera- gana and sarasvatagachcha, Senagane and Samandhabhadrageva.

Around 180 bastis spread all over Tulunadu. Hosangadi 8, Gerusoppe 4, Enuru 8, karkalla 18 and Mudabidure 18 were most prominent. But some are often in perilled condition. Nerebandihole, Kombaru, Nandavana,Uchitha, Ullala, Kalatturu, Mogaru, Bandadi, Chikkanagadi, Kannarapadi, Enigallu were some among them. One can find a network of Jaina temples through the length and breadth of Tulunadu. All these instances show that Jainism gain popularity and influence in Tuluva Country.

Apart from these, gifts and grants are made by monarchies, men of charity and religion were practiced. Danas like aradhana(gift of food), abaya-dana (protection) anushadhi- dana (medical treatment), sastra-dana (religious instruction) were given.

Jain Dialect

A greater portion of the Tulu speaking Jain population is found on the northern part of Tulunadu. Though the number of Jains are comparatively less, with a few peculiar features they could maintain their dialect of Tulu as distinct from other dialects. As they follow Jainism, the special words or technical terms relating to that religion have got a permanent place in the Tulu spoken by them.

Common Dialect

This is the dialect which is used in public speeches, mass, media public meetings etc and hence this dialect is commonly accepted and called the "Common Tulu". This dialect contains a less number of borrowed words especially from Sanskrit when compared to the Brahmin dialect. The oral poetry called the Paaddana is composed in the dialect, and journals, most of the Tulu writings, novels, dramas, poems ar generally written in this dialect. Thus the common Tulu is the most popular one among the Tulu dialects.

Harijan and Tribal Dialects

The Tulu spoken by the Harijan and tribal communities form another class of Tulu dialects. Though these communities are spread all over Tulunadu those who settled on the northern part of Tulunadu have almost adopted the common dialect and hence the difference between the dialect and the common dialects are negligible. Those who settled on the southern part of Tulunadu are still keeping up a clear distinction in their dialect.

The social affinity of Tulu speaking groups are Brahmins, Tulu, Bunts, Goudakumbaras, Mansa, Harijans, Mogaveeras, Billavas etc.[1] A reflection of speech habits amply certifies the social customs, habits, cultural traits, ecclesiastical practices of this community. The dialectical variations can be classed under following categories:-

a. Brahmin dialect; Shivalli Brahmins and Sthanika Brahmins stands prominent in this group.
b. Jain Dialect: The dialect of Jain community is reflected here.
c. Common Dialect: This group includes the dialect of Bunts, Gowdas, Billavas, Mogaveera, Kumbaras and other castes which do not come under other categories.
d. Harijan and Tribal Dialects-Mera, Manoa and other Harijan groups and tribal communities feature here.

(a) Brahmin Dialect

The Shivalli Tulu belonged to the 'main stem' of Brahmin dialect. They were highly influenced by the Sanskrit languages. They developed their own 'linguafranca with differing modes of ecclesiastical affairs and educational overtones. Caste was the impedimency among the Brahmins which isolated their dialects with other communities. It is a difficult task to pursue Brahmin dialect. Retroflex and non-retroflex sounds of indigenous group ie, Dravidian stock of language was frequently used. This dialect of Tulu displays remarkable variations between aspirated and unaspirated sounds.

CHAPTER TWO

Future Economy

Old-age economy

HARSHA V K

According to the study of Kerala Economic Review in 2021, by 2031, 21 percent of the total population of Kerala will be old age population. If the national average of the elderly is 3.28%, the average of the elderly in Kerala is 3.95% in the population census 2011. That means the average of elderly people in Kerala is higher than the national average.

According to a study by the Kerala Economic Review, by 2031 the elderly population in other states of India will reach a maximum of 16.5%. But it can be understood that Kerala's elderly population is more.

The old-age dependency ratio in Kerala can be calculated by dividing the total number of people above 65 years of age divided by the total number of people between the ages of 16 and 64.The old age dependency ratio in Kerala was 19.6% in 2011 and will reach 26.1% by 2021 and 34.3% by 2031. But,The old age dependency ratio in all India was 14.2% in 2011 and will reach 15.7% by 2021 and 20.1% by 2031.It can be understood from the study report of the population census that the old age dependency ratio in Kerala is higher than the national dependency ratio.

According to population survey, females are more than males in old age dependency ratio in Kerala. The male old age dependency ratio in Kerala is 18.8% and the old age dependency ratio in the female is 21.5%.

It is mainly said that the Elderly population is increasing due to global phenomena, but low birth rate, high mortality and high fertility are pointed out as important reasons for the increase of Elderly population in Kerala.

Fiscal challenge in aging Kerala

According to G20 estimates, the working age population will decrease globally and the old age population will increase by the time it reaches 2060.Demographically examined, fiscal challenges include the costs of aging and the inclusive growth that results from them. It is checked based on Kerala.This policy is set on the basis of social relations. Likewise, economic relationships are examined in greater depth.

1.The aim is to further improve the need for public pension implementation and the importance of providing it.

2.To increase personal investments in the elderly.

3.To enhance specialized health systems for the elderly.

4.To spend the coverage provided by the security.

5.To improve Work-based skills development in older people.

The number of young people going to foreign countries in search of employment from Kerala is increasing every year. Studies have shown that the number of students who go to foreign countries from Kerala to study after higher education is increasing.Those who come to a foreign country for education try to get employment there and at the same time try for permanent citizenship of the foreign country.Such reasons are causing the number of young people to decrease and the number of old people to increase in Kerala.

It can be understood on the basis of Kerala that the biggest feature is that when the number of elderly people increases, the number of working age people decreases. The increase in the number of elderly people in the Kerala society often becomes a shackle for the production in various sectors of Kerala and the income received from the working people and the developments in the business sectors.

As the number of elderly people in Kerala increases, wage inflation becomes less. When more money has to be spent for the health of the elderly, it often affects the family security of Kerala.

It is added that although the tax received from the elderly in Kerala is very low, the pension and services to be provided for them in the health sector should not be considered excessive and are an important factor in the welfare of Kerala.

Work from home: issues and challenges faced by working women in the it sector (during covid-19 pandemic)

AADITHYA PRAKASH

The Covid-19 pandemic has disturbed the working condition of people around the world. An unpopular style of work seen in developed countries started catching the minds of several companies worldwide to create a new space that could remove the barrier between private and public life. Working from home enabled people to work whenever possible. As the Covid-19 progressed, the companies started giving out permanent work from home jobs to their employees since the employees' productivity increased.

The employees' productivity has started increasing based on their time as WFH employees. As the time increases, companies can notice the employees' productivity improves since they are available most of the time (Choudary, 2020).

The technology and innovation 'helped' workers to connect with their members most of the time. However, these technology innovations also have the potential to introduce work-life conflict (WLC) to the employees. WLC is increasing in the life of the employees due to the globalisation of technology and the new capitalist mode of work where people have to give more time and dedication to work, making it difficult to focus on private life (Family).

Covid-19 Pandemic

As a precautious method to stop the spread of covid-19, Prime Minister Modi announced a nationwide lockdown on 24 March 2020. The announcement of the lockdown changed every aspect of the life of Indians. The economy had a massive collapse reporting a loss of 8.8 trillion rupees and badly affected workers worldwide, pushing around 5 billion people to do work from home (Borah, 2021; Jain, 2021).

The covid-19 pandemic economic loss made some of the firms in India shut down or liquidate, making jobless to millions of people, causing them to take any available jobs during the period. During the pandemic, the private firm tried to maximise their profit by making employees work within any time limit. The I.T. sector is one of the sectors where the timing of different countries is calculated to contact their clients. Due to the massive globalisation of work, I.T. sector people are required to work at irregular times, thus increasing WLC.

Work from Home and Social Life

WFH started in the 1970s when new policies emerged in western Europe due to increased fuel prices due to the war against Arabs. These policies allowed workers to work from home or in public areas. However, in the new era, work from home resumed its strength in 2015. Most IT- based companies have started giving out options to do work from home. It is imperative to balance work and family life for many employees today. This issue is specially taken up during this pandemic time (covid19). It is challenging for the employees to meet the demands of careers, child education, home care, work placement, and other long-term stress issues. On the other hand, this work from home does not affect a specific gender. It affects both genders; this work from home problem affects both men and women.

It is generally acknowledged that stress-related problems in the workplace are costly for human well-being and societies at large (European Commission, 2002). Works allow individuals to interact with many unknown people, which gives a lot of ideas about the country and the world. They will experience and learn about different cultures, and traditions and studies individuals' mentality from a particular area. However, the social relation reduced in the individuals' space because of the work from home.

The newly recruited worker directly placed from the college may find more problems. A sudden shift from college life (social interaction, sharing, relationship) to a closed room with strangers on the call can cause anxiety. Office groups play an important role in socialising people in the office. This includes "vocational training" and the transfer of specific organisational culture and current norms and practices to individuals and social symbols and required information to interpret the following scenario.

A 2015 study by Nicholas Bloom et al. cited by Choudary (2020) found that when employees opted into WFH policies, their productivity increased by 13%. Nine months later, the same workers were given a choice between remaining at home and returning to the office. Those who chose the former saw even further improvements: They were 22% more productive than before the experiment. Productivity has become an essential thing in work.

Work

Marx, Engels and Bellamy give the ideas of the Marxist perspective of work. Bellamy wrote 'work as a burden' in the capitalist model since Marxist viewed the capitalist society as using labour as a commodity with rigid timings and ages. Engels and Marx consider work as the essential part of man. They argue that legs, hands and other sense that they develop in due course from ape to man is for work. Further evolution of work led the path to the creation of society when people started to interact with each other while working. The emergence of industrialisation and capitalism led to the division of labour. The collective form of production changed into a private one. Marxists viewed that there is a hierarchical order in work. In the capitalist society, companies are at the top of the hierarchical order and control the workers, just like how upper-class people control their slaves and other paid workers during traditional culture (Magdoff, 2006).

Marxist-feminists analyse that capitalism and the introduction of private property made disadvantages to the women population of the society. They were forced to remove from their land-ownership and other paid work. Capitalism brought the notion of private property and patriarchy, and to continue this notion, women were discarded from owning any land and were asked to look into household works. At first, capitalism had only limited capacity to change the women's status in society with the allocation of jobs for women with paid wages. Their struggle continues to the date for equal pay and unbigoted approaches. "Women's reproductive functions have either limited their work to the home or created a "second shift" problem of unpaid housework and childcare as well as waged work" (Ferguson et al., 2021).

Work as a part of a Social Contract

Many workers, especially middle-aged women with older children, point out that their social relation is their main reason for finding work outside the home (Shamir, 1976). Giddens (2017) discusses the social importance of work in the modern-day. Work is considered a social relationship and to be kept in social content. Work in the office became a trend and later became a part of life due to the advent of industrialisation. Industrialisation brought the need for division between public life and private life. There existed a division between the public and private spheres during the industrial sector, making home a place of leisure and rest. Giddens (2017) mentions that work from an office provides a 'social contract' creating personal spaces to communicate with others and make friends. There was a division between the working hours and leisure period. Still, in working from home, the time for leisure and work became invisible, and the hours they worked became more challenging to find leisure periods. Now the public sphere has come into the space of leisure, making it very difficult to manage.

Burden of Double Work and Employment crises

The double work burden for women is due to the gendered division of labour. The gendered division of labour became rigid during industrialisation and capitalism. When the notion of paid work and private property came into existence, women were asked to do unpaid household work. Their work is considered voluntary due to their love and care for family and children (Sharma,2021). Unpaid household work are due to gendered inequality (Oakley,1974, cited in Bonney &Reinach, 1993). Household works are more when children or parents are present in the house. The burden of double work and heavy household duties make people resign from the paid work (Bonney & Reinach,1993).

The structure and the model of double work have changed due to urbanisation and modernisation. A shift in gender roles brought changes in marriage and family norms. The U.S. showed a decline in the rate of marriage and divorce rate from 1960 to 2008. Women entering the workforce changed their gender roles because of modernisation and urbanisation (Lindsey, 2011). These changes had an effect on 'traditional' families, and some groups have started against women in the workforce; for example, "A Justice of Peace announced that divorces were increasing because of male unemployment generated 'a false independence among the women'" (Salzinger, 2010, p. 328).

Women in the developed and developing countries show an increase in their overall status. An increase in women participating in the education sector helped them attain literacy. Technology training enabled them to attain jobs and start their own business, making women spend less on domestic household work. Men were needed to increase their time in domestic household work (UNDP, 2009; World Bank, 2009, as cited in Lindsey, 2011).Men increased their domestic period, but their activities remained under masculine jobs. For example, plumbing, car maintenance, garbage disposal, paying bills on time, etc.

Women are still left with gendered jobs like cooking, cleaning, child care, etc. Due to changes in the family structure, children also started helping their parents. However, gendered roles are passed on to the future generation where boys spend time with fathers to learn about cars and house maintenance, and girls spend with mothers to learn about cooking, cleaning and managing households. The situation is different when there is only one child in a family.

In India, women face employment crises. Like the rest of the world, women face discrimination, receive unequal wages, and become victims of sexual assault. However, jobs for women in India are also based on their caste and religion. Most unpaid labours are done by S.C. and S.T. women, and only a few percentages of women from S.C. and S.T. categories fall into high paying jobs (Neetha, 2014). After marriage, most of the job-related discussions of women are done by their spouses. Husbands have a voice in their wife's jobs, while the wife's interference in the husband's job decision is significantly less (Chauhan,2020).

Women's Work

Tradition forms of family and norms are changing because of industrialisation and its consequences. However, new jobs are created for women with poor economic status in developing countries. When husbands are addicted to drugs and other substances, they tend to leave jobs or get fired. Women are then required to take up the jobs they get to continue their living. They are making women from developing countries like India, Sri Lanka, Mexico etc., move to other countries to work as a maid. Thus, trying to break the ceiling of men as the family's breadwinners (Gamburd, 2012).

Men were required to take care of domestic work without their female companion, but men tended not to take care of any household chores since it affected the husbands' masculinity. Leaving the country for another job creates a vacuum in caregiving for their child. A new term is given to the mother known as 'transnational motherhood'. Grandparents then look after the children. Men increased their time with their children and drank alcohol to reaffirm their masculinity (Gamburd, 2012)

Women are employed more in factory assembly line-ups and most jobs which need patience and carefulness. Managers needed more women in place of men since they believed women do not form a union and pressure the company. If they fail to find women for work, their next option will be homosexuals, who are stereotyped as naïve. Women face inequality in wages and working hours. Families in the origin countries are against women working in foreign countries. Blame will be on women for leaving the family and children, and no pressure and no accountability on men who were fired or quit their jobs because of addiction to alcohol and other drugs. Children will blame mothers for abandoning them, have emotional uncertainty and will show disrespect towards mothers (Hondagneu-Sotelo, 2012).

Gender, Technology and ICT

Technology brought division between men and women in the case of communication and technology. Internet boom and the new invention of technologies brought technology-based communication known as e-communication. E-communication has become a vital part of modern urban life. (Lindsey, 2011; Castano and Webster, 2011). However, the effect of e- communication was different for different gender.

Men were able to capture the positives of e-communication. E-communication helped men to connect with their friends and families. More men use social media platforms in India than women in all age groups. For example, male and female Facebook users aged 18-24 as of January 2018 were 73.2 and 23.4 million, respectively (Basuroy, 2022). Statistical records show the gender division/gender gap in technology and e-communication. Men who failed to connect with family and friends were able to connect again. Internet and innovation created a virtual world where men can manipulate the environment and stage events (Lindsey, 2011).

According to Lindsey (2011), men are not good in non-verbal settings. Being in an environment where they control other things considers the virtual world as "Second Life" and gives satisfaction to their relationship in the virtual world. Women excel in non-verbal cues; however, the e-communication/ virtual world mirrors women's communication. The virtual world will be challenging for women since most of the platform's rules and other norms are made by men to control the virtual communities. Thus, creating gender gaps in technology and e-communication platform use. Women are feared to use internet platforms for e-business, e- communication etc., due to 'digital threat' (Michota, 2013).

ICT is considered the emerging sector in India, Africa and other developing countries. Women's participation in ICT is significantly less, and the number of women working in senior posts in ICT companies is considerably less. Musungwini *et al.* (2020), European Parliament's Committee on Women's Rights and Gender Equality, found gender inequality in the ICT and found that 95% of future jobs need ICT support. However, ICT jobs can help women find out employment in remote or desirable job places; International Telecommunications Union considers ICT jobs as the pathway to reducing the inequality in job opportunities (Musungwini et al., 2020).

One of the reasons for the minor participant in the ICT sector can be gender stereotypes within the families. Technologies and science-based jobs are considered for men and labelled as boys' toys (Castano and Webster, 2011). Science and technology are marked for men, and women are labelled to jobs which deal with service and care. Women's job career is not in a linear approach, i.e., women do not move from school to college, college to a job and from lower post to higher post. Women are tended/required by society to take breaks for child care. This led the women to move away from the job market (Castano and Webster, 2011). Due to women moving from the ICT job market, there are significantly fewer women to act as role models or mentors for younger women. A survey done by Musungwimi et al. (2020) on ICT in Zimbabwe found that 91.49% of women face discouragement from family, friends, and society, and 76.60% of women face difficulties joining ICT because of a lack of mentors and role models. Women get into lower roles after coming to the break from the ICT sector, making women quit the job (Castano and Webster, 2011; Musungwimi et al., 2020).

COVID-19 and I.T. sector Women employees

Covid-19 changed the way how people work. It has affected more in the I.T. Technology innovation made a huge difference in India after 1991 when the Government of India approved the liberalisation of markets and industrial opportunity. Technology innovation made people available even after their working hours. During Covid-19 employees are working from home and "this hybrid approach is expected to increase in the wake of change in Covid-19 pandemic, as many businesses are splitting staff into teams with alternative WFH days to ensure social distancing" (Darouei & Helen, 2020, p. 2).

Work from home and Covid-19 made a negative impact on most of the employees (Tams et al.,2020). Employees who are not having any control on their jobs are seen as the most unsatisfied Employees. Energy and time are considered as finite thus people can only give concentration to one. If one has to give concentration towards work, then employees have little or less time to focus on family. This can lead to WLC for the employees.

Women workers have to spend extra hours along with household workers due to burden of double work. Women are found to be engaged more in unpaid household chores during Covid- 19 period and no percentage of men were not found during the study in the highest hour group range women works. It affects the productivity of the women and increases the stress. These stress and WLC will be carried forward to the next day which again increases the difficulty to manage another day (Darouei & Pluut, 2021). Thus, making make psychological problem and other health issues (Ruysseveldt, 2011).

Marimuthu and Vasudevan (2020) studied about the problem faced by women in I.T. sector working in Singapore. They were out that women are facing difficulty to manage work life and family. One highly qualified working mother was facing very difficult to manage both work life and family life. Since schools were also closed during covid-19 children were present all the time and needs the attention of parents.

Operational Definition

I.T. sector is a service-oriented sector which deals with R&D, marketing and distributing client's product with minimum cost. Innovation in the field is the key for success in I.T. sector (Taganas, & Kaul, 2006).I.T. sector in India is a service exporting sector controlled by multinational and very large firms and brings economic disparities in the country because of the accumulation of wealth in a few hands (Hutchinson & Ilavarasan, 2008).

"I.T. sector means both software development and the hardware involved in the I.T. industry including everything from computer systems, to the design, implementation, study and development of I.T., I.T. based management systems, I.T. based service provider through- platform, and I.T. based Aggregator businesses and systems" (Anonymous, n.d.).

Case Summaries:

Case Summary-1

Gowri Kumar (name changed) is a 26-year-old woman working in an I.T. sector company. She is unmarried but is in a relationship. She is staying with her parents, sibling and her grandparents. She had a total of 1 year and ten months of work experience. She had an annual salary of 5 lakhs. She has completed her MBA and has a bachelor's in Commerce. She needed to quit her former company due to heavy work during covid-19. She was facing many problems in the family and her social relationship due to WFH.Her family was unhappy when she took marketing as a field of interest, and they wanted her to take the finance field since they consider it a women-friendly job. She could not talk to her parents about her problems because she decided to work in this field.

Case Summary-2

Elsa Sara (name changed) is a regional marketing executive of a well-known paint company. She is 28-year-old, married after the second wave of covid-19 in India. She has an MBA in marketing and a bachelor's in Engineering. She was chosen for the research because she can relate to the differences in work-life and family life when she was unmarried and married during the covid-19. Her husband is working (offline mode) in an insurance company in Kerala. She lives with a joint family with her in-laws. She has a work experience of 4 years in the I.T. field. She prefers the offline mode of working since it gives enough time to move from household and other domestic work.

Case Summary-3

Devi Sree (name changed) is a commerce graduate working for the last six years. She is a thirty-year-old divorcee who stays with her parents. She got divorced during the pandemic period. She believes the WFH and covid-19 have played roles in her divorce. They got married after having three years of relationship in the office. However, WFH forced them to live in separate house due to the connectivity problems, which later caused severe fights with them. Devi Sree is valuable to the research since it shows how WFH causes disturbance in the work- life balance and conflicts, leading to several repercussions.

Case Summary-4

Monisha Dileep (name changed) is a 25-year-old finance analyst in a Bangalore-based company with an annual income of 5.2 lakhs. She has only WFH experience. She is unmarried and stays with her family, consisting of five members, including herself. She has a Master's Degree in business Administration. She considered herself a joyful, energetic person who has a lot of friend's circle. She has done her schooling under graduation and post-graduation in hostels. This made her stay away from the family for most of her life, which caused the connection/relationship with the family to be very weak. However, WFH and the pandemic helped her re-establish a strong connection with her family.

Case Summary- 5

Devika Nambiar (name changed) is a 32-year-old working mother as a Project Management associate in a well-established firm in Chennai. She has been doing WFH for the last twenty months. She is married and living in her in-law's house in Kochi, Kerala. She has a five-year- old daughter. Her husband is working in another state. She is the one who has to take care of all the household work and manage everything in the house. Her mother-in-law herself takes charge of the cooking and the kitchen. However, she feels very guilty seeing her mother-in-law work, so she takes over her duties also.

Case Summary- 6

Aarthi BS (name changed) is the youngest respondent having 24 years old and having eight months of experience. She is working as an accountant process specialist associate. She has Masters in Business Administration (Finance) and a bachelor's in engineering. She has an annual salary ranging from 6-7 lakhs. She is unmarried and is the only child of her parents. She is very much attached to her family. She considered herself blessed to have WFH. She need not spend any money on travelling, room, etc., which she should pay for if she had an offline job. She spends her leisure time with her parents and friends. She went to have a workcation with her friend.

Work from Home Challenges faced by the working women (I.T. Sector)

The I.T. sector faced one of the most significant impacts on the work-life during the covid-19 pandemic. The I.T. sector was able to transform from offline work to online mode of work (WFH) very quickly since they had resources in hand. WFH brought work into the house, which disturbed the relationship between work and private life. Working women are now available 24*7 in the home and are required to work during office hours.

Other professions which turned their office into the home had some strict hours to work. However, the I.T. companies have started imposing more work on their employees. To finish off their work, they have to sit more time than their shift. covid-19 has brought the family together after a long time. Family members like husbands, in-laws, parents and siblings who were busy pre-pandemic were able to come close and started staying together. However, these changes also brought more household work to the working women. No matter the position or the job working women have, they are required to complete their household work since women's abilities are measured by the family members based on their competency in household work (Jain, 2021).

Work-Life Balance

People tend to choose jobs that give efficient time for work and their private life. Without Work-life balance, people tend to face problems in their personal life. There, they will face work-life conflict, which can negatively affect their relationship, mental health, and physical health. Out of six respondents, five were facing difficulty in balancing work and life. They have to satisfy not only one work but i.e., their careers and households.

The long working hour is one of the main reasons for the imbalance between work and life. Some of the respondents are required to start from 9 a.m. and extend up to 11 p.m.

I am required to work from 10 a.m. to 11 p.m. most of the time. Sometimes I don't get any time to take a break. More problem is that I have to keep my video on for all the people even when I am just an attendee. This is a kind of surveillance. Because of the presence of my family members in the house due to the pandemic, I am required to close my door to reduce sound from outside. This makes me feel isolated (Gowri, 26 years old).

Demand from the family and the company can make the life of the woman miserable whether she is unmarried or married. If the girl is unmarried, she faces difficulties having conversations or having time with their family, and if she is married, they will face problems maintaining a bond, and all the pressure from both works gets on. Respondents have a conflict with their husbands regarding the nature of the work. They question why companies are providing these hectic hours.

I have to work even on Sundays. They ask us to take one holiday except for Sundays. What can I do if one of the weekdays is a holiday? I cannot spend time with my in-laws or with my husband. They have holidays at the weekends. Even during my wedding time, I could not go out to shop for my dress. I have to ask my cousins and others for that. There are times that I have to attend a meeting in the middle of National Highways. I fought with my husband regarding the time I shut off my laptop. Now I have to reduce my sleep hours to spend time with my husband (Elsa Sara, 28 years old).

Women are supposed to find time to spend with their partners or with their family, while men can stay as long as they can for the work. Thus, maintaining a work-life balance is considered necessary, especially for women. Respondents are often tired of balancing work and life; they are required to sacrifice something to have a balance. Even during the marriage, the family tries to find women who have 9-5 jobs or no jobs. So, for having a quality of life, work-life balance is the key component. Thus, if a person can find a job in a company which respects work-life balance, then he/she/can have a quality life.

Strangeness within the team

Working from home is new to everyone, but some might have started their career by working from home. New members are added to the team every month. They have only contact with each other during official calls. In the case of offline work, they can mingle with each other and can know each other. Women are the ones who are facing this problem a lot. They are not able to have any official issues with their colleagues. Even if anything happens, they cannot discuss it with other members of the team. Since the number of women in the higher ranks is significantly less, women face opening up any sexual or verbal assault.Two of the respondents state that they have faced many problems in the office space, but they do not know anyone personally and do not know anything about the internal politics between the teams.

The company have arranged a get-together party in an urban area where all the members of the different teams were called. Everyone joined the party since they wanted to know each other personally. Drinks and food were provided. A male colleague who I know from an online meeting came near me, and after a few minutes, he started doing inappropriate things. I had no one to talk to about it. No women's head was there in my team. I had to speak to the other team's women's head and have to file against him. It is now difficult to have video calls with other members (Monisha, 25 years old).

The main problem is here two- people in the meeting are talking about official things and contain no personal matter. Listening to others' life stories or their perspective about an action help people to understand others. However, here women get no opportunity like other colleagues are. Another problem is the availability of a female head where women can openly talk about their office problems. This makes women come forward to talk about the issues complex.

Issue of Double Work

In society, women are needed to do household chores and manage everything. Even if both the partners are working, women are the ones who are required to work both in careers and in private life. The issue of double work can be corporate with the problem of long working hours. As discussed in the previous section, covid-19 brought the family back home. This made more workload for women. Respondents state that they are needed to cook for more people and have to make it at different timings. Women are required to do household work when they get free time from work; after that, they need to return to their job. Some people can't get time to move out of their workplace. This situation brings work-life crises/conflict. One of the respondents can be the perfect example of a double work burden.

I have been working for the last six-year. I got married three years ago. I was living with my ex-husband near our office. However, due to covid-19, we must move back to my in-laws. Our works are very hectic, and we have long working hours. Since I have clients in the Middle East and the USA, I have uneven timings making it very difficult to do household work. This caused severe tensions with my ex-in-laws. Ex-in-law started complaining about me to my ex-husband, which made us decide to live apart for a few days. The gap became large and got divorced (Devi, 30-year-old).

Some of the respondents tend to do household even if their in-laws help them. They stated they felt guilty about it. Not only guilt, but they also fear that making in-laws work more can affect their marriage and their relationship with their parents. It is a social stigma that women are the one who does all the thing. Respondents state that their parents teach them that they should do all the housework for their in-laws, and some believe society has put this pressure on them.Child care is another work which has to be done by women. During the WFH, the mother of small children suffered a lot. Mothers have to look after their children every time since day-care facilities were closed down. Children disturb their mothers while they are working. Mothers also need to find time to help children in their online classes. The productivity of the women is reduced due to the burden of double work. Women who excel in their fields are now facing difficulties to compete with men. They have to work than then men to excel since the field is designated for men. Pressure of leakage (discussed in chapter 2) also worsen the mental health of the women. If the women take leave from their career for a period of time for child caring or bearing, they get job only in the lower position than they had.

Restriction on Women

Since most of the I.T. sector jobs are found in urban or metropolitan areas, people are needed to migrate from other places to urban areas. Women move out from the family to settle in these metro cities. Here, they experience no restriction from family members. Women can move out at night; can work till they are needed and can have socialisation with others. They can have a relationship and can spend time with their partners. However, moving back to the house-made changes to their lifestyles. Restrictions are mainly put on unmarried women in every matter.

They are required to come back home before night. They have to take permission from their parents to move out. One of the respondents said:

I liked the stay with my parent. WFH brought more bonding with family, but it also took away my freedom. Now I have to find reasons to go out with my friends and cannot talk to my partner openly (Aarthi, 24-year-old)

Respondents state that once the people get the taste of freedom, it is very difficult to go back. Women often find the office a place to socialise and work for them. However, due to lockdown, they were focused on working inside the house's four walls.

Conclusion

The study's main aim was to discuss the challenges faced by working women in the I.T. sector during the covid-19 pandemic. Pandemics have affected nearly almost the people of India. Even during the pandemic, the sufferings were also gendered biased. Domestic violence against women and children has increased, and in every profession, women face more difficulties than men (Roy, 2020). In the I.T. sector, women were already facing discrimination in the industry since the field is marked for males. Female executives or heads are very few when compared to men. I.T. companies are situated in metropolitan cities or urban cyber parks. People migrate to these areas for a job where they live as a nuclear family or stay in P.G.

Due to the sudden lockdown due to the covid-19 pandemic, they are forced to move back to their parents' house or their in-laws. This transition from urban single or nucleated family life to the joint family has brought women physical and mental weakness. The companies have started giving out heavy workloads and targets. To meet the targets, they are forced to work more than usual.

As per the societal norms, women are the ones who should take care of the household work and manage everything about the house. An increase in the number of people put pressure on both the work. As discussed in chapters two and three, women face the burden of double work. Women have to cook, clean and take care of children when they get any break from the office. Due to taking breaks, they are forced to work more than usual times. This creates conflict in the relationship with partners. The mental health of working women during the period was so weak. They used to yell out to their family members when they could not control anything.

The difference between married and unmarried women is that the time unmarried women spend on household work is less when compared to that of married women. Out of three unmarried respondents, two liked WFH and are willing to continue even after the pandemic. They were able to save money and go out with friends whenever possible. Unmarried women face restrictions from their families on going out, having food, what to wear and what to do during free time. Control of the parents on unmarried working women can be seen. This felt comfortable by all three unmarried respondents.

Women having children are the ones who are facing the most difficulties due to WFH. Even mothers having infants are happy with WFH since they can spend time with them. However, mothers having young children are facing problems. They used to disturb mothers during worktime, especially during video calls. Mothers have to look after the online classes of the children and do the necessary actions to complete their activities and homework.

Most of the challenges women face can be removed when the company starts understanding the problem and gives work that can have a work-life balance. Some of the companies offer WFH for a lifetime but also ensure work-life balance. Some European countries like Portugal, Spain, Germany etc., have implemented the right to disconnect, which allows the worker the right to sign off after their prescribed time.

In the society, women needs to do more hard work and excels in everything more than men to get recognition from the society. Discrimination in the professional jobs starts from the salary itself. Technology and science field is considered as the "Boy's field" and women are not welcomed at all from centuries ago. Covid-19 brought families together and the bond between them have increased. However, the expectation of the family from women also increased. The burden of double work, child bearing etc. are meant for women by the society. Even when women holds important offices, they are still have discrimination in the family. The division of labour is unequal in the society. The main reason for the division of labour is the gender roles set by the society itself. It is very difficult to escape from gender roles set up from the society and life of the women continuous in a difficult stage.

CHAPTER THREE

Growth and Development

Growth rate,KIIFB,Kerala bank and Infrastructural Development

HARSHA V K

Growth rate of Kerala is mainly estimated by Growth Domestic Product (GDP).When checking the ranks of Indian states, Kerala ranks 9th in terms of GDP. Kerala's growth rate reached 12.1% during 2021-22. During this period itself, Kerala's GDP per capital reached ₹257,711.But, during 2020-21, Kerala's growth was 8.43%.

Ernakulam district is known as the richest district in Kerala. Ernakulam has this kind of advantage because it is also the industrial hub of Kerala. Kerala model developments have led to the increase in GDP growth rate.

The growth rate of the agriculture sector of Kerala was 4.6 during 2021-22 compared to 0.24 per cent in 2020-21. Kerala has achieved the highest growth rate in the agricultural sector during the period 2012-13. During the period 1970-71, 29,33,000 hectares of land for agriculture purposes compared to 25,79,000 hectares in 2017-18.

In the financial year 2021-22, Kerala achieved a growth rate of 17.3% in the industrial sector. Kerala has the 15th position in terms of industrial rank in India.Major contributions of the state are all related to the service sector. Kerala ranks 8th among the IT destinations in India. The people of Kerala have a high social standard of living and a high literacy rate.

KIIFB (Kerala Infrastructure Investment Fund Board)

KIIFB is an expansion of the Kerala Infrastructure Investment Fund Board. It came into existence as a corporate body under the KIIF Act, 1999. It was started on November 11,1999 as the Infrastructural Development Fund. All the primary components of development depend on infrastructure. Policy and initiatives have been included for the infrastructure development of Kerala.It is said that the main objective of KIIFB is to invest funds for various development projects in Kerala. KIIFB is an organization that works to invest funds in the fields of irrigation, road, power, water, port, navigation, solid waste management and drainage.

An important critical gap in infrastructure is the infrastructure requirements in the vital sector. It has grown into a special Infrastructural Department jointly with the Center and Kerala. The principal fund of KIIFB was first funded on November 11,1999 under this Act 4 of 2000.It is said that the act that came in 2016 is a project that modifies the Kerala infrastructure once again. Similarly, the scope and structure of this act are amended. KIIFB also includes social infrastructure development for sustainable development. All this is financially approved by the security exchange and Board of India (SEBI) and Reserve Bank of India (RBI).

Innovative Technology's Standard Quality Maintained in KIIFB. National and international financial agencies KIIFB gives a good external rating. KIIFB mainly deals with the health sector, water supply, power supply, education and transportation.The chairperson of KIIFB is the Kerala Chief Minister and the ice chairperson is the Kerala Finance Minister.The main member is the Chief Secretary to the Government. Also, it includes four other important members. Other important members are the Vice Chairman of the State Planning Board, Legal Secretary, Finance Secretary and Finance Resources Secretary. Apart from them, they are the main bosses of 7 independent institutions and all of them are related to the fields of finance, banking and economics.

KIIFB is a group of Non-Convertible and non-Statutory Lending Rate (Non SLR) bonds by private placement funds that can be backed by a government guarantee.Various infrastructural projects through deposits through the treasury of Government funds for KIIFB are also collected through schemes. KIIFB is helping to address criticism that large infrastructure projects in Kerala are taking too long to raise funds.

All bond systems and government approved general obligation bonds are used as Alternative Investment funds (AIF) to collect funds for long term and medium term. The Infrastructural Investment Trust (InVIT) and the Infrastructure Debt Fund (IDF) remain the institutional framework of KIIFB. Funds for purchasing Special Purpose Vehicles (SPV) required for the infrastructure development of Kerala are also provided through KIIFB. KIIFB will be remembered for giving a bright chapter to Kerala's infrastructure in times to come.

Kerala bank

Kerala State Cooperative Bank Banks later came to be known as Kerala Bank. State Bank was formed out of a concept that there was a need for a bank for Kerala following the merger of State Bank of Kerala with SBI.The mission of Kerala Bank is to work as a strong, sound and leading organization. Kerala Bank acts as a backbone for financial security in rural areas. Fulfilling social responsibilities, professional ethics and profitability are the main function of Kerala Bank.

Kerala Bank has been able to provide good value for money services to rural customers. Kerala Bank stands for good behavior towards customers. IFS code is provided in all branches of Kerala Bank. Similarly, the KSCB customer policy also exists. Account opening forms of Kerala Bank are available online. There are various types of deposit schemes available in Kerala Bank. Kerala Bank also provides necessary loans to fulfill the customer's dreams. Kerala Bank charges a small service charge.

The Kerala State Cooperative was formed in the early 20th century. Around 1914, the Travancore Co-operative Societies Regulation Act was enacted under the leadership of Sri Moolam Thirunal Ramavarma under the Maharajas of Travancore. In 1915 it was named Trivandrum Central Cooperative Bank.The bank became fully functional on 18th January 1916. The bank started with a capital of 100000 rupees and one thousand shares of 100 rupees each. In the beginning there were only 16 cooperative societies and 69 members in Kerala.

Infrastructural development

Infrastructural development is intended to carry out basic and advanced construction works to raise the economic growth of Kerala and raise the standard of living of the people.Thiruvananthapuram, Kochi, Kozhikode, Kannur have 4 international ports in Kerala. Kerala has eighteen sea ports. The International Port at Vizhinjam is under construction. There are also three intermediate ports and 14 minor ports in Kerala. The road density of Kerala is 446 km/100 km. The main roads in Kerala include National Highways with a length of 1457 meters and State Highways with a length of 4460 km. Kerala has a railway network with a network spread over 1148 km with 200 stations.

The renovation of schools and hospitals in the government sector in Kerala is going on. In some places, the renovation of schools and hospitals in the government sector has been completed. Infrastructural development related to the higher education sector has been very slow in the government sector. In many places, development work is not going on in the institutions related to the higher education sector.

Electricity is provided in Kerala in a low-cost manner for domestic and commercial purposes. It is said that 100% electrification has been done in Kerala. 2087.23 MW is provided by KSEB and 570.016 MW by NTPC.

Malappuram district is the district in Kerala with 100% computer literacy.KFON is enlarged by Kerala Fibre Optic Network.KFON is a low-cost network system under the leadership of the Kerala Government, came into existence in 2023.

CHAPTER FOUR

Tribal Poverty and Women

Tribal Poverty and Livelihood in Kerala

DEVI V

Kerala is a southern most state in India, known for its abundant natural resources and high levels of social development. It is home to several indigenous communities, commonly known as Tribals. According to 2011 Census data, the Scheduled Tribes population in Kerala is 4.75 lakhs, which is about 1.5% of Kerala's total population. Officially there are 36 tribal communities recognised in Kerala, and they are predominantly concentrated in the forest and hilly areas of the state, especially in the districts of Wayanad, Palakkad, Idukki and Malappuram (Kerala Public Service Commission, Government of Kerala).

Despite the state's overall social progress, the tribal communities still continue to face poverty and marginalization in the society. Here we try to explore the various factors behind tribal poverty in Kerala, the challenges faced by these communities, and possible solutions to address their issues.

Historical Context

Tribal communities have inhabited Kerala for centuries. They were popularly known by the name "Adivasis" or indigenous people. The history of the tribal communities in Kerala has been marked by a number of significant events and development. During the pre-colonial era, the tribal communities in Kerala were highly self-sufficient and maintained a strong relation with the land and the environment. They had their own culture and tradition, and their economic and social systems were based on a communal ethos. However the arrival of colonizers from Europe and the Arab world led to the displacement of tribal communities from their lands. In particular, the Britishers established large areas of tea, spices and coffee plantations in the state, which led to the large-scale deforestation. The British implemented the Forest Act in 1927, which restricted the movement of tribals in forest areas. The tribals were forced to work as laborers on these plantations, often under oppressive conditions and were subjected to exploitation by the British officials.

After independence, the Indian Government took steps to address the issues faced by tribal people, including the implementation of land reforms and introduction of special development programs for tribal communities. A significant piece of legislation that aims to protect the land rights of tribal communities in the state is the Kerala Scheduled Tribes (Restriction on Transfer of Lands and Restriction of Alienated Lands) Acts in 1975. But it has been limited and ineffective due to several reasons.

Current Scenario

The majority of the tribal population concentrated in engaging agriculture and forestry-related activities. According to a report published by the State Planning Commission, the ST population in Kerala has the highest poverty ratio among all the states in India. The districts such as Idukki and Wayanad have a ratio as high as 66%. The literacy rate among the tribal communities in Kerala is only 71.4% compared to the state's overall literacy rate of 93.9% (Census of India, 2011).

Understanding Tribal Poverty in Kerala

Poverty among tribal communities is a result of various factors including, lack of access to education, historical marginalization, health care, limited economic opportunities and so on. According to Census Data 2011, only 26.5%

of tribal households in Kerala have access to safe drinking water, compared to the state average of 68.5%. Also, only 10% of them have access to sanitation, compared to the state average of 75%. From this, we can understand that the tribal population still faces difficulties while accessing basic amenities.

Tribal population is no longer unique with the Human Development Indicators. Tribal groups such as Malayarayan, Kurichyar and Kuruman are forward tribes based on their better off HDI profile of 0.6 points. While the Muthuvan, Adiyan and Kattunaikyans etc have a low HDI profile of 0.4 points (Sunitha, 2014).

The poor among the STs in Kerala constitute 3% of the total BPL population in the state, while their total population is only 1.14%. With respect to the incidence of poverty among all sections, the ST community face severe poverty, which is about 3 times much higher than the overall population (GOK Report, 2008).

Several factors contribute to tribal poverty in Kerala, including:

- *Landlessness*: A significant proportion of tribal households in Kerala are landless or have small landholdings, which limits their capacity to generate income from agriculture and other rural livelihoods. According to the latest data from the Kerala State Planning Board, around 52% of tribal households in the state are landless.
- *Lack of access to health care facilities* is another challenge faced by the tribal population in Kerala. Many tribal communities live in remote areas, far from health care facilities. The lack of access to health care increases the risk of illness and disease, which can further exacerbate poverty. According to the National Family Health Survey-5 (NFHS-5), only 45% of tribal households in Kerala have access to basic health care facilities.
- *Exploitation and marginalization*: Tribal communities in Kerala often face exploitation and marginalization from dominant groups. This can take various forms, including exploitation in labor markets, denial of access to resources, and discrimination in social and political spheres. A study conducted by the Centre for Development Studies (CDS) in 2012 found that tribal households in Kerala often face wage discrimination, with lower wages than non-tribal households for the same work.
- *Dependence on forest resources*: Many tribal communities in Kerala depend on forests for their livelihoods, such as collecting and selling forest produce. However, with increasing deforestation and forest degradation, their access to forest resources has reduced, impacting their income and livelihoods.
- *Lack of Access to Credit and Markets*: Tribal communities in Kerala also face a lack of access to credit and markets, which limits their ability to invest in income-generating activities. According to a report by the Centre for Development Studies, Thiruvananthapuram, around 75% of tribal households in Kerala do not have access to credit from formal financial institutions.
- *Lack of Access to Education*: Tribal communities in Kerala also face a lack of access to education, which limits their opportunities for employment and economic mobility. According to the 2011 Census, the literacy rate among the tribal population in Kerala is only 71.4%, which is lower than the state average of 93.9%. This low literacy rate results in limited employment opportunities, as most of the jobs in Kerala require basic education and skills. As a result, the tribal communities are mostly engaged in low-paying jobs, such as agricultural labor and manual work.

For centuries, they have been denied access to education, healthcare, and other basic amenities, which has resulted in a lack of economic and social mobility. As a result, they have remained trapped in a cycle of poverty, where their economic and social status has remained stagnant.

Livelihoods of Tribal Communities in Kerala

The tribal communities in Kerala have traditionally depended on agriculture, forest-based activities, and hunting and gathering for their livelihood. They practice shifting cultivation, locally known as 'Podu,' where they clear a small area of the forest, cultivate crops for a few years, and then move to a new location. They also collect non-timber forest products like honey, medicinal plants, and bamboo. Hunting and fishing are also integral to their livelihood, but these practices are now restricted by conservation laws.

Tribal communities in Kerala are facing numerous challenges to their livelihoods, primarily due to the loss of their traditional lands and resources, as well as their exclusion from mainstream development processes. Here are some of the challenges faced by these communities:

- *Land Alienation*: Tribal communities have lost access to their traditional lands, which has impacted their livelihoods. According to a report by the Scheduled Tribes Development Department of Kerala, land alienation affects 90% of the tribal population in the state.
- *Lack of Access to Education and Skills Training*: Many tribal communities lack access to education and skills training, which limits their employment opportunities. According to the 2011 Census of India, the literacy rate among the tribal population in Kerala is only 76.48%, compared to the overall literacy rate of 96.2%.
- *Low Agricultural Productivity*: Agricultural productivity among tribal communities in Kerala is low, which affects their income and food security. According to a study by the Indian Council of Agricultural Research, tribal farmers in Kerala have a lower yield per hectare than non-tribal farmers.
- *Limited Access to Markets*: Tribal communities in Kerala have limited access to markets, which limits their ability to sell their products and generate income. According to a report by the Tribal Welfare Department of Kerala, only 12% of tribal households in the state have access to markets.
- *Vulnerability to Natural Disasters*: Tribal communities in Kerala are vulnerable to natural disasters such as floods and landslides, which can cause damage to their homes and crops. According to the National Disaster Management Authority, Kerala has experienced 18 major floods and landslides between 2005 and 2021.

As a result, many tribal communities have diversified their livelihoods by engaging in wage labor, small-scale agriculture, and other economic activities.

Government Interventions and Tribal Development Programs

The government of Kerala has launched a range of interventions and development programs to address tribal poverty and promote their overall well-being. These include the implementation of the Scheduled Tribes and Other Traditional Forest Dwellers (Recognition of Forest Rights) Act, 2006, which seeks to recognize and restore the forest rights of tribal communities. Other initiatives include the provision of healthcare services, the establishment of tribal schools, and the promotion of micro-enterprises and self-help groups. Some of the programs include the Tribal Sub Plan (TSP), the Integrated Tribal Development Project (ITDP), and the Vanitha Samrakshana Yojana (Women Protection Scheme).

- The *Tribal Sub Plan* is a special provision under which funds are allocated specifically for the welfare of tribal communities. The funds are used to provide education, healthcare, housing, and other basic amenities to the tribes.
- The *Integrated Tribal Development Project* aims to provide a holistic approach to the development of tribal communities in Kerala. The project focuses on providing education, healthcare, and economic opportunities to the tribes.
- The *Vanitha Samrakshana Yojana* is a scheme that provides financial assistance to women from tribal communities. The scheme aims to empower women and provide them with the means to become self-sufficient.

Impact of Government Policies and Programs on Tribal Poverty and Livelihoods in Kerala

Despite the implementation of several government policies and programs, tribal poverty and livelihoods in Kerala continue to face significant challenges. One of the key challenges is the lack of political will and commitment to effectively implement these programs. Other challenges include the lack of access to credit and markets, inadequate infrastructure, and the impact of climate change. Many of the programs suffer from inadequate funding, bureaucratic inefficiencies, and lack of accountability.

Another critical challenge is the lack of participation of tribal communities in the decision-making process. Many of the policies and programs are designed without taking into account the specific needs and challenges faced by these communities, which results in ineffective implementation and lack of impact.

However, there are also opportunities for tribal development, particularly through the promotion of sustainable livelihoods, the empowerment of women and youth, and the use of technology and innovation.

Conclusion

Tribal poverty and livelihood in Kerala is a complex and multifaceted issue that requires a holistic and integrated approach to address. While government interventions and development programs are important, they need to be complemented by a range of other initiatives, including the empowerment of tribal communities, the recognition of their cultural identity and rights, and the promotion of sustainable livelihoods. By working together, stakeholders can help to ensure that tribal communities in Kerala are able to live with dignity, respect, and prosperity.

Socio-Cultural amplitudes of Women's discriminations in rural societies

SREETHI KRISHNAN U & Dr. C. A. PRIYESH

Now a day Women Empowerment is a common term that widely used everywhere necessarily and unnecessarily. We make terrible speeches, discussions, plans and policies for women's empowerment, but does it ultimately seem to make any difference in the lives of the women around us? This is definitely a fact that needs to be analyzed. It is important to look at what has changed in the lives and outlook of women in society. To understand this, we need to study how different socio-cultural contexts affect the lives of women. This study examined various socio-cultural factors which influence the Empowerment of Rural Women. The objective is to analyze the role of socio-cultural factors on the empowerment of women among the rural area of Kerala. Random sampling method was employed in selecting 45 families in Pattazhy. From the rural areas of Kerala Pattazhy is selected through convenience sampling technique. The population for the study was 82 females from these families and this served as the sample size. A structured questionnaire prepared in 5-point Likert Scale was administered to the respondents for data collection. This study proves that different socio-cultural contexts have greatly influenced the thinking and life of women in rural areas. Women empowerment can only be fully extended to society if it gains the self-confidence to challenge all the cultural and social conditions that hinder its growth.

"Women empowerment is the provision of women with the means, skills, and opportunities to be independent, make their own choices and lead a life free of all sorts of violence and discrimination. (Nada Hamza, sexual and reproductive rights specialist, United Nations Population Fund). "There is no empowerment without rights, so women's empowerment needs to be anchored in human rights which provide a universal framework for monitoring. For women to be empowered, they need resources, respect, and voice. This requires redressing women's socioeconomic disadvantage, addressing stereotyping, stigma, and violence, and strengthening women's agency, voice, and participation." (Papa Seck, Chief statistician, UN Women).

"Women make up half of the world's population, and form a crosscutting group that overlaps all other groups in society. Compared to other disadvantaged or socially excluded groups, the household and family relations play a central part in women's disempowerment." (Boender, 2002). For an individual's development and functioning, there had a pivotal role for socio- cultural factors of their living environment. Socio-cultural factors are deeply rooted elements of a particular society and encompass the values, attitudes, norms, practices, institutions and related ways of a society (Maherukh Khan, 2017). They can have an influence on individual's behavior and lifestyle. Therefore, in order to assess the upliftment of women in a society, it is sufficient to study the socio-cultural components of that environment. This is because his surroundings play a huge role in shaping a man's thinking, wisdom and discernment.

Rural Urban difference in Kerala exists in women's empowerment also as in all Sectors. Therefore, a study of the current living conditions of women in the very hinterland of Kerala will help in overcoming the shortcomings of the existing women empowerment schemes and plans. The study examined socio-cultural factors on Economic Empowerment of Rural Women through primary research. This study was conducted in Pattazhy, an inland village in Kollam district in the state of Kerala. When we sit in the urban area where we live and think about the aspect of Woman Empowerment, all we see is progressive things. But when I had to live for a while in an inland countryside like Pattazy, the female community I saw around me prompted me to reconsider my thinking. It was that rethinking that led to this study. The purpose of this article is to assess the role of socio-cultural factors on the empowerment of women in the rural areas of Kerala.

Women empowerment refers to making women powerful to make them capable of deciding for themselves. But unfortunately, not every woman today lives in a situation where women can even decide their own thing.

Those who think that I am the one, who decides their own matter, will have to say that they are in a fool's paradise. This is because each woman finds her own place adventurously through the many constraints that the situation around them imposes. Women live their own life in a way that they think appropriate on the basis of their condition of family circumstances, qualities and capabilities of which they themselves are the best judges (Maherukh Khan, 2017). His socio-cultural factors play a crucial role in determining an individual's personality and character formation depending on one's social value. Socio-cultural factors are things that can affect our lifestyles as a society. Women can attain empowerment if they themselves challenge the prevalent traditions and culture of any society to effectively maintain their own well-being (Kabeer, 2001; Swain & Wallentin; 2009).

Socio-cultural factors are deeply rooted elements of a particular society and it directly and indirectly influence the lives of individuals. They are the facts and experiences that definitely had inculcating through generations. That is why injustice, discrimination and violence against women are being celebrated and passed down through the generations as our community cultural manifestations. Women's discrimination is reinforced by various socio-cultural norms which have been primarily created from the household itself. If each family adopts a progressive attitude towards the upliftment of the women involved, it will have the potential to make a difference in society as a whole. Therefore, by taking the lives of women in different families as the subject of study, it will be possible to assess role of various socio-cultural factors in the life of women and helps to take steps to address the shortcomings and to point out the changes in the attitude of women. The attitude of women is inextricably linked with the empowerment of women and hence the study of the various socio-cultural themes that shape the attitudes of each individual helps to measure the self-sufficiency achieved by women in a society.

Socio-cultural factors such as beliefs, social structure, economic structure, political structure, arts and entertainment all have a decisive influence on the life of the individual, especially women. Amongst important internalized social and cultural values are the general beliefs about responsibilities and behaviors deemed appropriate for women and men (Eccles et al., 1983; Eagly, 1987; Williams and Best, 1990; Corrigall and Konrad, 2007). Individuals holding traditional gender role beliefs support women's role as the caretaker at home and in the family and men's role is to provide financial support as the breadwinner of the family. Traditional cultural practices reflect values and beliefs held by members of a community for periods often spanning generations. Every social grouping in the world has specific traditional cultural practices and beliefs, some of which are beneficial to all members, while others are harmful to a specific group, such as women. These harmful traditional practices include female genital mutilation (FGM); forced feeding of women; early marriage; the various taboos or practices which prevent women from controlling their own fertility; nutritional taboos and traditional birth practices; son preference and its implications for the status of the girl child; female infanticide; early pregnancy; and dowry price. Despite their harmful nature and their violation of international human rights laws, such practices persist because they are not questioned and take on an aura of morality in the eyes of those practicing these (Harmful traditional practices, OHCHR).

The traditional gender social roles are consistent with stereotypical traits attributed to men and women. The traditional social roles of women and men have remained unchanged for many years (Barska, 2005; Diekman and Goodfriend, 2006). The traditional social role of women is that of the lady of the house, taking care of the family, being focused on children and their happiness. Traditional occupational roles attributed to women are related to caring for others (e.g., home keeper, nurse) and require communal characteristics (e.g., kind, sensitive) (Eagly et al., 2000).

A woman's personal preference is the key factor in determining whether she will seek out and engage in paid work or to continue in unpaid work. However, this preference is heavily influenced by socio-economic constraints and pressure to conform to traditional gender roles. Social Norms also plays a vital role in depriving women of their equal economic rights. Women in India are traditionally taught to be financially dependent, and independence acts as a threat to male dominance. Restrictions are imposed on them at an early stage of education itself. This ultimately leads to no professional or job-based skills. Women eventually lose their enthusiasm for participating in the workforce. Women's choices are suppressed, and many constraints are imposed on their participation in the economy, which results in their economic exclusion. Most women have no equitable access to assets, credit, capital or property rights

(International Center for Research on Women). What we learned from the survey for this study women want to be in paid employment, but a persistent set of socio-economic barriers keep them out of the workforce. Identifying and quantifying these barriers helps to develop smarter policy responses for eliminating them. The massive entry of women into active economic life has only rarely been matched by a corresponding improvement in their living or working conditions, says the International Labor Organization.

Socio-Cultural Barriers of Rural Women Empowerment

Infinite number of matters are prevailing in our society which knowingly or unknowingly influencing and questions the esteemed existence of the women folks in a society. Some major issues are like Social Barriers, Family Ties, Lack of Educational facility, Early Marriage, Male dominated society, Lack of family support, Lack of access to finance, etc. profound as which needed severe attention.

In this section with the help of my study, I concerned to explore how socio-cultural norms influence on women's discriminations based on women's own opinions, attitudes and experiences through depth-interviews and observation. It is generally we believed that discrimination between men and women occurs within the home, in a larger sense it does not originates from home and exists only within the home. It is simply an element in a system that subordinates women through social norms that define women's place and guide their conduct. From socio-cultural belief, sons are desired and valued for carrying forward the family name and providing security to their parents in old age. This indicates that parents and family give lower value to girls since their birth; and that this is translated into their lifelong neglect. These reflect on one of respondent's story to whom I interviewed:

"When I delivered my first daughter, my mother-in-law did not ready to meet or hold the baby. After giving birth, when I returned to my husband's house with my baby, they didn't perform the custom of performing an aarti for the mother and the new born baby, only because I had a daughter, they were not ready for that. But the second time I had a son, all these ceremonies were performed and I was greeted with joy."

Such stories are common in Kerala, especially in rural areas. Parents rarely want a daughter as a child. It is recognized that in rural Kerala most of the people live in absolute poverty. Conversely, due to socio-cultural practice, parents need to pay dowries for daughter's weddings. Sometimes, therefore, it is difficult to bear the expenses of daughter's weddings. In that case, poverty can be explained as the reason for discrimination against daughter.

The traditions and customs that exist in our societies towards women sometimes hinder them from growing and thriving. Caste and religions dominate each other and hinder women development, especially in rural areas they face more barriers. In our society women are very emotionally attached to their families. They are less practical so they need to do all the household works and look after children and other members of the family. They over burden themselves with family responsibilities like care of children, extra attention to husbands, and in-laws which takes away lots of their time and energy. One respondent she is my nearest neighbor told me several times that

"It is very difficult to meet household expenses, there is no fulfillment without going to work, but who is there to take care my two small children and aged mother-in-law".

Women in rural areas who are educated are provided either less or inadequate education than their male counterpart partly due to poverty, Early marriage, low socioeconomic status, partly due to son's higher education. Lack of education is one of the biggest obstacles for rural women for engaging in workforce. Due to lack of proper educational facilities rural women can't able to educate themselves and became unaware about new technologies. Culturally, especially in rural contexts girls were not given equal opportunity to study as boys; So, they had limited education and training, which would be affected effective performance in later life. It's result in early marriage of a girl child and it is one of the major obstacles in the rural areas for women empowerment and education. In some parts of the nation, guardians and parents think that girls are their burden. So, they always try to marry them.

In our constitution there are equal rights for men and women but in real sense equality does not exist in rural areas. Women are being neglected in many spheres of life. Women are not treated as equal to men. As far as rural areas are concerned, people have a set attitude that women are only for household work. Their entry to work force needs the approval of the head of the family. Earning bread for family has traditionally been seen as a male preserve and male dominated. All these put a break in the growth of women folks. In a patriarchal system where the man decides everything and the woman listens or accepts orders, it will be difficult for parents to decide who should go to school. Children's voices are not heard nor are they allowed giving their opinion, especially if they are girls. These reflect on respondent's story who shared with me:

"My parents allowed my brother to go to Bangalore for his degree but they did not even allow me to go to college in Thiruvananthapuram for my degree, and after my degree, they will marry me off and say that they will not be able to teach me more."

The support of the husband in fulfilling family responsibilities can be extremely helpful for those females who wants to do a job. Study says that husbands do not play an active role in the daily household responsibilities – the fact that females need to leave their family and children for pursuing their dreams. They receive no appreciation for their work and in most cases, they are discouraged. Researches emphasizing that lack of access to finance is also one of the major barriers that female population face in our society. A majority of the females does not own family property or personal savings and assets. It will badly affect their personal decision making and autonomy. Given table 1, provide numerical evidence that what I described in this article.

Socio-Cultural Factors influence Women Empowerment include that followed below it.

Male dominated society hinder the personal and economic development,Family ties affect individual development, Lack of motivation from family/ husband for achieving education and engaging in workforce hinder the personal development, Lack of progressive social attitude affect the empowerment of women, Marriage before getting a job hinder the individual development, Sole responsibility of childcare and elder's care hinder economic empowerment, Lack of personal property and assets hinder the economic independence and autonomy, Dowry and related issues can have a detrimental effect on a woman's self-esteem and life, Lack of educational facilities in rural areas hinder the empowerment of women,Socio-cultural factors that strongly persists in rural areas acts as a barrier against women development,Poor quality of road networks affects the ease of engaging in workforce,Lack of skills and awareness of new technology hinder the economic empowerment of rural women,Different socio-cultural contexts existing in rural areas hinder study and work abroad,Attitude of rural people disrupts health and beauty care and Inability to have access to credit facility is one of the major factors that affect the economic empowerment of the rural women.

Conclusion and suggestions

Through this study we have come to understand that a lot of socio-cultural factors in the rural areas are dragging down the empowerment of women to a great extent. The following are some of the important factors.

- Lifestyle based on religious superstition and tradition.
- Lots of traditional abuses and some social restrictions.
- Strict mentality related to cultural beliefs, religious thoughts and gender roles.
- Very narrow minded because they do not have much contact with the outside world.
- Lack of education and awareness about new information technologies.
- Less involvement and role in economic and social life and decision making.

The following are some suggestions to overcome the socio-cultural barriers that hinder the women's empowerment,

- If we want to change the lives of women in our patriarchal society, we must first take steps to improve men's attitudes toward women.
- Women are recorded in society as the bearers of culture and tradition, so if progressive and authentic knowledge is imparted to women, they will be able to correct themselves and nurture the next generation.
- Create an environment for women to work easily and live with self-respect by providing affordable childcare facilities, skill training and encouragement for women seeking employment after the break.
- Provide awareness about the legal system aimed at eliminating all forms of discrimination against women.
- Along with education, raise awareness about information technology and the progressive changes in the world around us.

- Changing community practices and social attitudes by active participation and involvement of women.
- Equal access to participation and decision making in all sectors of life.

In remote communities, training and employment opportunities are extremely scarce.

One issue is the lack of infrastructure to support training, education and employment. There was a clear message from women in regional and remote areas about the lack of opportunities to participate in the paid workforce. Other barriers to workforce participation in regional and remote regions involve limited transport options and a lack of training and development opportunities. Many women commented on the difficulty of re-entering the paid workforce after a

break to care for children. Issues raised included the availability of work at the same

level, control over the hours of work, lack of family/spouse support, lack of family friendly workplace policies and the need for skills development. Women particularly those in the rural areas need education, economic and social power to actualize their advancement.

After all, change is needed in the mental state of women. Violence and inequality against women can be completely eradicated only if girls have the knowledge and courage to recognize and break the shackles of tradition and belief that have bound them invisibly. It is the responsibility of every individual to dream of his own upliftment, regardless of socio-cultural circumstances. Without empowering every woman to acquire education and wisdom, understand her own mistakes and adapt to the changes of the times, society will not be able to achieve female empowerment.

Status of Women in Kerala

ASHNA

Kerala, a state located in the southwest of India, has made significant progress in terms of women's empowerment and gender equality. Kerala's literacy rate is among the highest in India with female literacy rates being almost equal to that of males. Women in Kerala enjoy greater access to education and healthcare compared to other parts of India, which has contributed to their increased participation in the workforce. Kerala has a high female labour force participation rate and women are employed in various sectors including healthcare, education, and information technology.

Kerala has also implemented several measures to promote gender equality, such as the introduction of a 50% reservation for women in local government bodies, and initiatives to address issues such as gender-based violence and discrimination.

Despite these positive developments, there are still some challenges that women in Kerala face, such as a persistent gender pay gap, limited representation in higher levels of government, and continued discrimination and violence against women. However, overall, the status of women in Kerala is relatively high compared to other parts of India.

Empowerment is a continuous process of realising the goals of equality and human liberation and freedom. Women's empowerment implies equality of opportunity and equity between the genders, ethnic groups, social classes and age groups, collective participation in different spheres of life etc. The major landmark in the field of women empowerment was brought about by 73rd and 74th amendments in the first half of the 90's in which 33% reservation to the women in the Panchayats and Municipalities was made mandatory

Sex ratio in Kerala

As of 2021, the sex ratio in Kerala, India is 1,084 females per 1,000 males. This means that there are more females than males in the state. The sex ratio in Kerala has been consistently higher than the national average, which is 933 females per 1,000 males. The higher sex ratio in Kerala is attributed to several factors, including better healthcare facilities, higher literacy rates, and increased awareness and education about gender equality. However, it is important to note that sex ratio alone does not necessarily indicate gender equality or women's empowerment, as there are many other social, economic, and cultural factors that contribute to women's well-being and status in society.

The Gender Inequality Index (GII)

It is the latest index for measurement of gender disparity which was introduced by UNDP in the Human Development Report, 2010. Gender inequalities in three important aspects of human development are measured by this index. The three aspects are,

1) Reproductive health which is measured by maternal mortality ratio and adolescent birth rates

2) Empowerment is measured by the proportion of parliamentary seats occupied by females and proportion of adult females and males with secondary education.

3) Economic status expressed as labour market participation.

The GII of 155 countries has been calculated and according to the value of GII, these 155 countries have been ranked. India's rank in Gender Inequality Index is 130 and the GII value of India is 0.563 while that of the top ten countries is below 0.05. The indicators highlight areas in need of critical policy intervention and it stimulates proactive thinking and public policy to overcome systematic disadvantages of women.

Literacy Rate and Education

Female Literacy Rate in Kerala (92%) is the highest among Indian states. However, the Male Literacy Rate in Kerala is still higher at 96%. Hence a small gender gap exists. (Census, 2011) in table 4.1.

Year	Persons	Male	Female
1951	47.18	58.35	36.43
1981	78.85	84.56	73.36
1991	89.81	93.62	86.17
2001	90.92	94.20	87.86
2011	93.91	96.02	91.61
2012	93.95	96.21	91.99
2013	94.01	96.41	92.09
2014	94.36	96.67	92.65
Source: Kerala State Literacy Mission Authority, 2014			

Table 4.2 Girls in Enrolment- at Different levels-2015-16

	Boys	Girls	Total	% of Girls
School Education	1907811	1864910	3772721	49.43
Higher Secondary	168191	187606	355797	52.73
Graduation	226500	155520	70980	68.66
Post Graduation	14029	22883	30294	75.54
B Tech	4022	2348	6370	36.86
M Tech	607	768	1375	55.85
Total Engineering	4629	3116	7745	40.23
Polytechnic	10518	21587	32105	32.76

Source: DPI, DCE and DTE, 2015

In the case of education, enrolment is universal at the primary level and gender parity has been achieved. Girl students constitute 49.4 % of total student enrolment in schools,

showing more or less uniformity. Girls outnumbered boys in terms of enrolment in higher secondary education at 52.73%. Dropout rates are low for both boys and girls. At the tertiary level also, the enrolment of girls is higher than boys. For example, girls constitute 68.66 percent of total enrolment for degree courses in various Arts & Science colleges under the four general universities in Kerala during 2014-15. When Post Graduation is considered, the girls" position is highest with 75.54%. Hence, girls are well off in terms of education in Kerala. But when the intake of girls in engineering colleges and polytechnics is considered, the situation is different. Out of the total enrolled students, girls constitute only 40.23% in engineering colleges and 32.76% in polytechnics.

Women's Participation in Employment

Women of Kerala outperform their counterparts in many developmental indicators. But in the case of economically independent indicators, it is not favourable to women. In countries with high human development, the share of economically independent women seems to be high. The Labour Participation Rate (LPR) of women in 10 countries having the highest Human Development Index is around 60 and that of men is around 70 as per the Human Development Report of 2015. But as per the 68th Round of NSSO, a wide gap between male and female LPRs is seen in the State. The female LPR in Kerala is 35.4 and that of male is 82.4. It means that the difference between Male and Female LPR is very high in Kerala.

As per Census of 2011 the last decade the FWPR of the state has increased by 2.8 points . Four districts in Kerala such as Kannur, Kozhikode, Malappuram and Pathanamthitta have FWPR is lower than that of the State as a whole. The performance of Kozhikode and Malappuram is too pathetic. Two districts, Wayanad and Idukki have FWPR is higher than the all-India rate. Idukki has the highest FWPR in the State as the women in the rural sector of the agrarian district are more economically active and independent.

It is to note that Female LPR is much higher in some of our neighbouring countries, whose HDI rank is lower than that of India. For example, Female LPR in Bhutan is 66.4, in Cambodia it is 78.9, in Bangladesh it is 57.3, in Nepal it is 54.3, and in Myanmar it is 85.7 as per the Human Development Report of 2014. It argued that, it may not be possible to increase the LPR of a country beyond a particular level due to various educational and family commitments of persons. So, a very high FLPR of this kind may not be feasible. However, it cannot be ignored that less women in the labour force means under-utilisation of human resources. That says the back productivity and economic growth.

When we consider the Work Participation Rate (WPR) of women in Kerala, it is lower than that of many states in India as well as all India average. According to Census 2011, the average WPR is 25.21 in India and that of Kerala is only 18.23. The FWPR of Kerala is one of the lowest in the country and also far below the national level.

Work Participation Rates of Males and Females in Kerala

In Himachal Pradesh the female workforce participation rate of 44.82 is the best performer. It is surprising that the North-eastern states like Nagaland, Sikkim, Manipur, Mizoram, Arunachal Pradesh and Meghalaya have higher FWPR than Kerala as the NSSO Report of the 68th Round. Hence it is high time to have a relook at our strategies in this direction and learn from experiences elsewhere.

Self-employment plays an important role in enhancing the share of economically active and independent women in Kerala where the educational level is very high. Even with the large number of opportunities for self-employment, the share of female self-employed workers is significantly lower in Kerala than in many other states in India. The percentage of female self-employed workers (FSEW) in Kerala is 36.4 in rural areas and in urban areas is 36.3. But in rural areas, the percentage of FSEW is 89.5 in Arunachal Pradesh, 87.9 in Himachal Pradesh, 94.9 in Nagaland and 90.2 in Sikkim. In all these North Eastern states, FWPR is above 35% as per the NSSO Report of 68th Round.

Gender disaggregated data on employment can give a clearer picture of women's economic empowerment. The sectoral distribution of employment of women in Kerala presented in figure the table 4.3 shows that women are more engaged in agriculture but more males are engaged in service and industry.

Sectors	Agriculture	Industry	Service
Total	25.5	31.8	42.7
Female	31.9	30.4	37.7
Male	22.8	32.4	44.8

source:-Work participation rate of male and female (NSSO Report)

The analysis of figures makes it clear that women's participation in traditional industries are very high in which wage or remuneration are comparatively low. For example among the cashew workers and beedi workers if the women constitute 95% and 99% respectively.

Political Leadership of women

Political representation is an important indicator to measure Gender position in many of the Indices. For example, the Gender Inequality Index developed by UNDP measures empowerment, by the proportion of parliamentary seats occupied by females. The Global Gender Gap Report brought out by the World Economic Forum measures political empowerment in terms of percent of women in parliament, percent of women holding ministerial positions, and years of women in executive office. Health and education achievements have played a major role in the empowerment of the women of Kerala and enabled them to take part in the practices of democracy. It is an essential condition for Equal Democratic Citizenship but not a sufficient one. Equal Democratic Citizenship will be complete only when the women get equal participation in direct decision making and also it is regarded as the representation of women in legislative bodies becomes important.

Political participation must not be restricted to casting votes during elections to decision making bodies and women must occupy the leadership positions in decision making bodies. Women in the state can be empowered through their direct participation in policy making. A fitting example is the local governments in Kerala, where 50% of seats are reserved for women.

Crimes against Women

As per the report of State Crime Records Bureau, the total cases of crime against women for the year 2015 was 9344 which registers a decline from 10690 in 2014. It shows that cruelty by husband or relatives constitutes a major component in crime against women. According to the data of National Crime Records Bureau, Kerala is a state where the Rate of total cognizable crime incidence per one lakh female population is much more than the national level. Even when women come to their homes and employment places, the insecurities within the family always remain.

Schemes

Saranya

Self-Employment Scheme Registered for the Unemployed Widows or Divorced or Unmarried Woman and Unwedded Mother. The scheme is to support the unemployed widows or unmarried women and unwed mothers by providing financial assistance for self-employment. 50% of the project cost is subsidised and the remaining 50% is disbursed by way of interest free loan. The application for this purpose is collected by the District Employment Officer.

Seethalayam

The Women Health Care Centre Scheme provides Homoeopathic aid for suffering women. It provides Outpatient services and a comprehensive approach towards women development. It also combines the activities of other supporting departments for women development like Social Welfare Department, State Women Commission, Home Department. It also provides the infertility clinic services and de- addiction treatment facilities.

Conclusion

Women in Kerala are valuable, healthy and educated resources and can contribute effectively in all aspects of development of the state. An attitudinal change can be by highlighting successful endeavours of women and providing support systems for the multiple tasks they can take up. This paper suggests that women have equal participation in the field of human development. Lot of crime against women is seen in modern society and the constitutional provisions are not sufficient to get a respectable position for women in society. Many new tribunals and public institutions are to be established to guarantee for women effective protection against discrimination. Kerala women have mastered anything and everything which a woman can dream of. But she still has to go a long way to achieve equal status in the minds of men.

CHAPTER FIVE

Educated Unemployment and Underemployment

Educated Unemployment

HARSHA V K

According to the Kerala Economic Review of 2021, educated unemployment has reached 16.7 percent. 14.1% male and 21.1% women are unemployed in rural areas of Kerala. Similarly, 15.3% males and 20.4% females are unemployed in urban areas. Educated unemployment is caused by more opportunities for education and less education-related job opportunities.

Around: 25% of postgraduates and 17% of technical degree holders are unemployed in Kerala. Lack of industrial training and learning methods using old curriculum and old methodology are affecting the modernity of education. Health reports indicate that hypertension, heart issues, psychoneurosis, depression, and suicide are increasing in Kerala among educated unemployment people between the ages of 22 and 40 years.

Improvements in the areas of location tourism IT health sector will help reduce education employment to some extent. Education unemployment in Kerala indicates that post-degree and doctoral (PhD) holders are more unemployed than degree holders.

Mismatch between job opportunity and qualification is another cause of educated Unemployment in Kerala. Educated unemployment is another cause of not acquiring the required skills for the site and not utilizing it as such. Although the service sector knows how to reduce educated Unemployment in Kerala to some extent, there are not many opportunities in that sector. Urban areas in Kerala are facing more educated Unemployment.

According to the 2020 Periodic Labor Force Survey (PLFS) survey, 40.5% of youth between the ages of 15 and 29 are unemployed in Kerala. Enable job seekers in Kerala to find self-employment. The self-employment for that should be in accordance with their educational qualification.

Underemployment

Underemployment is a situation in which a job seeker is forced to do work below his qualifications. Underemployment can be seen even in government services in Kerala. Underemployment has occurred in Kerala's economy as a result of educated unemployment.

There are three important conditions for underemployment in Kerala. They are added below.

1. A situation where a person who is well-skilled in a job has to work for a low wage.

2. A situation in which a person cannot get a job according to his/her qualification and has to do a job with a lower qualification than that.

3. The condition of having to work part-time in places where full-time work existed.

Below are examples related to under-unemployment.

1. The person who has to work in engineering has to work as a delivery boy.

2. A degree holder has to work as a driver.

3. A person who is supposed to be a financial advisor has to occupy a clerical post.

4. A post graduate is required to work on a part-time contract position in a small scale industry.

Socio-economic and industrial factors become important causes of underemployment. Social factors include problems within the family and communication problems. Due to the state of the economy in Kerala facing major fiscal crises, there is a significant shortage of job opportunities in Kerala society.

Governments from time to time failed to create the required employment in the industrial sectors of Kerala. This has led to growing economic poverty among the youth. As a result of that, there is a possibility of increasing psychological imbalance in the society and increasing diseases like stress, anxiety and depression among the youth. Fiscal deficits, the main problem facing the government, have left it unable to find new ways to raise revenue.

Below are the ways to eradicate underemployment from society.

1. New sector related initiatives should be initiated.

2. Diversify academic syllabi and develop industrial skills.

3. Put industry skills to practical use.

4. Infrastructural development should give more importance to transportation communication and more employment opportunities should be created in the society.

Rising Educated Unemployment: A Concern in Kerala

SHIBIN. Y & VIJITHA S VIJAYAN

Kerala, the southernmost state of India, has carved a unique identity for itself on the global stage, not only for its picturesque landscapes but also for its outstanding achievements in education and literacy. The state's development process is a beacon of hope, setting an exemplary standard for universal literacy, schooling, school-pupil retention, and social inclusiveness in education. Kerala's journey from a modest literacy rate of 47.18 percent in 1951 to a staggering 94 percent in 2011 stands as a testament to its relentless pursuit of knowledge and empowerment. Kerala's commitment to education and social inclusiveness is evident through its top position in the country for literacy, with a 94 percent literacy rate in 2011. The state prioritizes the education of marginalized and vulnerable sections, offering tailored programs and extracurricular activities for holistic development. Education is accessible to most households, both in urban and rural areas, fostering a culture of learning. Recent initiatives like '**Vidya Kiranam'** and the **'Kerala Knowledge Economy Mission'** have significantly improved the quality of education in public schools and higher education. Additionally, Kerala's efforts to bridge the digital divide during the pandemic and the 14th Five-Year Plan's focus on enhancing connectivity to school education and offering new-age learning opportunities demonstrate the state's determination to ensure equitable access to education for all.

Despite Kerala's laudable achievements in education, the state faces the paradox of educated unemployment. The unemployment rate has marginally increased from 10.0 percent in 2019-20 to 10.1 percent in 2020-21, but the situation is particularly concerning for educated individuals, especially in rural areas, where the unemployment rate is substantially higher than the national average. This phenomenon, termed "Educated Unemployment," poses significant economic and social challenges for Kerala's youth. In this phenomenon, individuals with educational qualifications are unable to secure jobs that align with their skillsets and qualifications.

As per the Kerala Economic Review 2022, Kerala continues to grapple with the challenge of educated unemployment despite its impressive literacy rate and educational achievements. The unemployment rates among educated individuals aged 15 and above in the state are notably high, standing at 16.6 percent overall, with 16.0 percent in rural areas and 17.3 percent in urban areas. This rate is significantly higher than the national average of 9.1 percent for educated individuals.

Gender Disparities: The issue of Educated Unemployment is further compounded by gender disparities. Female unemployment, especially in rural areas, remains a matter of concern, with rates as high as 22.4 percent in Kerala, in contrast to 12.2 percent among urban females at the national level. Although Kerala boasts a higher female labor force participation rate (LFPR) compared to the national average, the high unemployment rates among female youth in the state pose significant challenges.

Youth Unemployment in Kerala: The youth in Kerala comprise around 23 percent of the state's population, but the unemployment rate among this age group is disproportionately high compared to other age groups. The youth unemployment rate stands at 33.0 percent in rural areas and 34.5 percent in urban areas, far exceeding the national average.

The live register of employment exchanges in Kerala indicates a significant increase in the number of job seekers over the years. As of December 31, 2015, there were 34.9 lakh job seekers, which rose to 38.3 lakh by December 31, 2021, and further reduced to 28.4 lakh by July 2022.

Notably, Kerala's job seekers comprise a higher proportion of women compared to the national scenario, with 63.1% of the total job seekers in 2021 being women. The educational distribution of job seekers shows that a vast majority, 93.5%, have qualifications of SSLC (10th standard) and above, while only 6.4% have qualifications below SSLC.

Regarding professional and technical job seekers, as of December 31, 2021, there were 2.9 lakh individuals seeking such employment. Among them, 57.4% hold ITI certificates, diplomas, or engineering degrees. Specifically, there were 56,540 registered engineering graduates, 11,103 medical graduates, and 1,09,984 other professional candidates (such as those with PG second class and above, LLB, Ph.D., etc.).

Examining district-wise data, Thiruvananthapuram District had the highest number of job seekers, totaling 4.5 lakh individuals, of which 2.9 lakh were women and 1.6 lakh were men. Kollam District followed with 3.1 lakh job seekers, while Kasaragod District had the lowest number of registered job seekers, with 0.7 lakh individuals.These statistics underscore the pressing need for comprehensive policies and targeted interventions to address Educated Unemployment in Kerala, particularly concerning gender disparities and the disproportionately high unemployment rates among the youth. The state government must focus on industry-relevant skill development, promoting entrepreneurship, and creating a conducive environment for job creation to fully harness the potential of its educated workforce and drive sustainable economic growth.

The consequences of Educated Unemployment are profound. The frustration and disillusionment among educated youth lead to social and economic implications, including underutilization of human capital, decreased productivity, and potential social unrest. Addressing this challenge is crucial for Kerala's sustainable development and inclusive growth.

The high unemployment rates can be attributed to several supply-side issues that need to be addressed.

- **Lack of employable skills:** One of the key reasons for the high unemployment rates is the lack of employable skills among the youth. Many young individuals may possess academic qualifications but lack the necessary practical skills and training required by industries. This mismatch between education and industry needs hinders their ability to find suitable employment.
- **Outdated curriculum:** The curriculum in educational institutions needs to be updated to align with emerging trends and demands in the job market. An updated curriculum that focuses on relevant skills and knowledge can better prepare students for the changing job landscape.
- **Sector focus:** The report suggests that the majority of employment opportunities are expected to arise from sectors like building and construction, trade, hotels, restaurants, and manufacturing. To create more opportunities, the government should invest in technical and professional education, health tourism, and IT sectors, which have the potential for growth.
- **Skill ecosystem:** The state government is taking steps to build the skill ecosystem through initiatives like the Knowledge Economy Mission and ASAP (Additional Skill Acquisition Programme). However, it is essential to ensure that the skill courses offered are based on academia-industry associations to cater to the expanding sectors in the state.
- **Relevance of education:** The education system needs to be reworked based on the New Educational Policy 2020, incorporating practical training during semester breaks and a robust credit system. This should include credits for online certificate courses to encourage continuous up skilling and reskilling.
- **Addressing teaching quality:** The quality of education in higher educational institutions is crucial. The lack of appraisals for government lecturers may contribute to a decline in teaching quality. Implementing appraisal mechanisms and curriculum revisions can help ensure that teachers remain up skilled and maintain enthusiasm

for teaching.
- **Industry-specific standards:** Skilling initiatives must be designed to meet industry-specific standards and be accessible and efficient. Simply announcing skilling missions and budget allocations may not be sufficient unless they address the actual requirements of the job market.

In conclusion, to tackle the issue of high unemployment rates among the educated population in Kerala, a multi-faceted approach is required. This includes focusing on relevant skill development, updating the education system, addressing teaching quality, and aligning the skill ecosystem with the demands of the job market. By implementing these measures, the state can improve its economic opportunities and employment prospects for its educated population.

An analysis of Kottayam District to Determine Why People are Unemployed Despite all have Degrees

ALFIYA K S AHAMMED

Kerala has made great strides in the area of infrastructure, basic health, and literacy, but the state hasn't been able to significantly address its unemployment issue. Despite, a greater supply of educated workers, employment possibility of the state have not expanded. The biggest obstacles to further human development in kerala are the issue of educated unemployment. The study draws attention to the role that socio-economic position plays in determining unemployment as well as the challenges faced by educated job seekers. The main focus is on the nature, scope, traits and cause of educated unemployment in Kerala, with particular emphasis on Kottayam. The sample size is 50, young adults with college degrees who are unemployed have been randomly chosen from the Kottayam district. Survey conducted based on well structured questionnaire. The study discovers that respondents' socio economic level and income affect their job preferences and the majority respondents prefer government jobs. They not ready to choose private sector. It is abundantly obvious from the study that this is the cause the area's high unemployment rate.

Keywords: unemployment, educated youth, socio economic status

Unemployment refers to a situation when a person actively searching for employment cannot find work. Unemployment includes all persons who are without work, seeking work and able to join a job if offered. When someone actively seeks job but is unable to do so, this is referred to as being unemployed. One important indicator of the state of the economy is unemployment. The unemployment rate is the most often used indicator of unemployment. It is computed by dividing the total labour force by the number of jobless people. Numerous governments provide unemployment insurance to certain unemployed people who meet the criteria. The role of education in bringing social status and its linkage with employment has attracted the attention of researchers and social scientists from very early times. The reduced chance of unemployment at greater levels of education is a significant benefit of education. The growing unemployment of the educated has hindered the state from reaping the full social and economic benefits of its educational progress. Unemployment should not be interpreted simply as a lack of opportunity for individuals. It amounted to denying unemployed people opportunity to participate in the state's economic activities and contribute to its economic development.

In Kerala's situation, despite having progressive socioeconomic policies, the state's economy is constrained since it is unable to utilize the full potential of its labour force. As a result, Kerala is experiencing a severe problem in educated unemployment. Numerous societal issues, such as frustration, social unrest, and political instability are brought on by the growing number of educated unemployed people. The states flawed and insufficient educational manpower planning is evident in the absence of employment prospects, especially for young people who have finished their higher education. Kerala's youth were emotionally strained by the jobless crisis. According to data from the PSID (Panel Study of Income Dynamics) on the male labour force1, the incidence of unemployment has been found to be far more important than the duration of unemployed in causing differences in unemployment rates based on schooling. Accordingly, the lower unemployment rate of highly educated workers is largely attributable to both their stronger bond with the companies that employ them and their lower risk of losing their jobs should they leave the company. Highly on-the-job training is mostly responsible for decreased job churn among more educated individuals, which results in fewer periods of unemployment. In order to explain the reduced conditional unemployment of educated workers and the marginally shorter duration of their unemployment, indirect evidence is offered that (1) the costs of on-the-job search for new employment relative to costs of searching while unemployed are lower for more educated workers; (2) that these workers are also more efficient in acquiring and processing job search information; and (3) firms and workers search more intensely to fill more skilled vacancies.

Kerala's socioeconomic indicators, which represent increased female empowerment in the state, have undergone notable progress. However, a recent trend indicates that women's labour force participation is not up to par. The NSSO data from 2011-2012 show that, Kerala's total unemployment rate is 6.7%, with a significant gender difference of 14.1% for women and 2.9% for males. Additionally, the data reveals a significant salary gap. In Kerala, it is widely held that women can only benefit from general education because it promotes understanding of health, education, and better child care. However, some people who advocate for greater education later pursue low-paying professions. The prevalent societal norms, however, do not view this adversely. However, in accordance with the societal norms already in place, this is not viewed negatively.

Kerala shows remarkable development in the socio-economic parameters that reflect greater empowerment of women in the state. But recent trend shows the contribution of women to the workforce is not up to the mark. According to the NSSO data from 2011-2012, the overall unemployment rate in Kerala is 6.7 with a wide gender gap of 14.1% for women and 2.9% for men. The data also shows a huge disparity in wages. The prevailing belief in Kerala is that only general education is beneficial for women as it fosters knowledge about education, health, and better child care. Although others who urge higher education later get into low-paying occupations. But this is not seen negatively according to the prevailing social norms.

Development of human resources is the process of creating and enhancing a workforce through formal education and training. As a result, it is a crucial requirement for achieving national development. University-educated people who have had some work experience are essential to the prosperity of a country.

Almost everyone in the new generation aspires to graduate because they need high-paying employment to develop their careers, yet for a variety of reasons, these highly educated young people remain unemployed. Kerala's youth are well educated but unemployed. The data also demonstrates a gender imbalance in employment, with educated women underemployed when compared to their counterparts' job status. As a result, this research focuses on unemployment among highly educated people in Kerala, with a particular emphasis on Kottayam.

1. E T Mathew in his work "Educated unemployment in Kerala: Socioeconomic aspects" examined that educated unemployment in Kerala has assumed alarming proportion in recent times. Some of the reasons for educated unemployment are the opening of many private arts and science and ITI colleges and the preference for paid jobs over self-employment.
2. Raj Krishna in his article "Unemployment in India" points out that the country has not defined a solution despite two decades of planned development. He attempts to explain the phenomenon of a positive growth in unemployment associated with positive output growth.
3. B A Prakash in "Urban unemployment in Kerala" examines the incidence, type, and characteristics of urban unemployment in Kerala's second-largest city, and offers some reasons to explain the high rate of joblessness. Joblessness is the basic problem of educated youth, leading to migration abroad in search of employment.
4. Mukherjee, Chandran in his work "The market for the educated in Kerala" describes the importance of the job market for the educated in Kerala. According to the author, the main form of employment for the educated is the well-salaried one.
5. Allan T Udall in his work "The luxury unemployment hypothesis" pointed out the hypothesis that unemployment rates are low in very poor countries since workers cannot withstand the long period of job search.
6. Rajeev. P.V examined in detail the problem of unemployment in Kerala in his work 'Economic Development and the Unemployed.' According to him the employment generation in Kerala demands more investment in productive sectors and in public sector undertakings compared to investment in public administration and social

services. In his view restriction of entry into higher education will be a solution to the problem of educated unemployment.

7. Mark Blaug's (1973) work, 'Education and Employment Problems in Developing Countries,' deals with the principles of educational planning, particularly in developing countries. According to the author, educated unemployment is caused by a misalignment of desires and opportunities. Underemployment becomes open unemployment as a result of education. Blaug emphasized that public education subsidies invariably result in an excess demand for education and thus an excess supply of educated labour.

The classification of respondents based on age, out of 50 respondents 40% of the respondents belong to the age group that comes between 24-29 ages whereas 24% are between the age group 18-23. That is, most of the respondents are those who completed their higher studies and looking for a job. 20% are of the age group 30-35 and remaining 6% are from the age group 42 and above. Here, we can say that the study is focused on the youth.The gender-wise classification of respondents. As per the table, out of 50 respondents, 76% are female and 24% are male. It can be concluded that the majority of the respondents are female.69.2% of the total unemployed are female and only 30.7% constitute male.78% of the respondents belong to BPL and the remaining 22% belong to the APL category.The out of 50 respondents 24 are employed where 16.6% are satisfied and 83.3% are not satisfied with their current job. It can be concluded that most of the respondents are not finding satisfaction in their job.The educational qualifications of the respondents. Out of 50 respondents, around 32% are degree holders, 24% are postgraduates, and others completed school education. It can be concluded that the majority of the respondents have attained higher education.All respondents have a preference for government jobs. No one is interested to work in the private sector.

Findings

- Majority of the respondents, 40% belong to the age group that comes between 24 to 29, and 24% comes under the age group 18-23.
- Most of the respondents are female, that is 76%
- 52% of the respondents are unemployed, out of that more than 60% of unemployed are female.
- Majority of the respondents, that is 78% belong to the BPL category.
- Most of the respondents have higher education, 32% are degree holders.
- Out of the 48% employed, most of them are unsatisfied with their current job. Only 16.6% are satisfied with their job.
- All respondents prefer government jobs.

Suggestions

- Educational system should conduct skill development programs to enhance the soft skills of the students.
- Encourage the youth to come up with startup ideas.
- The occupational outlook of women should be changed so that more of them will attain higher education to get jobs and thereby ensure equality of opportunity.
- Jobs should be given only based on ability and qualification, not on recommendations, caste or influence.

Conclusion

Everyone aspires to find employment through education, but when jobs are few, applicants become upset. In this time, it is critical to comprehend the concerns of educated unemployed people in a state like Kerala, which excels in higher education. The study's goal is to discover the socioeconomic conditions of unemployed youth in Kottayam and to investigate the causes of educated unemployment in the study area. It has been discovered that the majority of the kids in this area have had access to higher education, and the majority of them are graduates. However, because of their economic level and educational qualifications, they exclusively express preference for government jobs. As a result of this trend, they are currently jobless, and educated labour is wasted.

CHAPTER SIX

Service Sector

Service Sector Role and Perfomances

KAVEYA P

In modern economies, service sector performs many important roles. First, it represents a major share of the developed economies and is increasingly integrated into the overall production system. Second, it plays an active role in market integration and globalisation. Third, the creation of employment, value added, income and exports are increasingly related to the good performance of the services.

Service Sector: Concept and Meaning

The economy has basically three sectors. First, the primary sector comprising of agriculture, fishing, and extraction such as mining. Second sector is the secondary sector comprising of manufacturing. Third sector is the tertiary sector also referred to as service sector.The tertiary sector involves the provision of services to other businesses. Services may involve the transport, distribution and sale of goods from producer to a consumer, pest control, entertainment or hotel industry. The goods are transformed in the process of providing the service. However, the focus is on people interacting with people and serving the customer rather than transforming physical goods.

The explanation for this shift is as follows:

- Income elasticity of demand for agricultural products is relatively low; as a result,
- with rising levels of income, the demand for agricultural products relatively declines
- and that for industrial goods increases and, after reaching a reasonably high level
- of income, demand for services increases sharply. Accordingly, the shares of
- different sectors in the national product get determined by the changes in the
- pattern of demand. On the supply side, agriculture, being mainly dependent on a
- fixed factor of production, namely land, faces a limit on its growth and is subject
- to early operation of the law of diminishing returns.
- Composition of GDP
- For the past few decades, there has been a considerable shift from the primaryand secondary sectors to the tertiary sector in the Indian Economy. The tertiarysector is now the largest sector of the economy and is also the fastest-growingsector. Examples of service sector employment include: Government, hospitals,public health, waste disposal, education, banking, insurance, financial services,
- legal services, consulting, news media, hospitality industry (e.g. restaurants, hotels,casinos), tourism, retail sales, franchising, real estate, and sales.

Performance of service sector in Kerala

Performance of service sector in Kerala can be assessed with the help of three parameters as follows:

1. Sectoral composition of GDP Growth
2. Employment contribution of Service Sector
3. Productivity Growth in Service Sector

- Sectoral Composition of GDP Growth
- This trend is projected to go further in wake of liberalisation of the economy. This may happen primarily because of the following factors:

a. reduced restrictions on private sector involvement in areas like software development and information services,

   (b) technological advances, and
   (c) lower fixed capital requirements.
   Causes of rapid increase in tertiary sector

- The tertiary, i.e., the non-commodity sector, has been growing at a much faster rate than the commodity sector. This in essence means that income generated in the process of circulation grew at a much faster pace than that in the directly productive process, and thereby resulting in an increase in the share of the no commodity sector. This trend can be attributed to a number of factors, among which, the more important are as follows:

i. A very important factor has been the advent of information technology and the knowledge economy. This has enhanced the growth of the high productivity segment of the services sector as well as a variety of service activities involving low productivity activities catering to a large mass of people.
ii. A large part of the service sector consists of infrastructure such as banking, insurance, finance, transport and communication and social and community services such as educational and medical facilities.
iii. Operation of the demonstration effect as a consequence of the growing mobility due to expanding foreign trade, tourism and cultural and educational tours is another important factor.

Lottery

HARSHA V K

Gambling has been declared illegal in India but the lottery is considered legal in India. India's largest and oldest lottery system exists in Kerala.It can be said that Kerala is the casino of India. According to the state government figures, the number of lottery tickets sold in a day is close to 1 crore out of a population of 3 crores in Kerala. Similarly, the number of lottery tickets sold in a week is around 7.92 crores. If so, let's say a year's worth Kerala has a turnover of 10000 crore rupees.

Lottery system was first introduced in Kerala in 1967. In the early days, lottery in Kerala was sold for Rs. 1.The prize money at that time was around 50000 rupees. Many types of lotteries were sold in Kerala but after 2008 lotteries from many other states were banned in Kerala. Hence, a monopoly system of lotteries by the Kerala government has emerged. Therefore, in 2008, 500 crores worth of lotteries were sold, but by 2020, Kerala had a revenue of 10,000 rupees from the sale of lotteries.

The revenue from the Kerala lottery is mainly 15 to 20 percent for the government. The three main reasons for such a high lottery revenue are trustworthiness, transparency and popularity. Lottery draws are held every day of the week in Kerala. Winwin, Streeshakti, Akshaya, Karunya, Nirmal, Karunya Plus and Fifty Fifty are all lotteries in Kerala every day of the week. Apart from this bumper lotteries are also conducted several times in a year.Bumper lotteries like Vishu, Thiruvonam, Puja, Christmas Monsoon and Summer are also conducted in a year. A person also has the opportunity to buy multiple lotteries.

The Central government does not say that the lottery should be conducted, therefore, the income of the lottery comes from the state governments. Lottery exists in 13 states in India itself. It is said that Kerala stands first in that. Starting with a lottery prize of 50000 rupees, today Kerala has reached the level of giving a prize of 25 crore rupees.At least 1500 crore profit is available to Kerala from lottery every year. 80 percent of the non-revenue tax that Kerala receives comes from the lottery.

Kerala State Lottery is given a good promotion through movie, Web ad and TV advertisement. It is mainly an effect of the governments that led to the lottery industry gaining more importance in Kerala. Educated and high-minded people have to change their lives suddenly and save their lives through some shortcut, which has become the reason for the progress of the lottery in Kerala.

To give an example, if 90 lakh people buy an Onam bumber priced at Rs 500, they get about Rs 450 crore from this. Chance of success in Onam bumper is 5 percent people. That is, about 4 lakh people will be winners and 12 people will get a huge amount of money as a prize. If we say so, 126 crore rupees will be given as prizes.Then the government has 324 crore rupees. 200 crores out of which the state government gets the profit of Onam Bambar. Now there is likely to be a major doubt. That is, there is a possibility that 95% of the money you pay to buy the lottery is wasted. That means the money you pay for the lottery goes either to the winners or to the government.

Probability of significant price amount =12÷90 lakh=0.0001%

Probability significance means that one in 10 lakhs has a chance of winning.

Below are the reasons why a person might say buying the lottery is a good idea.

Kerala Lottery is making a good contribution to the economy of Kerala through the Non-Ras revenue category. Kerala's lottery system is transparent, popular and trustworthy. Many phases of lottery sales are going on in Kerala as a means of livelihood for a few people. Kerala Lottery profit proceeds are used for the development of Kerala's infrastructure as well as for various charitable activities. Unclaimed prize of Kerala Lottery is used by State Govt. In this way, in 2022, the state government has received Rs. 638 crore as unclaimed prize. Similarly, the state government has received Rs 10 crore as unclaimed prize for Vishu 2022. In short, the biggest lucky winner is the state government.

The reasons why buying lotteries is not a good idea

Addiction becomes a habit among regular lottery buyers.It is good for people with higher incomes to develop addiction habits. A lottery ticket even if a person has no income and has taken out a loan If you buy it, it can be called an addiction habit.It is not written in the lottery that buying the lottery is an addiction habit, and it cannot be written like that. Buying lotteries without thinking about a person's financial capacity can be considered as a social evil. The main power of the lottery is to create a sense of hope or excitement in individuals.

Real estate

If we look at the last three months of 2022, more than 50 percent of the growth rate of the real estate sector has been acquired in Kerala. Flats have come up for sale at an offer price in Kochi, the metro city of Kerala. Investing in real estates is a safe bet these days in Kerala.

Owning a house is every symbol and builders turn it into a valuable investment in Kerala. Demand for houses is also increasing among consumers in Kerala. The growth in the real estate sector is due to the advancement of industrial, education and infrastructure in many cities of Kerala. A house buying a plot is possible after various document checks.

More profit is obtained from the sale of commercial real estates for retail, office and parking purposes. 2023 is a likely price hike year in Kerala real estate sector. Kochi, the industrial hub of Kerala, is at the forefront of the real estate price hike.More builders are attracted to Kerala due to good availability of land, low price, resale value and construction cost is less.

The infrastructural developments and potential in the real estate sector of the nearby areas such as Technopark in Thiruvananthapuram, Infopark in Kochi and Cyber Park in Kozhikode are significant. Known as the Golden City of India, Thrissur also has the potential to make leaps and bounds in the real estate sector. Sharing the border with Kochi is another reason for real estate growth in Thrissur. A water-friendly real estate is taking advantage of the opportunities in Kochi.In Kochi and Thiruvananthapuram, about 70% real estate-related share stocks have been sold. In Thrissur district, 75.8% share stocks of estates in residential areas have been sold through unorganized developers.

A study on consumer perception towards high-priced drugs and pricing by pharmaceutical companies

ABIN ABRAHAM

Marketing concept that incorporates a customer's impression, awareness, or consciousness about a firm or its offerings.' Customer gathers information about a product and interprets it to generate an opinion. Customers form opinions based on product ads, promotions, customer reviews, social media input, etc. Consumer perception begins when they see or learn about a product. This continues until the customer forms a product opinion. Everything an organisation does affects consumer perception. The logo, colours, product placement, ads, and discounts all affect client perception. Perception is "discerning, realising, and becoming conscious of through the senses."

Consumers are king in any industry, but the pharmaceutical industry is different. Doctors influence consumer purchases. In India, the pharmaceutical industry is the most technically skilled in drug manufacturing and invention. With cheap production costs, inexpensive R&D, competent workers, and world-class national laboratories specialising in cost-effective technologies, India's industry meets all demands. India has the world's cheapest generic medications, yet they are costly and leave patients sleepless because they can't afford them. Customers also buy popular branded medications. The study examines brand-name and generic drug buying determinants. It examines consumer acceptance of high-priced medications and beliefs about price drivers.

Price is one of the most interesting and contentious issues in pharmaceutical marketing. Understanding consumer perception is critical for marketers in this industry because their goal is to obtain as many customers as possible. As a result, research on this topic is required. This study aims to better understand customers' attitudes towards high-priced pharmaceuticals as well as their beliefs about the factors that contribute to higher drug prices. It also tries to identify the characteristics that encourage the purchase of both branded and generic drugs. In this regard, the study can also provide important insights for pharmaceutical managers and marketers.

Each company's success is determined by its ability to persuade customers to make purchases and take action. Marketers must understand consumer perception in order to do so. Only when a corporation recognises the consumer's view can it design appropriate plans. This is especially true in the pharmaceutical industry, where price is a critical issue and pricing strategies play an essential role. The survey gives managers and marketers with information about customer perception, which they may utilise to better position the medicine in the market.

Saxena (2010) in his article has presented the changing marketing strategies when a pharmaceutical company moves from an acute base to a chronic base. The author also gave an insight into the shift in the supply chain process and the perception of customers and end- customers which is the basis for framing of various marketing strategies. **Yadav (2010)** in his report analyses available literature on differential pricing, examines successful and unsuccessful examples of differential pricing, and recommends actions for advancement. Through implementation of differential pricing, quality improvement and enhanced accessibility of medicines together with achievement of higher profits for pharmaceutical manufacturers is noted. It also mentions about the difficulty of pricing drugs and affordability for the people of India. **Khanna (2013)** in his PhD thesis has attempted to examine consumer perception towards ayurvedic drugs vis-à-vis allopathic drugs. The study focused on consumer attitudes, beliefs and opinions related to ayurvedic drugs as well as their availability and distribution system to devise a marketing strategy for the marketing of ayurvedic drugs in India to be successful.

Ahire et al., (2013) conducted a survey-based project which revealed that irrespective of whether consumers belong to science background or not, they want economic alternative to branded medicines. Further the study shows that doctors do not prefer generic medicines, pharmacists have too little business through it and that significant number of consumers do not have knowledge of generic drugs. At the end, more stringent rules and regulations were recommended to make drugs available to masses at affordable cost. **Khoso et al., (2014)** in his study has mentioned price as the most interesting as well as controversial matter in pharmaceutical marketing. The study was an attempt to present possible pricing approaches and strategies for pharmaceutical industry in Pakistan. Nature of market and demand was shown as an external factor affecting pricing decision. Internal factors included company's costs and marketing mix strategy among others. **Shekhar et al., (2019)** in their paper examined the features that consumers look for when they reach the pharmacy to purchase a drug. The paper underscores the importance of factors such as price, trust and brand in making important purchase decisions. It has been found in the study that consumers try to be well aware of the drug before buying or consuming it. Further, price sensitivity was found to be the most dominant factor influencing the consumer buying behaviour.

Review shows that only few studies have been conducted in relation to this topic and most of the studies have been carried out outside Kerala. Identifying the need to address this gap, the study makes an attempt to investigate the consumer perception towards high- priced drugs and pricing by pharmaceutical companies through analysing various factors influencing purchase of medicines.

It is clear that majority of the respondents belongs to age category of 20-30 (70%) and 21.8% percent of belongs to 30-40. Only few percentages of respondents belongs to 40-50 (8.2%) and no respondents belongs to above 50 category.According to majority (73.6%) of the respondents has expressed that advertisements and other promotional strategies of medicines affect the pricing scenario.The most important factor that influence purchase of branded medicines is the quality (40.10%) followed by awareness (26.70%), brand name (26.20%) and rest of them choose high price (7%).According to 39.1% of the respondents are neutral with regard to purchase decision of renowned drug in market without having sufficient consideration. Almost similar percent of respondents (40.9%) either agreed or strongly agreed (28.2% and 12.7% respectively) that they are influenced .Rest of them disagree with the statement.

The value of the test statistics is 1.944 at the degree of freedom 2.The table value is 5.991.So the table value is more than calculated value .Therefore we will accept the null hypothesis and reject the alternative hypothesis .Thus consumer age of respondents do not have the significant impact on perception relating to contribution of promotional strategies to higher drugs prices.

The value of the test statistics is 27.230 at the degree of freedom 16.The table value is 26.296.So the table value is less than calculated value .Therefore we will reject the null hypothesis and accept the alternative hypothesis .Thus there is significant difference between brand name and level of preference towards branded drugs.

The majority of the respondents fall under the age category of 20–30. The majority of the respondents (73.6%) expressed that advertisements and other promotional strategies affect the pricing scenario. Most of the respondents are neutral with regard to the purchase decision of renowned drugs on the market without having sufficient consideration. A similar percentage of respondents agreed that they are influenced. It has been found that the most important factor influencing the purchase of branded medicines is quality. The chi square test on age of respondents and perception relating to the contribution of promotional strategies to higher drug prices accepted the null hypothesis, i.e., that there is no significant relationship between age of respondents and perception relating to the contribution of promotional strategies. The chi-square test on brand name and level of preference for branded drugs accepted the alternative hypothesis. Therefore, brand name and level of preference for branded drugs are significantly related.

Conclusion

Consumer perception has a significant impact on corporate success. Understanding consumer perception is essential in the pharmaceutical industry since price is a major concern and pricing tactics are critical.The study sought to better understand consumer attitudes regarding high-priced pharmaceuticals as well as their beliefs about the factors that contribute to higher drug pricing. Furthermore, it was an attempt to identify the characteristics that encourage the purchase of both branded and generic medicines. The findings were reached after assessing areas such as medication awareness, basic pricing facts, and media sources utilised.The vast majority of respondents choose branded medications. The study discovered a significant association between brand name and level of preference for branded medications. The primary motivator for purchasing branded drugs is quality.To compete and enhance sales, pharmaceutical companies must conduct market research and understand consumer perception. Companies can use reputable market research service providers to track consumer attitudes and business performance.To summarise, pharmaceutical businesses must perform market research and understand consumer perception in order to better position themselves in the marketplace and drive higher customer and sales numbers. Companies can assess their business performance by analysing the influence of consumer perceptions with the help of reputable market research service providers.

Upshots of Reverse Migration during Pandemic

MUZNA MUHAMMED P

History of human life is exactly attributed to history of migration. Migration is an important factor that changes demographic profile of a region. The push and pull factors make migration as a necessary step to overcome existing difficulties as in the case of push factors and to achieve some better opportunities in the case of pull factors. Migration is a broad concept which entails emigration, immigration, in-migration, return migration Reverse migration etc...Reverse migration is a hot topic today because of the Pandemic Covid -19 and subsequent Lockdown imposed in the country. The following paper discusses the effect of reverse migration on the life of migrant workers and impact of such migration on Kerala economy which is regarded as rainbow country of migrant workers.

Now we are living in a year which may demarcates the history of world into Pre Covid and Post Covid period. There is nothing wrong in saying that every walk of human life is under miserable condition during Covid 19 pandemic. Almost all countries are trapped in the Pandemic and trying to recover from it by issuing restrictions especially in the form of lockdown. Our country also adopted lockdown. All layers of social hierarchy are affected by it. In the case of India one of the most vulnerable categories, among them are migrant workers. India's image in front of whole world was faded little due to miseries and difficulties inflicted upon migrant workers who return home during lockdown due to mismanagement o authorities during lockdown. Several hundred migrant workers stranded across the country started to depart on foot back to their states. Most of them started walking along railway tracks without taking any precautions. Most of them returned with their children and old parents by carrying on shoulders. They were compelled to do so because of the hardship they faced during lockdown. The unexpected lockdown urged **reverse migration. It is a situation when labourers, workers and people start migrating back to their native place in the back drop of non availability of livelihood and job opportunities.** Reverse migration might seem to be the most logical coping mechanism available to them. The first national lockdown (March 25s, 2020) created panic among migrant workers who were suddenly left without any income security. Most of them left with no income, food and no shelter and they were threatened by loss of life due to hunger and starvation. Central government's intervention by arranging Shramik Express trains gave some solace to the plight of migrant workers, but that too late. As per the data shared by the Railways, 2600 such trains had been run carrying around 35lakh passengers out of these workers more than 40%(48.5%) belong to Uttar Pradesh and 31.3% were to Bihar.

Status of Kerala after Reverse Migration

Kerala holds a significant position in accommodating migrant workers. Kerala is one among the attractive destinations of migrant workers .They are ubiquitous. Their numbers are astonishing in Kerala. "According to the 2011 Census, there are 457 million internal migrants in India accounting for 37.8 per cent of the total population and in Kerala this percentage was 48.9 per cent. One out of two persons in Kerala is an internal migrant. Over the decades, Kerala's external (international) migrants were replaced by internal (in) migrants"(Paper by Irudaya rajan). As per 2001 Census there were 31.5% crore migrants in the country which constitutes 31% of the population.While population grew 18% during last tw census periods the number of migrants increased by 45%.The prominent factors influencing for in migration to Kerala include Relatively higher wage rates, better job opportunities particularly semiskilled and un skilled works, shortage of local labourers, comfortable living condition etc.. These factors altogether made Kerala as a lucrative labour market for migrant workers. They had been flowing into the state and state heart fully welcome this "guest workers". They had filled the vacuum created in the labour market due to emigration of large number of Keralites to Middle East countries in the wake of oil boom during 1970s. Earlier period Kerala witnessed in-migration of workers from neighboring states. But recently workers from far off states also arrived here. These migrants have outnumbered the local workforce and their numbers particularly outweigh in sectors such as constructions, hotels, plywood and jewelry-making industries. A study by UNO agency in collaboration with state govt of Kerala in 2018 estimated there are 35 lakh migrant workers in the state. According to Gulatti Institute of Finance it was 25 lakh in 2013. It shows that within a span of five years number of migrant workers in the state increased by 40%.Number of registered workers in Awaz scheme is 5.08 lakh.

A trend of internal migrants as a share of total population in Kerala since 1971 in which a migrant is defined according to the criterion of place of last residence. The share of migrants in the total population of Kerala more than doubled over the period between 1971 and 2011.As far as in-migration concerns it also shows increasing trend. In-migration into the state in terms of individuals originating from others states of India, have been increasing. During 2001, in-migration into Kerala accounted to 0.45 million which increased from 0.43 million in 1991.

The migrant workers return due to Pandemic and consequent lockdown created another void in the labour market. During 1970s they have filled the vacuum created in Kerala labour market due to emigration of semi skilled and unskilled labourers(Keralites) to middle east countries. Now their return to native states made almost similar condition here after fifty years later. An estimate given to Supreme Court reveals that 4.48 lakh migrant workers live at 21,556 camps in Kerala.1.67 lakh returned, 1.20 lakh willing to go back home and 1.61 lakh reluctant to return (june 13, Mathrubhumi Newspaper).

The construction sector, industrial units, agriculture sector, manufacturing sector, number of service sectors as well hit by their return. They were engaging in almost all fields of works. There is a saying that they are doing 3D jobs, dangerous, demeaning and degraded Jobs. When the lockdown lifted up; production commences and business operations started in the state with full of uncertainty. It is impossible to ensure that production process and services go into full stride without their presence

Impacts on Kerala Economy

The unprecedented journey of migrant workers to home town undoubtedly affects Kerala economy in several ways. As the state host number of workers from several states in the country, the phenomena of reverse migration has deep rooted consequences in the development process of Kerala economy. Some important consequences are given below:

- Construction sector in the state face shortage of manpower.
- Return of workers to home caused suspension of industrial activity in the state.
- Agriculture sector experience shortage of hard working farm labor. Workers from Andhra Pradesh, Bengal and oddisha were predominant in agricultural activities especially in paddy cultivation, their return made difficulties in cultivation.
- Number of works such as farming, masonry, Hair cutting, cleaning in chicken shops etc hit hard

Several key projects in the state have been punch with the return of migrant workers amid Covid

1. Completion of Some projects has compelled to stop and commencement of some has delayed. Only the construction of Pulimuttu (sea wall) was pending in Vizhinjam project. This work will have to be suspended during mansoon when huge waves will be generated. The construction of Kazhakkoottam -Karode national highway is also moving at snail's space. Most of the works have pre monsoon preparative works which have been affected by their absence.

Some major works that are halted

- The construction of Kazhakkoottam karode national highway is moving slowly.
- Construction of 2 buildings of Govt Medical College Manjeri as covid care center has been delayed.
- Vyttila and Kundannur Flyovers,
- Kochi metro's extension to Pettah
- Vizhinjam project.
- Punalur- Ponkunnam Road.
- Restoration of TB junction-Vattappadu road costs 8 crore
- KIIFBI road construction at Kunnathur.

- Construction of Super Specialty block at Govt Medical College Aleppey.
- Railway works

Initiatives to be taken for welfare of return migrants

There has to be a holistic approach for the labourers (returned migrants) in order to lift them from clutches of poverty and financial stress .Both the states should implement welfare schemes for them. Some of the measures ought to be taken by state are given below:

- Issuing of a smart card for every migrant worker is needed. Such card should contain personal details, work details, contractor's name and other details and it should be linked to Adhar or any other identification document. There must be facility in railway stations and Bus stand to swipe the card when they return home. This kind of imitative will help state to get an idea of estimate of reverse migration and prepare facilities to bring them back.
- Launching of mobile app in every states to register stranded migrant laborers is to be recommended(example: 'Chief Ministers Special Assistance Scheme' a mobile app launched by Jharkhand Government)
- A fiscal stimulus for the demand side must be formulated so as to provide immediate monetary support.
- The central government can keep aside more money for the well being of migrant workers.
- The one nation one ration card scheme must be issued as early as possible.
- The state government should implement employment guarantee programs in cities like MGNRGEGA.
- Job guarantee programs must be initiated from district level as consider it as a primary unit.
- Social security schemes should enlarge to include migrant workers.
- Health insurance package is needed.
- The unique wage structure for migrant workers is advocated. So that they can avail it when they return home too.
- To tide over the financial difficulties of migrant workers, cash transfer to all inter- state and inter district migrant worker is advocated. This will inject purchasing power and thereby increasing demand which will ultimately leads to increased production and increase in income.

- The FCI must transfer its excess grain stored to the demand hotspots so that there is no hunger and starvation in the states which are taking migrant incomings.
- A special package should be given to landless seasonal migrant labourers.
- Government should come up with livelihood programs and asset creation.
- Skill acquisition programs must be initiated and the state should frame rules to pave the way for hiring of workers on hourly basis so that both the stakeholders benefit from the arrangement. Competition in the labour market and increase in productivity can be attained.
- A proper movement strategy should be devised for future action if the migrant return again to work states.

The Novel Corona Virus pandemic induced migration to home cities by migrant workers is absolutely a serious issue for almost all states n the country. The states with high out-migration face problems regarding with engrossment of large number of incoming migrant workers. They have to re-structure their labour policies to trickle down to its effect on migrant workers. The states with high in-migration now face shortage of experienced work force. Its implication is present in every sectors of the economy. The central government intervention for rehabilitation of migrant workers is the need of the hour.

CHAPTER SEVEN

Health and Tourism

Declining Child Sex Ratio in India and Kerala – An Examination

DHANUSREE ULLAS K

India, a country of cultural diversity, is the seventh largest and most populous country in the world. The World Population Review (2023) projected that 17.85 per cent of the world population is residing in India followed by China (17.81%). As per the provisional figures of the census 2011, the total population of India is 1210.19 million of which 586.46 million (48.46%) are female population and 623.7 million (51.54 %) are male population. Even though India is at the forefront of world population figures, the sex ratio is observed to be unfavourable to women. The adverse sex ratio will affect the development of India's economy in general and women in particular. The sex ratio in the country has seen a drastic decline from 972 in the year 1901 to 927 in the year 1991 whereas in the year 2011, it was 943 women per 1000 men (Census of India, 2011). The sex ratio is expected to increase to 952 women per 1000 men in the year 2023 (Women and Men in India, 2022). In India, 13 per cent of the population constitutes of children aged below 6 years (Census of India, 2011). When it comes to Child sex ratio, the situation is dire; the Child sex ratio has been declining over the years and majority of the Indian states have a low Child sex ratio. Kerala is an exception to this and has achieved a higher sex ratio among the Indian states long before. Unfortunately, the state of Kerala also has a skewed child sex ratio, which is alarming. At this juncture, it is significant to examine the child sex ratio of India and Kerala in detail.

Child Sex Ratio in India

The Child sex ratio is a significant indicator in understanding the status of the girl child in society. As per the definition of the Census of India, 2011, Child sex ratio is 'the number of girls per 1000 boys in the age group of 0-6 years. Though the sex ratio in India is low, it has increased from 933 in the year 2001 to 940 in the year 2011. On the contrary, the Child sex ratio has observed a sharp decline from 927 in the year 2001 to 919 in the year 2011. Generally, female children and girls have been found to have higher survival rates than boys (Waldron, 1998). But in South Asian countries, including India, the girl child have no such advantage (Rajesh Kumar Rai et al., 2013). India, being a male dominant society, the preference is always given to the male child. As a result, India has a deteriorating sex ratio in the case of both adults and children.The adult and child sex ratio is miserable in the country. Even though adult sex ratio manifested a lower sex ratio, it has seen a meagre increase from the year 2001 to the year 2011. According to the population census 2011, the higher sex ratio was observed in Kerala (1084) while the lowest was in Haryana (877). In the case of union territories, Puducherry (1038) has the highest sex ratio and Daman Diu has the lowest sex ratio (618). On the other hand, the Child Sex has deteriorated from the year 1951 to the year 2011. According to the census 2011, child sex ratio has shown an increasing trend only in six states and two union territories. The top three states having the highest child sex ratio are Mizoram (971), Meghalaya (970), and Chhattisgarh (964). Among union territories, Andaman and Nicobar Islands (966), Puducherry (965), and Dadra Nagar Haveli (924) come in the top three places respectively. On the other hand, the lowest child sex ratios are observed in the states of Haryana (830), Punjab (846), and Jammu Kashmir (859), and among union territories, Delhi (866), Chandigarh (867) and Lakshadweep (908).

One of the main reasons for the skewed sex ratio is female foeticide. The sex selective abortions and female foeticide are common in India. The socio-cultural and religious factors such as the dowry system and the expectation that male children would look after the family were the main reasons for female foeticide. Apart from this, biological issues and diseases like prematurity and low birth weight, Diarrheal diseases, injuries, Pneumonia, Acute bacterial sepsis and severe infections, non-communicable diseases and malnutrition disproportionately affected infant female children (Annual Report, Ministry of Health and Family Welfare, 2019-20).

As per the census of 2011, Child Sex Ratio in rural areas in the year 1991 was 948 and it decreased to 933 in the year 2001 and further to 919 in the year 2011, whereas in urban areas the figures were 935, 906, and 902 respectively. The decline in rural areas was three times higher than the decline in urban areas for the year 2011. The decline in Child Sex Ratio in 27 states/UTs in the year 2011 calls for urgent action from the government of India (Census of India, 2011).

Child Sex Ratio in Kerala

Kerala is a peculiar state which outperforms other states of India in all human development indicators. Kerala achieved the highest sex ratio, literacy rate, lower maternal and infant mortality, and fertility rates three decades ago. Higher literacy of the people in Kerala has enabled lower female foeticides and infanticides, including a higher adult sex ratio. From the years 1901, Kerala has seen an upward trend of adult sex ratio. Unfortunately, despite being the state having a higher adult sex ratio, Kerala failed to maintain a higher Child Sex Ratio among Indian States. As per the 2011 census, Arunachal Pradesh has the highest Child Sex Ratio of 972 while in Kerala it is only 964.

The increasing trend of favourable sex ratio in Kerala from the year 1901 to 2011. Except for the years 1961 and 1971, there is a steady increase in the sex ratio in the state. In Kerala, the outmigration of younger males for employment is high. In addition, the survival chances of women in Kerala and sex ratios of above 50 age groups are higher when compared with their male counterparts. These are significant factors for the high adult sex ratio in Kerala (Vibhuti Patel, 2002). On the contrary, the Child Sex Ratio displays an adverse sex ratio in the state.

As per the census of 2011, the total child population of 0-6 years of age in Kerala was 3,472,955 in the year 2011 compared to 3,793,146 in the year 2001. The data depict a negative growth rate (-8.44 %) of child population in the state during a decade. In the year 2011, the per cent of child population in Kerala was only 10 while during the year 2001 it was 12 per cent. Among the districts in Kerala, Malappuram has the highest number of Children and the highest proportion of children to total population, while Wayanad has the lowest number of children and Pathanamthitta has the lowest proportion of children to total population in the year 2011. The child population has decreased in all the districts between the years 2001 and the 2011. All the southern districts except Kollam (-1 %) saw a decline of 2 per cent in the proportion of child population. On the other hand, all the northern districts, except Wayanad (-2 %), saw a decline of 1% in the proportion of child population in Kerala. From table 3, it is obvious that the southern districts have seen a bigger decline in child sex ratio than northern districts.

In a state like Kerala, the contradiction between the adult child sex ratio and child sex ratio has to be discussed in detail. Several studies on child sex ratio in Kerala found that the child sex ratio is alarmingly low in the state and emphasized the need for the formulation of policies and schemes by the government. On the other hand, the studies of demographic and health researchers rejects the notion of alarming child sex ratio. In Kerala, the sex ratio at birth dropped from 1407 in NFHS-4 to 951 in NFHS-5, while the overall sex ratio manifested a rise from 1049 in NFHS-4 to 1121 in NFHS-5. Generally, for biological reasons, boys are more tend to be born than girls. As per United Nations World Prospects Report 2019, normally, 107 boys per 100 girls are born in the world. Hence, 951 girls per 1000 boys at birth is normal according to demographic and health researchers. At the same time, boys are more prone to death. In all stages of life, males die more than females. This is the reason for the favourable sex ratio in many countries. But in India, girls die more than boys and this is mainly due to the gender discrimination existing in the country. But in Kerala, there is no evidence of gender bias at birth like sex-selective abortions. The prospective adopters prefer a girl child more than a boy child, though preferences for boys against girls can be seen in some cases. A couple with two girls may try again for a boy, and at the same time, a couple with two boys may not prefer another girl child. But, the possibility of this scenario is also negligible due to the lower fertility rate (Total Fertility Rate :1.8) in Kerala.

Welfare Schemes, Policies and Acts regarding Women and Child Health in India and Kerala

The government of India has put forward many laws, welfare schemes, and policies for the prevention of female foeticide and for fostering Child sex ratio. The fundamental rights unified in Part III of the constitution of India, part IV of directive principles of state policy and Part IV A of fundamental duties play a crucial role in the development and progress of a child. In the year 1951, Child Health and Reproductive Programme were initiated to provide quality endured primary health services to women. It also focused on immunization and family planning. The Integrated and Child Development Scheme (ICDS) launched on October 2^{nd,} 1975 was one of the important schemes for child development in earlier times. It aimed at reducing mortality, morbidity, malnutrition, and learning capacity among children aged 0-6 years along with their mothers. ICDS provided services of supplementary nutrition, immunization, health check-ups, referral services, and services on pre-school education. During the 1990s, India had higher Infant Mortality Rates and the government of India introduced the Reproductive and Child Health (RCH) programme to diminish Infant, Child, and Maternal mortality in the year 1997 (Centre for Public Impact, 2017). Under the RCH scheme, ORS kits were supplied to all sub centres in the country every year.

The pre-natal and Diagnostic Techniques (Regulation and Misuse) Act 1994, was enacted and implemented on 1st January 1996 to eliminate female infanticide in the country. The act prevents the disclosure and determination of the sex of a foetus. A breach of the act is punishable with fine and imprisonment. The government is extending financial support for all states and UTs for the operation of PNDT- cells, education and communication campaigns, capacity building and also stands as a pillar for the easy implementation of the Pre-Conception and Pre-natal Diagnostic Technique (PC-PNDT) Act under the guidance of National Health Mission (NHM).

The government of India has implemented different schemes for improving the health and nutrition among women and children through National Health Mission (NHM) and Integrated Child Development Schemes (ICDS) etc. Under NHM, the schemes like the Janani Suraksha Yojana (JSSK), 104 health helpline, 108 ambulance service, and weekly iron and folic acid supplementation (WIFS) programme are notable initiatives that helps to improve the health status of women and children. The national campaign "Beti Bachao, Beti Padhao" was launched on 22nd January 2015, in 100 gender critical districts under the guidance of the Ministry of Woman and Child Development and the Ministry of Human Resource Development with the goal of celebrating the girl child and providing her education. The other objectives of the scheme are to check gender biased sex selective abortions and safeguard the existence & safety of the girl child in addition to the education of the girl child. The scheme also cares for the health of mothers by providing different health care facilities in government hospitals.

The Ministry of Women and Child Development has taken various measures to address the declining child sex ratio and improve the status of the girl child. In addition, January 24 has been designated as "National Girl Child Day" since 2009. A sectoral Innovation Council was set up to examine the various issues related to the declining child sex ratio, recognizing the interventions which have functioned and not, an-d suggesting new strategies, procedures, and methods for addressing the diminishing child sex ratio. The council has undertaken several meetings and the members of the council have to make proper recommendations under the following heads: 1. Policies& programmes for the girl child and their implementation 2. Legal framework and the related issues like technology, violations and enforcement, and 3. Advocacy, awareness, and ethical issues-innovative approaches. All three subgroups have to arrange meetings and give a final report to the ministry.

A new scheme, 'Care and Protection of Girl Child', a Multi Sectoral Action Plan to prevent the diminishing sex ratio, has been formulated by the government to improve the child sex ratio by selecting the most critical 100 districts with the worst CSR across 12 states in the country. The other important initiative taken for improving the child sex ratio is the 'Beti Janmohotsava' under Mission Poorna Shakti in Rajasthan, for upgrading the value of the girl child in the community. The government of India also started various campaigns including 'Save the Girl Child' and telecasted a serial called 'Atmaja' for creating awareness of the value of girl child in society. In addition, health schemes like Janani Shishu Suraksha Karyakram (JSSK), Rashtriya Kishor Swasthya Karyakram (RKSK), Janani Suraksha Yojana (JSY), Rashtriya Bal Swasthya Karyakram (RBSK), Universal Immunisation Programme, Pradhan Mantri Surakshit Matritva Abhiyan (PMSMA), Navjeet Shishu Suraksha Karyakram (NSSK), LaQshya Programme (Labour Room Quality Improvement Initiative), Mission Indradhanush and National Programme for Family Planning. In addition, the national nutritional programmes namely MAA (Mother's Absolute Affection) Programme for Infant and Young Child Feeding, the National Programme for Prevention and Control of Fluorosis (NPPCF), the National Iodine Deficiency Disorders Control Programme and the National Iron Plus Initiative for Anaemia Control were also implemented.

In addition to the central schemes, various welfare schemes and policies were formulated by the Government of Kerala for the safety of women and children. The important schemes for women and children operating in Kerala are the Supplementary Nutrition Programme, Aswasanidhi, Beti Bachao Beti Padhao, Pradhan Manthri Mathru Vandana Yojana (PMMVY), and First 1000 days. NIRBHAYA, GIS based Mother and Child Health Tracking System in Mananthawady, Attapady and other backward blocks, Kaithangu, and Marriage assistance to inmates of women welfare institutions are other schemes implemented by the government of Kerala for the sake of women and children.

Conclusion

Sex Ratio is a key issue in the development of girl children and women, and thus the over-all development of a society. Without increasing the welfare of women and children, the nation will not progress. India is a country having the largest population in the world. Unfortunately, in India, the sex ratio is not favourable to women and girl child. This is mainly due to the female foeticide, infanticide, and ignorance of the girl child. Though Kerala is the state having a higher sex ratio among Indian states, the number of girl children is far behind their male counterparts. This contradictory phenomenon in Kerala has to be studied in detail and the government should implement proper laws, schemes, and policies to tackle this problem.

Development and Growth of Kerala Tourism

SEENA V

Kerala state situated on the tropical Malabar Coast of southwestern India is one of the most popular tourist destinations in the country. It is named as one of the ten paradises of the world by the National Geographic Traveler Kerala is famous especially for its ecotourism initiatives. Its unique culture and tradition coupled with its varied demography, has made Kerala one of the most popular tourist destinations in the world. Several international agencies, from UNESCO to National Geographic, have recognized the tourism potential of the state. Kerala has been selected by TIME Magazine as one of the 50 Extraordinary Places to Explore in the list of World's Greatest Places in 2022. In 2023, Kerala was listed at number 13 on The New York Times' annual list of places to visit, and was the only tourist destination listed from India.

Kerala is the first Indian state to declare tourism as an industry. Kerala's tourism brand, namely "Kerala - God's Own Country", was the first to be registered as a brand in the Trade Marks Registry of the Government of India. Kerala tourism has won several national and international accolades, mainly due to the scenic beauty of the region and the state's responsible tourism projects.

History of Kerala Tourism

The history of Kerala tourism dates back to 1900. It is associated with two names; Halcyon Palace in Kovalam and Colonel Godavarma Raja of the Poonjar royal family. The Travancore royal family took the initiative to promote Kovalam as a tourist destination. In 1929, His Highness Ramavarma of the Travancore royal family built the Halcyon Palace at Kovalam to attract tourists. Since then many foreign tourists frequently visited Kovalam and the palace. Foreign tourists started flocking to Kovalam from 1930s onwards. Col. GodaVarma Raja, a multi-talented man, took over the reins of Kerala's tourism development in 1934. He is named as the 'father of Kerala tourism'. He tried to remove obstacles in the development of Thiruvananthapuram International Airport. In 1960, GV Raja started Travancore-Kochi Cooperative Travels, today's Kerala Travels, the first tour operating company in Kerala. He promoted exhibitions in order to gain foreign markets for Kerala handicraft products. As a promotional measure the Travancore govt. started an Art Emporium in Mumbai in 1936. Periyar Wildlife Sanctuary was developed as a tourist destination by G.V. It was opened to tourists in 1931.

After Kovalam Beach, new places like Kochi have emerged as new tourist destinations. If GV Raja sparked the growth of tourism in Kerala, it was the Gulf boom of the 1970s that fueled it. Air service started between Kerala and Gulf countries opened the door for international tourists to reach Kerala. At that time, Kerala had no air connectivity with Europe and America. Air India started marketing tourism products in these countries in the 1980s. Air India operated low-cost flights and brought tourism professionals from abroad.

Until the early 1980s, Kerala was an unknown tourist destination, with most tourism circuits centered in the north of the country. Aggressive marketing campaign launched by the Kerala Tourism Development Corporation, the government agency to oversee the state's tourism potential, laid the foundation for the growth of the tourism industry in the state. By 1996, tourism was given the status of an industry. Kerala Tourism later adopted the tagline "God's Own Country" in its advertising campaigns. Aggressive promotion in print and electronic media has managed to invite substantial investment in the hospitality industry. By the early 2000s, tourism had grown into a full-fledged, multimillion-dollar industry in the state. The state has managed to secure a niche in the world tourism industry, thus becoming one of the 'highest brand recall' destinations. By 2003, a hitherto unknown tourist destination had become the fastest growing tourist destination in the world. National Geographic Traveler, a magazine published by the National Geographic Society in the US, has selected Kerala as one of the 'Ten Paradises of the World'. Today, Kerala is one of the most visited tourist destinations in India.

Kerala's model for success in Global Tourism

- Strong Brand positioning
- Thinking out side of the Box
- Product Differentiation
- Model public/private partnership
- Tremendous political support
- Public Acceptance
- Vibrant Private sector
- Safety and security for tourists

Major Tourism Products in Kerala

Kerala is far ahead of many other states in India in terms of diversity of tourism products. Major tourism products in Kerala are divided into six categories: (1) Heritage / Cultural / Religious places and events, (2) Backwaters, (3) Beaches, (4) Hill stations, (5) Forest and Wildlife tourism, and (6) Ayurvedic tourism. These are supported by the development of related tourism products such as eco-tourism and responsible tourism.

Table 7.1 Diversification of Tourism Products in Kerala

Tourism Product Categories	Domestic tourists (Percentage)	Foreign tourists (Percentage)
(1) Heritage / cultural /religious	65	40
(2) Backwaters	15	20
(3) Beaches	8	25
(4) Hill stations	7	5
(5) **Forest & Wildlife**	5	10
(6) Ayurvedic tourism*	Negligible	Negligible
Total	100	100

Source: Kerala Tourism Executive Summary- Tata Economic Consultancy Services, Bangalore, (2012)

The following section presents a brief picture of the major tourism products in Kerala.

1, Cultural & Heritage Tourism

Kerala's cultural heritage is about 5000 years old. The culture of Kerala is an amalgam of native art forms, language, literature, architectural style, music, festivals, cuisine, archaeological monuments, heritage centers and so on. There are many cultural institutions dedicated to protect these as well. Cultural and heritage tourism is an important tourism product of Kerala today. The main language spoken here is Malayalam and the people here are called Malayalees. Their traditional clothes include saree (for women) and mundu/lungi (for men). The staple cuisine here is sadya - vegetarian food served on banana leaves. Other delicacies include various vegetarian and non-vegetarian dishes.

Kerala has a distinctive architectural tradition. Places of worship and ancient houses are examples of that architectural style that gave importance to simplicity. They were built according to "Thachushastra." Kerala has about fifty unique classical dance forms. Among these, Theyam, Tiruvathirakali, Chakyar Kooth Koiyattam, Ottamtullal and Kolkali are prominent traditional dances in Kerala. Kerala is popular for two classical dance forms 'Kathakali' and 'Mohiniyattam' which attract tourists from all over the world. The musical culture of Kerala includes folk music (folk songs, ritual songs, Thiruvathira songs, Vanchipattu) and classical music comprising Carnatic music, Kathakali music and Sopana music. The traditional musical instruments of Kerala include among others Panchavadyam, Chendamelam, and Thayambaka. Kalaripayat is a martial art developed in Kerala.

Thrissur - "Cultural Capital of Kerala", its name is derived from "Thiru-Shiva-Peru" meaning, the abode of Lord Shiva. The best heritage sites in Kerala are Guruvayur - the historic Sri Krishna Temple, Cheraman Juma Masjid - the oldest mosque in India, Kerala Kalamandalam - famous for Kathakali training center and St. Thomas Monument which houses ancient relics. Sabharimala temple, Malayattoor church, Krishnapuram Palace, Mattancherry Dutch Palace, St. Francis Church, Kodungallur/Kranganoor, Pazhassiraja's tomb, St. Mary's Florance Church, Poonjar Palace, Bekal Fort, Sripadmanabhaswamy Temple, Jewish Synagogue, Bolgatti Palace, Thalassery Fort, Gundert Bungalow, Anchuteng Fort, Palakkad Fort, Edakkal Caves and rock-cut temples are places of historical importance in Kerala.

2, Backwater Tourism

Backwater tourism emerged as the backbone of the tourism sector of Kerala. While other types of tourist attractions abound in various parts of India, the extensive backwaters are a distinct feature of Kerala, providing a unique opportunity to position itself as an exotic tourism product. The geographical extent of backwaters makes it convenient and conducive to spread tourism activities across the state, thereby dispersing the accompanying economic benefits and mitigating negative impacts.

The backwaters of Kerala are one of the most captivating attractions for the tourists in Kerala. The palm-lined, serene backwaters were once the only trade routes of Kerala. The backwaters represent the largest inland lakes in Kerala. Kerala lives along these backwaters. The backwaters and lakes of Kerala narrated its history, shaped her present and offering unparalleled beauty and outstanding experiences. The whole of Kerala is blessed with rivers and the resources of many are still untapped. Waterways in Kerala play an important role in the state's economy. In the past, backwaters served as Kerala's main state highway. Passengers and goods were transported from one place to another through these backwaters. But today the tourism industry mainly uses these backwaters to introduce tourists to the hidden places of the state.

The Backwaters of Kerala are also a venue for the annual boat races that take place in the different parts of the state. Every year from July to November boat races are conducted across different backwaters in Kerala. The most famous boat race held in Kerala are Nehru Trophy Boat Race, Aranmula Boat race, Champakkulam Boat race, Payippad Boat race, Kallada Boat race, Sree Narayana Jayanthi boat race or Kumarakom Boat race, President's Trophy Snake boat race, Marine Drive Boat Race etc. Backwater tourism in Kerala is centered mostly around places like Alleppey and Kumarakom (Vembanad), Ashtamudi Lake at Kollam, Kavvayi Backwaters, Kochi Backwaters,

Chandragiri, Kumbalangi, Vallyaparamba etc.

3, Beach tourism

Kerala is a prime haven of beach tourism in India, and has one of the long coast line of 580 km (360 mi). Kovalam beach near Thiruvananthapuram is one of the first beaches in Kerala to attract tourists, and is today the most visited beach in the state. Other popularly visited beaches in the state are Kappad, Alappuzha, Kozhikode Beach, Marari Beach (Mararikulam, Alappuzha), Thumpoli (Thumpoli Beach) Alappuzha, Alappuzha, Natika (Thrissur), Vatanapilly Beach (Thrissur) and Cherai. Beach, Ponnani Beach, Bekal, Kappad Beypur Beach, Marari Beach, Fort Kochi, Varkala. Muzhappilangad Beach in Kannur and Thikkodi Beach in Calicut are two drive-in beaches in India. Marari Beach has been rated as one of the top five hammock beaches in the world by the National Geographic Survey. Beaches of Kerala offer a variety of options such as swimming, boating, wind & board surfing, water skiing, para-sailing,scuba diving and sport fishing. It is a fact that most of India's finest beaches are in Kerala.

4, Hill Station Tourism

Eastern Kerala is the land encroached by the Western Ghats. The region consists of high mountains, canyons and deep valleys. The Western Ghats is a UNESCO World Heritage Site and is one of the 36 biodiversity hotspots in the world. Wild lands are covered by dense forests, while other areas are under tea and coffee plantations (mainly established in the 19th and 20th centuries) or other forms of agriculture. The Western Ghats are at an average height of 1500 meters above sea level. There are more than 50 hill stations in the state. Some of the famous hill stations in this region are Munnar, Thekkady, Vagamon, Ponmudi, Lakkidi, Vythiri, Idukki, Peermade, Malampuzha, Mattupetty, Ayyampuzha, Gavi, Athirapally, Charalkunnu, Malayattoor, Thiruvambadi, Malakkappara, Vithura, Ranipuram, Paithalmala, Wayanad, Nelliampathi, Nilambur, Ponmudi.

5, Forest & Wildlife Tourism

The Western Ghats are a range of mountains that run almost parallel to the Arabian Sea through the states of Kerala, Tamil Nadu, Karnataka, Goa and Maharashtra. Out of a length of about 1800 km, about 450 km is in Kerala. The Western Ghats region of Kerala covers about 21856 square kilometers or 56% of the total geographical area of the state.

Kerala has 9,400 km² of natural forests, which include tropical moist evergreen and semi-evergreen forests, tropical moist and dry deciduous forests, montane subtropical, temperate or shola forests as well as 24% of Kerala's grasslands. It includes trees such as Anjily, Cassia, Fig, Rosewood, Teakwood, Bamboo, Palm etc and also includes the smaller bushes of spices and medicinal herbs like Pepper, Cardamom etc. Overall, Kerala's forests are home to more than 1000 species of trees and plants. Kerala is home to a variety of species such as the Asian elephant, Bengal tiger, leopard, Nilgiri tahr and grizzled giant squirrel, endangered species such as the lion-tailed macaque, Indian sloth bear and gaur. Other commonly found species include Indian Porcupine, Chital, tailed Macaque, Indian Sloth Bear and Gaur or Indian Bison, Sambar, Gray Langur, Flying Squirrel, Boar, Gray Wolf, and Common Palm Civet. These are found in the state's numerous wildlife reserves, sanctuaries and national parks that form prime biodiversity zones. There are about 453 varieties of birds in Kerala covering rare species such as Sri Lankan Frogmouth, Oriental Bay Owl and Indian Grey Hornbill as well as the more common and widespread ones like Peafowl, Cormorant, Hill Myna, Oriental Darter, Oriole, Drongo, Bulbul, Kingfisher, Woodpecker, Jungle Fowl, Water Fowl and other migratory birds. Reptilians include King Cobra, Viper, Python, and the more common Turtle and Crocodile. Insects like Butterflies and Ladybird Beetles are also found in plenty in these parts.

6, Ayurvedic Tourism

Health tourism is a new sector of the tourism industry and has been recognized as an important component of Kerala's economy. The terms medical tourism and health tourism are used interchangeably. But in Kerala it is known as Ayurvedic tourism. Medical tourism is a growing concept mainly due to cost-effective quality treatments available in Kerala. Health tourism mainly includes Ayurvedic treatments, yoga therapy, herbal treatments and indigenous systems.

Ayurvedic tourism is a craze for tourists visiting Kerala and has become an important component of health tourism. Kerala offers two types of health vacation options such as rejuvenation and treatment programs that come in four categories: health care (treatments), body care, beauty care and special treatments. The different ayurveda treatments are Abhyangam, Dhanyamla Dhara, Dhara, Kativasthi, Kizhi, Ksheeradhoomam, Ksheeradhoomam, Lepanam, Nasyam, Njavarakizhi, Pizhichi, Sirovasthi, Snehapanam, Thalam, Udvarthanam, Urovasthi, Vasthi etc.

7, Ecotourism

Ecotourism is a new concept in tourism. Ecotourism stands for green or conservation or sustainability. There is a relationship between living things and the environment, thus linking tourism development and the environment. Tourism helps in environmental development. Ecotourism is therefore purposeful travel to natural areas to understand the cultural and natural history of the environment, to preserve the integrity of the ecosystem, and to create economic opportunities that benefit local people in the conservation of natural resources.Kerala offers maximum potential for promoting ecotourism. Miles and miles of endless serene beaches, serene stretches of emerald backwaters, pristine valleys and mountains, rare flora and fauna, wildlife sanctuaries and national parks, fascinating art forms, magical festivals and cultural monuments are all unique to Kerala.

The Forest Department in Kerala where identified 60 ecotourism destinations in different parts of Kerala giving emphasis to conservation, ecological sustainability, environmental education and sharing benefits to the local community. With this objective in mind, Kerala Tourism has constituted a special Ecotourism wing to provide policy support for the development of ecotourism destinations in the state. The ecotourism project aims at the development of products such as trekking and bird watching trails, enabled by the constitution of Eco- Development Committees / Participatory Forest Management Committees (Vana Samrakshna Samithi). This will help to bring the benefits of ecotourism to the local people, which will ultimately gain the support of the local community for forest conservation.

Thenmala Ecotourism, India's first planned ecotourism destination was inaugurated in January 2001 in the foothills of the Western Ghats in Kollam district. Ecotourism practices were started in 59 other places, but the program was not a huge success, except in Thenmala and Parambikulam, Iravikulam. The Tiger Trail (guided trekking programme for tourists) in the Periyar Tiger Reserve is projected as a model success story in eco-tourism in forest areas. Here, local people organize trekking along designated forest routes. It is said that poaching and other illegal activities have reduced in the area due to the presence of trekkers.

Growth of Tourism in Kerala

This section furnishes an analysis of the growth of tourism in Kerala during last 12 years (2011-2012). This has been performed by focusing attention on three important aspects of tourism growth as:

1) Trends in tourist arrival in Kerala,

2) Earnings from tourism and

3) Plan allocation and expenditure to tourism sector.

1. **Trends in Tourist Arrivals in Kerala**

As a favorite tourist destination, Kerala receives both domestic and foreign tourists. Table 3.1 explains the trends in domestic and foreign tourists arrivals in Kerala during 2010 t0 2021. It also depicts the percentage variations of tourist arrivals over previous years (both domestic and foreign tourists).

Table 7.2:- Trends in Tourist Arrivals in Kerala

Year	Number of foreign Tourists	% variation	Number of domestic Tourists	% variation
2010	6,59,265	18.31	85,95,075	8.61
2011	7,32,985	11.18	93,81,455	9.15
2012	7,93,696	8.28	1,00,76,854	7.41
2013	8,58,143	8.12	1,08,57,811	7.75
2014	9,23,366	7.6	1,16,95,411	7.71
2015	9,77,479	5.86	1,24,65,571	6.59
2016	10,38,419	6.23	1,31,72,535	5.67
2017	10,91,870	5.15	1,46,73,520	11.39
2018	10,96,407	0.42	1,56,04,661	6.35
2019	11,89,771	8.52	1,83,84,233	17.81
2020	3,40,755	-71.36	49,88,972	-72.86
2021	60,487	-82.25	75,37,617	51.09

Source: Kerala tourism Statistics 2020, 2021, Department of Tourism, Government of Kerala Economic Review 2020, 2021 GoK

The table 7.2 depicts the gradual increase in the domestic and foreign tourist arrivals during 2010 to 2021. The domestic tourist visit in the State marked an annual growth rate of 8.61per cent with 85,95,075 lakhs tourists in 2010 which increased to 1,83,84,233 crores tourist with an annual growth rate of 17.81 per cent during the year 2019. There was a 18.31 percent increase in the foreign tourist arrivals in Kerala in 2010 with 6,59,265 lakhs tourists in 2010 which increased to 11,89,771 lakhs tourist with an annual growth rate of 8.52 per cent during the year 2019.

The percentage increase in foreign tourists reached its maximum in the year 2010 with an increase of 18.31 per cent and minimum in the year 2021 with a decrease of -82.25 per cent. The past ten years of data (2010-2019) of the domestic tourist arrivals shows that the state has achieved a double digit growth during the Years 2017 and 2019. During the pandemic the number of foreign tourist arrivals was declined from 11,89,771 to 3,40,755 and domestic tourist arrivals was also declined from 1,83,84,233 to 49,88,972 in the year 2020.

2) Earnings from tourism

Foreign exchange earnings from tourism have shown a steady growth over the years. In 2019, Kerala has earned Rs.10271.06 crores as foreign exchange earnings from tourism against Rs.8764.46 crores in the year 2018 showing a growth of 17.19 %. Table 1.3 throws light on the earnings from tourism in Kerala from 2010 to 2021.

Table 7.3 Earnings from foreign and Domestic tourists for the last 12 years

Year	Foreign Exchange Earnings	% Variations	Earnings from Domestic Tourists	% Variations	Total revenue generated from Tourism (Direct & Indirect)	% of Increase
2010	3797.37	33.09	9282.68	30.33	17348	31.12
2011	4221.99	11.18	10131.97	9.15%	19037	9.74
2012	4571.69	8.28	10883	7.41%	20430	7.32
2013	5560.77	21.63	11726.44	7.75%	22926.55	12.22
2014	6398.93	15.07	12981.91	10.71%	24885.44	12.11
2015	6949.88	8.61	13836.78	6.59%	26689.63	7.25
2016	7749.51	11.51	15348.64	10.93%	29658.56	11.12
2017	8392.11	8.29	17608.22	14.72%	33383.68	12.56
2018	8764.46	4.44	19474.62	10.60%	36258.01	8.61
2019	10271.06	17.19	24785.62	27.27%	45010.69	24.14
2020	2799.85	-72.74	6,025.68	-75.69%	11335.96	-74.82
2021	461.5	-83.52	**12285.91**	**8.38**	12285.91	8.38

Source; Kerala Tourism statistics 2021, 2022 Handbook of Statistics on Indian state

Foreign Exchange Earnings from Tourism

Earnings from tourism have shown a steady growth over the years (2010 to 2019). The table given above shows the foreign exchange earnings and domestic earning from tourism during 2010 to 2021. It also depicts the percentage variation of foreign exchange earnings and domestic earning over previous years. While analyzing the table it is found out that the percentage variations in foreign exchange and domestic earnings showed a mixed trend throughout the period. It becomes negative in the year 2020. **During the time of Pandemic** the foreign exchange earnings from tourism in 2020 was rupees 2,799.85 crore and domestic tourist earnings was rupees 6,025.68 crore. The total earnings in 2020 was only rupees 11,335.96 crore, registering a decline of (-) 74.81 per cent over 2019. In the year 2021 foreign exchange earnings was rupees 461.5 crore and percentage variation became -83.52%.

3) Plan allocation and expenditure

Kerala has taken the lead among Indian States in making substantial allocations in the government budget for the tourism sector which indicates the importance given to the tourism sector. The allocation of funds to tourism industry in the planning time and the original expenditure of fund to the tourism sector are revealed in the table below. The details of Plan allocation and expenditure of tourism sector during the period 2010-11 to 2019-20 are given in Table 7.4.

Table 7.4 Plan allocation and expenditure of tourism sector from 2010-11 to 2019-20

Financial Year	Amount Sanctioned (Rs.In Lakhs)	Expenditure (Rs. In Lakhs)
2010-2011	14528.43	13306.54
2011-2012	18249.48	17654.22
2012-2013	18053.28	17443.17
2013-2014	21489.8	21257.23
2014-2015	24535.61	22435.13
2015-2016	23045.45	20273.15
2016-2017	31931.96	29610.67
2017-2018	35010.38	30894.57
2018-2019	30249.6	28931.4
2019-2020	39237	19550.78

Source: Kerala tourism Statistics 2019

Impact of COVID-19 on Kerala Tourism

This section analysis the impact of COVID-19on Kcrala Tourism sector by comparing with 2019 and 2020 data, and State Intervention against COVID-19

As tourism alone contributes 10 per cent to the state's economy and employs 23.5 per cent of the total workforce. The outbreak of the epidemic has seriously affected the economy of Kerala. According to the Kerala Tourism Department, The foreign tourist arrivals in the state slumped by 72% from 11.89 lakh in 2019 to 3.40 lakh in 2020. Similarly, the domestic tourist arrivals declined by 71% from 1.83 crore in 2019 to 49.88 lakh in 2020. Consequently, the earnings from tourism declined by 75%, the revenue generated from tourist footfall were 11,336 crore last year as compared to Rupees 45,019 crore in 2019. All these shown in the Table 1.5

Table 7.5 Kerala Tourism at a glance 2019 and 2020 year - a comparison

1	Total tourist arrivals in 2020	53,29727 (Nos)
	Total tourist arrivals in 2019	189,84,233 (Nos)
	% Variation	72.8%
2	Foreign tourist arrivals in 2019	1189233 (Nos)
	Foreign tourist arrivals in 2020	340755 (Nos)
	% Variation	72%
3	Domestic tourist arrivals in 2019	18384233 (Nos)
	Domestic tourist arrivals in 2020	4988972 (Nos)
	% Variation	71%
5	Total Earnings from tourist arrivals 2019	Rs. 45,010 crore
	Total Earnings from tourist arrivals 2020	Rs. 11336 crore
	% Variation	75%
6	Earnings from Foreign Tourists in 2019	10271.06 crore
	Earnings from Foreign Tourists in 2020	2799.85 crore
	% Variation	72.74%
7	Earnings from Domestic Tourists in 2019	24785.62 crore
	Earnings from Domestic Tourists in 2020	6,025.68 crore
	% Variation	-75.69%

Source: Kerala Tourism Department

The shocking collapse of the tourism industry in Kerala is reflected in the livelihoods of the people. According to figures released by the Travel Agents Federation of India (TAFI) Kerala, over one lakh people have lost their jobs in 2020-21 and more than 20,000 shareholders have terminated their ventures. More over the state's tourism industry is estimated to have incurred a loss of Rs 20,000 crore in 2020-21. (Source: Directorate of Tourism)

State Intervention on Tourism Sector against COVID-19

The tourism sector has been hit hard by the Covid-19, since it has direct effect on employment and livelihood of rural people involved in the sector directly and indirectly. In a bid to revive the State's travel and tourism sector, the State Government has announced the Chief Minister's Tourism Loan Assistance Scheme (CMTLAS), Tourism Working Capital Support Scheme, Tourism Employment Support Scheme, Tourism Houseboat Support Scheme and Tourism Guide Support Scheme for the stakeholders in the tourism industry in the wake of **COVID-19**. Few of them are discussed below-

1, Tourism Houseboats Support Scheme (THSS): Houseboats are one of the favorite products of Kerala Tourism. Houseboats provide employment to a large number of people, thereby providing a livelihood for their families. Like all other segments of the tourism industry, houseboats suffer severe setbacks as a result of the COVID-19 pandemic.

Although there are over a thousand houseboats plying in various backwaters in Kerala, the COVID-19 pandemic has been docked or inoperative for several months now. These vessels are already exposed to severe damages. This will require additional investment to repair the damage caused to the houseboat entrepreneurs and to bring the houseboats back. So the government has implemented a financial assistance scheme (Tourism Houseboats Support Scheme) to help the houseboat sector. Houseboat owners can avail this Scheme (THSS) to obtain one-time financial assistance for emergency repairs and maintenance of house boats. Financial assistance for repair and maintenance of the houseboats shall be provided in three categories up to a maximum of Rs80000, Rs100000 and Rs120000 respectively.

As per this scheme, Financial Assistance for repair and maintenance of the house boats will be provided as follows.

For houseboats with 01-02 bedrooms up to a maximum of Rs. 80,000 / -

For houseboats with 03-04 bedrooms up to a maximum of Rs. 1,00,000 / -

For houseboats with 05 bedrooms and above up to a maximum of Rs. 1,20,000 /-)

The validity period for applying for financial assistance was till 30.11.2020. As a result, the additional financial commitment of the Government is `9.90 crore.

2, Tourism Working Capital Support Scheme (TWCSS): The government has approved the Tourism Working Capital Support Scheme to help entrepreneurs in the tourism industry overcome the crisis following the outbreak of Covid-19. As per this, tourism entrepreneurs will get a loan of `25 lakh as per the approved policy of the concerned banks. Department of Tourism would absorb 50 per cent of the interest, subject to a maximum of 4.5 per cent for the first 12 months. The remaining 50 per cent will have to be borne by the borrower concerned.

Repayment duration will be 42 months, including six months repayment holiday.

The total loan amount under this scheme is limited to Rs. 355 Crore.

Resorts and hotels, Ayurveda centres, Tour operators/travel agents, Transport operators, Houseboats, Restaurants, Serviced Villas, Grihasthali Units, Homestays and Tourist motor boat operators that are Licensed/ Classified/Approved/Accredited by State/Union Governments are eligible to apply.

Validity of the scheme: 31.03.2021

3, Tourism Employment Support Scheme (TESS): The Covid-19 pandemic devastated the tourism industry as a whole with an estimated loss of Rs 20,000 crore. The ban on all domestic and international air services, trains and all local transport has made the tourism industry bookings almost zero. All stakeholders, including tour operators, hotels / resorts, ayurvedic centers, home stays, houseboats, restaurants, tourist guides, and transport providers, have lost their daily bread due to this problem. Many employees working in various tourism establishments have been made unpaid or underpaid, causing them severe hardship. Therefore, to protect and support the interests of the employees, the government has proposed Tourism Employment Support Scheme (TESS) for employees to the State Co-operative Bank of Kerala. Under this scheme, Kerala Bank will provide short-term loans (up to 18 months) at an interest rate of 9% up to Rs. 30,000 / - per annum to tourism employees. The Department of Tourism will bear 6% of the interest and the remaining 3% will be borne by the total and the remaining 3% will be borne by the concerned borrower. For this the employer has to submit a list of permanent or daily wages working in their establishments.

4, Tourism Guides Support Scheme (TGSS): Tourist guides are an essential part of the tourist industry and act as a bridge between the destination and the visiting tourists. It is through them that tourists learn about destinations, and like many other partners, they have been instrumental in making 'Destination Kerala' a popular tourism brand. Like all other segments of the tourism industry, tourist guides suffer severe setbacks as a result of the COVID-19pandemic. Since the entire tourist center remains dormant for about fifteen months, it is very difficult for the tourist guides to make their living. In this context, the Government of Kerala has decided to provide financial assistance to tourist guides working in Kerala. The scheme aims to provide financial assistance to tourist guides until the tourism field returns to normal. National Level Tourist Guides approved by the Ministry of Tourism of India, State Level Tourist Guides approved by the Department of Tourism, Government of Kerala and Local Level Tourist Guides approved by the Government of Kerala are eligible for financial assistance under this scheme. The Department of Tourism has decided to provide a one-time non-refundable financial assistance of Rs. 10,000 each to the guides in the above categories.

5, Bio bubble tourism: Bio bubble tourism is a positive response of Kerala tourism in the COVID-19era. The Bio Bubble is a sanitized, safe and secure environment that provides immunizations to people who are likely to come in contact with tourists. Tourists landing at any airport in Kerala can only see the vaccinated ground staff. From the airport, they can drive to their chosen destination in cabs provided by authorized tour operators, and their drivers are vaccinated. This applies to the hotels, resorts and homestays where they stay during the holidays.

Through these relief measures, the Government of Kerala extended help to all the stakeholders of the industry to tide over the current crisis and start functioning as soon as the pandemic gets controlled. The State Government has always been actively supporting tourism sector.

Aspects to consider on the way forward

- Kerala must maintain its reputation as a leading tourist destination, a world-renowned brand and a continuously growing business.
- The focus should be on destination development, tourism infrastructure, tourism products, information technology, hospitality, investment and funding in the tourism industry.
- Heritage Tourism, Cultural Tourism, Health Tourism, Adventure Tourism, Monsoon Tourism and MICE Tourism need to be prioritized.
- Other issues like health, sanitation, urban-rural planning and connectivity need to be addressed.
- There is a need to focus on promoting rural tourism and extending responsible tourism practices to all destinations.
- The state should strive to accelerate tourist arrivals in a sustainable and responsible manner.
- Provide a warm, safe, clean, hygienic and accessible destination that offers unique experiences for all.
- Kerala should develop different strategies to meet the needs of international, domestic and local tourists.

CHAPTER EIGHT

Agriculture and Industrial Sector

Kerala agriculture

KAVEYA P

Kerala is the 21st largest Indian state. It comprises of 38863 sq. Km. With a GDP growth rate of 12 per- centage in agriculture the GDP position originates as the 8th position. The Kerala model of development regards high importance to the agricultural sector around 12.5 per cent are employed in the primary sector of the economy. Around 7 per cent of the GSDP of the economy is contributed by the Indian agricultural area. Around 97 per cent of the national output of the pepper production and 85 per cent are contributed by the natural rubber.90 per cent of the total cardamom production is being undertaken by the Kerala economy in India.

Animal husbandry and home gardens comprises a significant proportion of the agricultural sector practices. Majority of the labour force which includes around 3.2 million people are employed in feeding, milking, breeding, management, health care and concomitant. Top most production in case of Kerala is in the area of rice or paddy production. About 600 varieties of rice are available in Kerala and it exists as an important contribution in the area of productivity. The kuttanad region of the district of Kerala stands as a significant one in the area of agricultural productivity. Tapioca stands as the next most important one in the area of agricultural productivity. Other important crops include cardamom, cinnamon, clove, turmeric, nutmeg and vanilla. In 1960-61 Kerala accounts to almost 71 per cent of the country's total coconut production .Agricultural programmes concentrate mainly to upload the section that is the primary sector and the programmes includes Pradhan Mantri Krishi sinchai yojana, national scheme of welfare of fisherman, vibrant village programmes etc.

Private and public sector industries

The public private discussion has always been a burning discussion of the recent dates. The Liberalisation privatisation and globalisation tendency of 1991 has promoted the growth of private sector entity which ease the operation of establishment of a particular industrial unit. Public industry by meaning refers to those industries which functions on the basis of welfare consideration considering each and every sector of the economy. On the other hand, private sector entity includes those industries which functions in accordance with the means of profit motive.

Role and growth of private and public sector industries

It was with the rapid liberalisation tendencies that there was rapid growth of the private sector industrial units. There was the existence of public sector industrial units initially with rapid contributions in almost all areas of operation. The public sector industrial units where basically classified into three which included financial institutions, departmental undertakings and non-departmental undertakings. Most of the industrial units basically lie upon the principal of welfare motive but their contributions to the economy was minimal. This marked the beginning of a new phase with private sector industrial units contributing significantly towards the development of the area. The basic idea behind the formation was development of capital goods industries and that of basic goods industries[1].

Objectives of public sector industrial units

1. To develop a strong industrial base for the economy

2. To create more and more amount of employment opportunities
3. To develop and prosper the infrastructural base of an economic unit
4. To provide and augment social and economic resources of a particular country
5. To promote export and reduce the level of import of a particular country
6. To reduce the level of inequalities that exist and move for a rapid span of development opportunities

Public sector and economic progress

1.Public sector and capital formation: capital formation refers to rapid development of capital basis of an economy. Addition of capital stocks, saving and investment adds a lot to the economic progress of a nation adding more to the GDP base of an economic unit.

Role of public sector in economic growth

The public sector industrial units are an important backbone for the augmentation of the industrial productivity of an economic unit. Around 14 per cent of the contribution to the economy are being made by these public sector industrial units. The role of the public sector could be analysed considering various factors which includes:

1. Generation of income
2. Capital formation
3. Employment
4. Infrastructure
5. Strong industrial base
6. Export promotion and import substitution
7. Contribution of central exchequer
8. Concentration of income and wealth
9. Removal of regional disparities

1. **Generation of Income:** Public sector plays an important role in generation of income of a particular country. The share of public sector in the net domestic product of an economy has increased tremendously augmented from 7.5 per cent to 21.7 in 2003-04.
2. **Capital formation**

Role played by the public sector industrial unit always stands as an important one in the area of contribution of gross domestic production of a particular economy. The contribution of public sector shows an increasing tendency from 7.6 per cent to 22.7 percent at 2002-2003.The liberalisation process even though had paved the way for the establishment of private sector industrial units their contribution to the total productivity of an economy stands as an important thing to be discussed with.

1. **Employment**

Public sector plays an important role in mobilising the employment situations of particular economy. The employment level in the public sector industrial unit could however be divided into two which mainly comprises of public sector employment situations in the government departments and administration situations. Employment in the public sector units both of the central and state governments. Figures postulates that around 11 million employment situations are being provided by the public sector industrial units in 1971.Around 18.6 million employment opportunities are being provided by the public sector industrial unit with swapped levels of potentiality in the employment situations generated. At the end of march 2004, about 51.7 per cent of the employment situations are being provided by theses public sector industrial units incurring and concentrating more for the development of government departments, administration centres and personal services.

1. **Infrastructure**

Infrastructural facilitates plays an important role in mobilising the GDP contribution of an economy. Development of a society highly depends upon the social and economic infrastructure of a particular economy. Ample amount of investment in all sectors lays great emphasis on agricultural and industrial development of an economy. private sector and public sector investment opportunities invite massive levels of investment options leading to over all development of the economy.

1. **Strong industrial basin**

Public sector industrial basin plays an important role in building a strong industrial unit in an economy. It was with the in initiation of five-year plan and development of iron and steel industry massive contributions in the field of industrial development occurred. Second five-year plan too laid great emphasis on industrial development with the plan mechanism called MAHALNOBIS MODEL of development. It also laid great emphasis on development of chemical industries, coal and copper industry at that time period. The maximum growth was seen in the railway sector and minimum in case of housing and urban affairs. capital outlay contribution was also rapid in the field of ministry of petroleum and natural gas too.

1. **Export promotion and import substitution**

Public sector industries plays an important role export promotion and import substitution pattern of an economy. The foreign exchange earning had increased from 35 crore to around 6000 crore in the near century. Important public sector industrial units include Hindustan steel limited, Bharat electronics etc. With the initiation of Liberalisation. privatisation and globalisation even though the private sector progressed massive levels of progress was seen in the area of public sector industrial basin.The share of the public sector industrial basin in the area of important public sector industrial units. Massive levels of trend were seen in the area of engineering goods and lower export trends was seen in the area of organic and inorganic chemicals with a ratio of 29.15. Key import trends were seen in the area of petroleum and crude oil products with a contribution of 160.7 and lower in the case of machinery, electrical and non-electrical component with a share of 39.9.

Role and growth of private sector industry

Liberalisation privatisation and globalisation 1991 tendency marked the beginning and establishment of private sector industrial basin. Role and growth of private sector plays an important role in contributing towards the economic growth and development of a particular economy.The share of private sector industrial growth rate. The number of private sectors in 2000-01 was 1,10,634 in compare to total number of companies 1,28,549.

1. **Employment Generation**

Private sector plays an important role in creating employment generation of an economy. private sector industrial basin starts as an important one in area of small scale, medium and large-scale industrial basin.The contribution of public sector, joint sector, private sector and employment in other sectors. The employments sector development in public sector accounts to 3430, in joint sector it accounts to 309, private sector it includes 3965,others constitute 46 and in total it makes up to 7750.

1. **Development**

Private sector employment helps in the over all development of an economy. It helps in the development of industrial basin, plants and job hubs. Recent studies postulates that the contribution of private sector in developing the Gross Domestic Product of an economy shows a developing tendency. About 90 per cent of its potential contribution are contributed by them.

1. **Making use of technology**

Technological factors play an important role in development of private sector industrial units. Making use of both labour intensive and capital intensive technological progress leads to employment of resources in an efficient manner leading to over all development of an economy. The fourth industrial revolution led to massive levels of development in the area and move towards a digitalised platform lead to prosperity of the economy as a whole. Industry led initiatives widened the scope of operation and created a network platform through which massive levels of developmental strategies where initiated.The share of Indian economy in India's global innovation index shows a declining trend which is due to fault adoption of good and ample technological progress. The global innovation index shows a decline from 66 to 60,then to 57,52,48 and 46 from 2016 to 2021.Proper selection of technology hence matters a lot. The economic survey of 2021-22 revealed that China basically depends upon labour intensive technology as it was easily available for them employing and swapping much more human capital formation. Identifying the potential group matters a lot.

1. **Fostering innovation and entrepreneurship**

Private industrial units mainly focus on the development of GDP contribution of an economy. Modern century is governed by innovatory practices and trends which positively results in the over all progress of an economy. There are both labour intensive and labour-intensive technical progress but representing them in a perpetual way matters mostly. private sector positively results in a sustainable technology based innovatory practices resulting in massive level of prosperity. It provides way for a sustainable developmental progress resulting in adaptation of innovatory practices in an economy. In most of the developed countries massive research and development activities are initiated so that positive human capital formation takes place.The growth of public and private sector industrial units. The trend from 1981 to 2006 shows that up to 2000 public sector shows a progressive trend and latter it declines. Private sector increases up to 2002 and later shows a minimum decrease and latter it shows a positive contribution.

Problems of Rubber Cultivation in Kerala

SHABNA S S

Kerala's Natural Rubber cultivation is region-centric and covers 88% of the area and production in Rubber production. Natural Rubber has a vital role in the development of the socio-economic lifestyle of the rural poor. The economic position of small rubber growers is miserable due to price instability, labor costs, Resource constraints, tree disease attacks, unskilled labors, low productivity, poor processing quality, weak marketing system, etc... Majority of smallholders including men and women in traditional rubber areas are not a member of RPS, hence not availing any kind of assistance and at the same time, suffering from middlemen exploitations. Small farmers are less aware of ICT-based interventions, tapping systems, varieties of trees to be cultivated, preventive measures to be taken for disease attacks, scientific manuring for productivity enhancement, etc. They are illiterate to adopt technological readiness. Rubber is a chief outlet for automobile industries. Due to insufficiency in rubber production, less import duty and reduction in demand, India depends on other rubber-producing countries which may result in a declining trend in GDP. Here, the researcher identifies the need for an in-depth analysis of how the problems in NR cultivation impact the socio-economic profile of the rural poor and the Natural rubber productivity and what are the suggestions to promote these scattered unorganized farmers at the grass root level, thereby improving them with technological readiness for the overall growth of the economy.

Keywords: Natural Rubber; Rubber cultivation; women empowerment; ICT; GDP; Socio-economic profile; Rural poor; Technological readiness; livelihood

India is in a prominent position through the dominance of small sectors structural transformation of 88% of smallholders. The Natural Rubber tree was found by Christopher Columbus, during his visit to South America in

1493. The name 'RUBBER' came from the first use of Rubber, it was used to rub off charcoal marks or graphite on paper, hence the name 'RUBBER' came. Rubber is dynamic, and versatile which is an indispensable part of our life. Indian Rubber industries use Natural Rubber (NR) as a basic raw material to manufacture a variety of products such as Automobile spare parts, Consumable goods, Industrial goods, medical equipment, etc. through diversification and modernization of Natural Rubber products. Rubber is the backbone of Commercial Agricultural activity. India has a fast-growing domestic market in Natural Rubber. The dependency on Natural rubber is more in India. Rubber industries are the emerging ones that changed the lifestyle of Human beings. Rubber products have a place in the international market too. India has the best availability of foreign exchanges through this. Rubber has strategic importance as a Raw material in the level of cultivation, production, Processing, and Marketing of Natural Rubber. Rubber cultivation has great importance in the creation of economic opportunities and rural employment. Automobile parts are the chief outlets of Rubber, which are the largest consumable goods. Today's world cannot imagine a world without Rubber. As a cash crop or plantation crop Rubber growers experience the usage of Natural rubber in Domestic, Industrial, and technological. So, it is the most profitable plantation cash crop in today's scenario. India's Domestic market is dominated by small-holding sectors and the Production of Natural Rubber is highly focused on regional concentration, i.e., in traditional regions in Kerala. Rubber plantation improves the social and economic status of the Rural population. Rubber Producer Societies (RPS) are the village-level self-helping group that functions under the guidance of the Rubber Board. RPS empowers small growers by assisting with new planting, replanting, finance, and Rubber Board grants. Cooperative societies are district-level organizations entitled to the marketing and promotion of the Natural Rubber and Rubber Board at the National level. The Rubber Board, which is an apex controlling body of the Rubber plantation industry, promotes Rubber industries through scientific, technological, or economic research and provides technical advice to improve Rubber productivity. There was a tremendous growth trend in the production of rubber industry after the Second World War. 'Indian Rubber Board' was set up by the Government on the recommendation of the Ad hoc committee in 1945. Later, the Rubber Production and Marketing Act of 1954 replaced the name with 'Rubber Board'. Kerala produces more rubber in Kottayam District, so the Government of India selected Kottayam as the headquarter of the Rubber Board.

Rubber cultivation: statistics

The World's largest producer of Rubber is in Thailand. Apart from Thailand, the production and consumption of Rubber is more in Vietnam, Indonesia, and India. Asian Countries dominate 93% of the total area in Rubber cultivation. A statistical report shows that Kerala, the chief producer of Asia produces 3207100 tons of NR and in the list of state-wise production of Rubber, Kerala's productivity is between 438630- 490450 tonnes. In 1902, on the banks of the river Periyar in Kerala, the British government started Rubber production in India. In India, Rubber is cultivated in 16 states. India is the second largest producer of Rubber. India has a structural transformation of 88% of the area and production is in small farmers. The largest consumable goods are tires and tubes, and more than 50% of rubber production is engaged in Automobile parts. In ancient India at the year of 1886, the Government of Travancore state introduced Rubber cultivation in Calicut and Panchor as an experimental basis. The first Commercial cultivation of rubber started in 1902 at Kerala. In Kerala, Rubber production contributes 74% of India's Rubber production. Apart from Kerala, Karnataka and Tamil Nādu also contributes well. In Report of the Rubber Board, states that during the period of 2017-20, there seems a decline in Rubber production in Kerala. It means during 2017-18, the Rubber production is 5.40 lakh tonne which is reduced to 5.33 in 2017-18. But at the same time, it increased in the northeast states of India such as Nagaland, Assam, and Tripura. Therefore, the planning authority of Industry Body Automotive Tyre Manufactures (ATMA) invested 1100 crores to enhance additional rubber production in 200000 hectares of land in Northeast India.

Rubber horticulture: geographic characteristics

Rubber as a plantation crop adopted Horticulture as a farming practice. The exclusive provider of Natural Rubber is Hevea trees. Propagation by seeds and propagation by bud grafting are the two methods used for the propagation of rubber plants. Rubber plants are obtained by seeds or bud grafting. The growth and yield of a Rubber tree depend on the suitability of the soil and its proper management. The climatic conditions of Kerala are well suited for the Rubber vegetation. Kerala receives rain from southwest and northeast monsoons. Alluvial soil or deep and laterite soil with an Acidic PH value of 4.5 to 6.0 is considered best suited for the Rubber plantation. In India Rubber is cultivated on porous, well-drained laterite soil which is mostly concentrated in remote rural areas. Rubber tapping needs skilled labours who know tapping and preventive mechanisms for disease attacks. Tapping seems easier when the land is gently sloppy and Soil erosion is experienced as a major problem on steep slopes. The prevention of soil erosion is better seen in flat lands. So before cultivating, growers use machines for the preparation and better harvesting of tress. Kerala is rich in the availability of cheap labours. Rubber trees require an equatorial or Tropical climate with

an annual rainfall of 2000 to 4500 mm and a temperature of above 25 $^{\circ}C$ is suitable. Rubber is grown gradually at a higher elevation which is more than 1500 feet. Rubber is effectively planted mostly in slope and undulated land or slightly high elaborated flat land, where there is no possibility of water stagnation and well drainage, thereby it can be grown up successfully to the elevation of 450 meters from sea level. Kerala's Rubber cultivation is fully region-centric; therefore, rubber is productively grown in regions which is hot and moist. The rubber tree is sown in June-July and cut in Nov to Dec. The planting structure of Rubber trees on land is not similar to other trees, rubber trees are planted in rows with a density of 100 to 300 trees per acre or 2 trees in a cent, and a fact that not all trees are fit for cultivation. For Rubber growers, the plantation of rubber is an art and it requires skill and patience. **Cover cropping** is a cultural practice that benefits soil erosion protection, reduction in nutrient leaching, weed suppression, water quality, improve soil fertility, and integrated pest management. The leguminous plants which are grown between the seedling tree of rubber plants conserve the soil by adding humus and nitrogen content. **Intercropping** is an agricultural practice of planting multiple species in a single land along with a plantation crop. Small growers grab benefits from this practice through increasing profit, protection of cash crops, prevention of soil erosion, getting nutrients to the main crop, natural suppression of diseases, and reduction in fertilizer applications. **Rain guarding** in Rubber trees acts as a tool for diverting the stem flow of water from the tapping panel and bark area of the tree for protecting the tapping area from fungal infection. It enhances latex productivity and income generation for small growers. For the healthy growth of trees, the cultural practice of Cover cropping, weed controlling, mulching with dry leaves, grass cutting, and Intercropping is essential. The traditional practice of Hand weeding is popular in Kerala.

Rubber tapping and processing

Rubber Tapping is the process of making a 2 mm deep cut at an angle of 300 in a rubber tree for collecting milk juice or latex or it is a process of obtaining sap/ latex from the rubber tree. But during the process, tappers should ensure that the cambium of the tree is not damaged. Cambium is a paper-like thin skin seen between the wood and bark of the tree. Tapping is a skillful job and hard work, it requires special care, In-depth knowledge, and patience. Maturing period of the rubber tree is about 7-8 years and thereby it becomes a source of income for farmers. In a year, Rubber trees are tapped for between 200-300 days and a rubber tree gives latex/milk juice for 25-30 years. Latex is seen in the bark area of the tree and the small growers collect it from the cells of several plants by using the appropriate tapping method. A rubber tree becomes productive when it begins to provide Latex. The appropriate time for Rubber tapping starts at 2 AM, overnight. Due to the coolness of the morning air, the latex drips smoothly, thus improving yield. It is done by a spread tapping knife, which is used to shear off a thin layer of the tree. Cutting deeply would cause injury, thereby reducing the rubber-yielding capacity. When the latex flows, Farmers collect it in a coconut shell or plastic cup, which is attached via a short sharp stick in the tree. The latex will be stopped flowing by noon or early afternoon. Tapping should not be done during rain, the mixing of water may dilute latex. Rubber tappers carry latex to the rubber factory by collecting it from all coconut shells into tins. In the Rubber factory, Rubber processing is done by the pooling of small holdings of small growers. Tapping can be easier if the land is gently sloppy. For flat or gentle slopes, machines are used for the preparation and clearing of the land. On steep slopes, experienced soil erosion is a major problem but on flat land, this problem is not there. Terraced farming is an add-on factor for small growers. Latex, Sheet rubber, and scrap rubber are the main crops of Rubber plantations. According to the market demand, Rubber manufacturing industries further processed these crops in the forms required. Natural Rubber is soft and sticky and the properties of natural Rubber are improved through vulcanization. The latex is poured into moulds, then formic acid and acetic acid are added. To squeeze out water, latex passes through rollers or rubber pressing machines, and for removing excess water, wet sheets are hung on reapers. Smokehouses are used for the final drying of sheets. The sheets are then graded and packed in bales and marketed. Smallholders market sheet rubber and latex through village-level dealers and the price is determined by the demand and supply prevailing in the market.

In Kerala, more than 88% of the area and production is famous for its Agriculture and farming practices and it is covered by small rubber growers. Rubber cultivation is region-centric, a source of livelihood for small farmers in rural areas. But the crop profitability and annual income of smallholders are exploited by middlemen interventions. They are suffering from poor processing, low pricing, and weak marketing systems. The rural rubber economy experiences price instability in the domestic market. It negatively impacts their livelihood. A rubber tree only matures after 7-8 years so, Rubber cultivation needs a long time period for returns of its investment. Small farmers work hard to improve the productivity of rubber. They are difficult to bear the cost of production and price instability. Most of the farmers stop tapping rubber because of fluctuations in demand and supply. The preparation and management of Natural Rubber is highly labor-intensive. Crop profitability and productivity of rubber crops are fully dependent on the quality, hard work, and skill of labors. During rubber tapping, the tapper should be careful not to cut the cambium of the tree. It should be done with utmost patience and in-depth knowledge. Kerala has the availability of cheap labors but the rural economy faces insufficient skilled labor as a complicated labor issue. Most of the Rubber tappers seem unaware of the tapping methods, Manuring and practicing slaughter tapping affects tree productivity. Around 75% of middle-class and 20% of high-class rubber cultivators possess a high degree of labor expenditure. But 10% of the vulnerable category of small growers afford self-labor. Dependence on hired level is an operational-level problem of cultivation. Due to low educational status, small growers in rural area are less aware of ICT, technological interventions, the latest productivity hormones, and trends in modern rubber plantations. The global demand for natural rubber increased especially due to technical advancement. Countries generate income through rubber exports. Automobile industries are the chief consumers of rubber products. As domestic production does not meet the entire consumption, India imports from other rubber-producing countries. The foreign exchange spent on these rubber imports results in cash outflow and impacts low economic development. Tapping can be easier if the land is gently sloppy. For flat or gentle slopes, machines are used for the preparation and clearing of the land. On steep slopes, experienced soil erosion is a major problem but on flat land, this problem is not there. The rural population spent a huge expenditure on the preparation and maintenance of the land. The formation of steeper slopes on terraced farming needs additional labor. Cover cropping, intercropping, rain guarding, and beekeeping are the other allied activities done along with rubber cultivation. It is an add-on factor of cost, but depending on the climatic conditions, income may be increased up to an extent. Another important issue is that rubber harvesting is highly susceptible to bacterial degeneration. Most of the Small growers are less aware of the preventive measures for diseases. Due to fewer management trees become immature early. Rubber board statistics show that rubber productivity is comparatively lower. Most of the rubber growers are not a member of RPS, so they are not getting any assistance from the government or the Rubber board. A sector of Rubber growers are still remaining marginalized or unorganized, scattered throughout the country. They are facing problems from the planting stage to the marketing stage.

CHAPTER NINE

Trade,Export,Survey and budget

Trade sector

HARSHA V K

The system of buying and selling goods and services is called trade. There are various types of trade within (internal) and outside the country (international). If the trades are classified into five categories, they are Domestic Wholesale, Foreign, Import and export. Trade is said to be a necessary factor for the growth of Kerala. Trade mainly advocates more employment opportunities and eradication of poverty. All this contributes to the growth of Kerala's economic opportunities. Kerala's middle class spends the most money on food and clothing. If we talk about the Kerala market, the situation here is that in the trade sector, low price items are sold more and expensive items are sold less.

There are many types of trade sectors in Kerala. Food, clothing, jewelry, hardware shop, electronic shop, handicraft shops, medicine shops, mobile shops, wood shop, agricultural shop, flower shop, bakery, thrift shop, hotel, vehicle shop, book shop, supermarket, mall ,Thattukada, vehicle repair shops, steel shops, beauty parlors, petrol or diesel pumps, unused household items shops, vegetable shops, stationery shops,fish markets,meat shops, Clock shops,Street vendors, fruits shop, Akshaya centers,Driving Training Institutes Tourist bus service center, educational institutions etc. The trade includes various types of shops.

<u>Rural Development and Local Markets</u>

PARVATHI RENJU S

Production and consumption are the basic traits of homosapiens. In the evolution of human civilization, a one to one correspondence can be observed between the basic economic activity and human progress. In the science of Economics use value and exchange value constitute a central premise in economic theorising.

Logically it is production, which precedes consumption. The question of 'what to produce?' thus assumes priority in any theorizing. This question is tackled in different societies at different times in different ways.

In a rudimentary economy, it is natural that production will be organized for consumption purposes. Thus, use value occupies a central place in the organization of production. In any traditional society production of use value will be a basic concern and in the Economic History we call such economies as 'subsistence economy'. One would normally ask the question how the link between production and consumption would be established. In other words, one may reflect upon the distribution of use value among different users. In a traditional society, which is of a rudimentary type, this link is accomplished by the collective sharing. Thus, the distribution mechanism assumes a particular form of economic organization in a particular society.

Complexity may increase as the quantum of use values and differences in use values change. This complexity takes a particular economic form while in its attempts to build the gap between production and consumption. Exchange becomes a specific issue in this complex milieu. Unfortunately, the exchange relations which emerge at this particular context entails a series of other dimensions stretching over other organizational patterns in the society. We may think about the implications of exchange relations not only on consumption realm but also transcend into issues like distribution including equality.

Economic theorizing emanated from this plank of exchange value constitutes a major chunk in the science of Economics. Right from Adam Smith's "Wealth of Nations" onwards upto the present globalization paradigm economic literature is concerned about exchange relations. In modern economics, all the exchange relations are assorted into the concept of markets.

The concept of market assumed different meanings and assigned different roles. A well knit body of theorising has emerged in the discipline of Economics relating t markets.

In economic theory, it is generally argued that free operation of the market forces ie, free competition will ensure the optimum or most efficient allocation of all the existing resources resulting in he situation of Pareto optimality. That is, it will be impossible to increase the welfare or any one individual without reducing the welfare of others. However, in the global scenario, the invisible hand does not operate as expected and quite often it ends up in market failures. Unfortunately, as we have pointed out earlier, the impact of such failure is not confined to the realm of mere exchange but even extends to wrecking the life systems.

The functioning of the markets facilitates exchange but this exchange need not be a fair exchange. Economic history reveals that the merchandise exchange ended up in resource transfers culminating in dividing the global economy into a well-defined grouping of developed and less developed countries.

While functioning of the market during the colonial period caused this division, the progress of the market in the post-colonial period went up in such a way that suitable structures where evolved in the global economic relations facilitating the resource transfers continuously form less developed countries to developed countries. Even in the present international economic relations, no change has happened in the biased functioning of the markets. Moreover, it has emerged as an inevitable paradigm from which no country can keep away, thus pushing he less developed economies in a perpetual loosening of economic sovereignty. Thus what we see in the functioning of the markets is that while it has been adorned and praised as perfectly neutral

and unbiased, the real functioning of the markets has taken humanity on a discriminating plane, always forcing the citizens of LDCs to bear the burden of the functioning of the market.

While markets functioned generally in the way mentioned previously, we must be cautious in appropriating the strength of the markets in putting economies at a higher and better productive level. In other words, we could organize the production and consumption realms by integrating into it market forces. A rudimentary economy, which was normally a subsistence economy, can be turned onto a highly materialised consumer economy by appropriating the forces of markets. However, the success of such a move depends upon not only the internal economic organization but also on external economic conditions. In the present study, we focus on the internal economic organization a d exchange relations. Hereto complexities may emerge because market forces constitute an abstract system where it can function on different planes. Therefore, we focus specifically upon one category of markets – Rural Markets / Local Markets.

In the third economy like India, the primary production constitutes a major component in the national income. According to 1994 estimates, for example, the primary production constitutes

27.7 % of national income (Tandon BB and Tandon KK, Indian Economy, 1997, 133). Also, the primary constitutes 62% of working population. Obviously, the functioning of the market in this particular economic scenario should be learned. This constitute and important element urging one to look into the functioning of rural / local markets. For the primary produces, rural market centers are the first contact linking their production system with the marketing channels. Therefore, rural / local markets may be considered as the nerve centers of economic, social and cultural activities of the rural folk. Having highlighted the importance of rural / local markets in India this study focuses on how a rural market functions in a specific area in order to find out the ways the market forces changes its role and facilitates rural production, and also to analyses the different agents involved and their motives in the working of rural / local markets.

The method of study was the direct observation of the phenomenon associated with marketing activities. Secondary data were also used. The sample data was collected by five field visits to Sasthamcottah biweekly market. In addition to this some cases personal discussion and observation was also adopted.

The study reveals that all the forces existing in the rural / local market make the system for their enrichment and thus resources are not used for the development of rural / production system. This always leaves the rural farmers in a subsistence level and makes the rural / local economy a subsistence one.

From the analysis, it is found that middle aged participants are more active and male participants are more, when the analysis was made it was found that irrespective of age, education etc. the rural people are interested in production and marketing of commodities. About 96% of the participants are educated.

Shows that 50% are depending on primary sector. Of these 40% of the market, participants are producer sellers and 60% are buyer sellers. This establishes the existence of agents or forces in between producers and consumers. As 50% of the rural population depends on the primary sector, the existence of agents or forces will divert the resources for the rural folk and leave them always in poverty and unemployment.

The perishable nature of products also contributes to the farmers getting as far lower price for the products. The over dependence on moneylenders is also a source of exploitation and locking the rural production system in subsistence level.

Thus the analysis proves that there is no integration between rural / local production and marketing. The rural / local market centers and paving way for the emergence of new market structures, forces and agents such as buyer sellers, money lenders etc. Thus, the producers are subjected to all kinds of harassment and exploitation from the agents.

The study thus revels that the rural / local production system is related to the marketing process, the marketing structure has been dominated with forces and agents who always put the local production system as a means for enrichment. Thus, the link between rural / local production and marketing is not integrated leading to the impoverishment of the majority and enrichment of a minority of the rural population.

Thus, the hypothesis that 'the link between rural / local production and rural / local marketing is increasingly disintegrating' proves to be true.

Exports of Services

KAVEYA P

Exports of services supplement the merchandise-exports as a source of foreign exchange earnings. Services encompass telecommunications, transportation, tourism, banking, insurance, construction, computer-related services and professional ones. But as with trade in goods, the nature of services, too, is daily changing, acquiring fresh dimensions. Trade in services, and high technology industries are also virtually symbiotic.

- **World Trade in Services**

World trade in service exports has taken a big leap forward with service exports growing at a rate of 10 per cent in recent years. There are factors both on demand and supply sides that have contributed to this trend.

On the demand side, world trade in services is certain to accelerate in the coming years with advances in generic technology of computers and telecommunications. It is considerably influenced by the emerging demand for a whole range of business services due to innovations, new technology, sophisticated buyer needs, opening of new markets, service-based inputs and globalisation strategies.

- **Balance of Trade in Services**

The present trends indicate that there is not much parity between service exports and imports. This is especially true of items like transportation and business services coupled with a factor service like investment income. The latter has grown fast on account of interest and service payments on foreign loans and credit. As a result, trade in services has suffered from trade deficits, and these deficits have been widening.

- **Determinants of Exports of Services**

A recent study identifies the following as the principal determinants of exports of services:

i. Travel receipts have been mainly dependent on expansion of tourist facilities in the country.
ii. Transportation receipts have been dependent on merchandise exports originating from the country.

Kerala Budget

KAVEYA P

Budget Highlight 2021- 22
▪ The Gross State Domestic Product (GSDP)
▪ Expenditure (excluding debt repayment
Policy Highlights 2022-23
▪ Tax proposals
  ▪ Environment
  ▪ Skill development
  ▪ GSDP: Kerala's GSDP (at constant prices) saw a growth of 6.8% in 2021-22. In comparison,national GDP is estimated to grow at 8.9% in 2021-22
  1.Sectors: In 2021-22, at current prices, agriculture,manufacturing, and services sectors contributed to 12%, 23%, and 66% of the economy, respectively
  ▪ Per capita GSDP: The per capita GSDP of Kerala in 2021-22 (at current prices) is estimated to be Rs 2,36,093; 9% higher than the corresponding figure in 2020-22
  ▪ In 2022-23, the state is estimated to observe a revenue deficit of Rs 22,968 crore, which is 2.30% of its GSDP. In comparison, in 2021-22, the state is expected to observe a revenue deficit of Rs 23,176 crore (2.57% of GSDP).

Revenue expenditure in 2022-23 is estimated to be Rs 1,57,066 crore, which is an increase of 5% over the revised estimate of 2021-22 (Rs 1,49,803 crore). This expenditure includes the payment of salaries, pensions, interest, and subsidies.
  ▪ Capital outlay in 2022-23 is estimated to be Rs 14,891crore, which is an increase of 22% over the revised estimate of 2021-22. Capital outlay comprises expenditure towards creation of assets. This includes expenditure on building schools, hospitals, and roads and bridges.

Committed expenditure: Committed expenditure of a state typically includes expenditure on payment of salaries, pensions, and interest. Allocation of a large portion of the budget towards committed expenditure items limits the state's flexibility to decide on other expenditure priorities such as developmental schemes and capital outlay.

Sector-wise expenditure: The sectors listed below account for 47% of the total expenditure on sectors by the state in 2022-23
  ▪ Total revenue receipts forfor 2022-23 are estimated to be Rs 1,34,098 crore, an increase of 6% over the revised estimate of 2021-22. Of this, Rs 85,867 crore (64%) will be raised by the state through its own resources (tax and non-tax revenue), and Rs 48,230 crore (36%) will come from the centre
  ▪ **Devolution:** In 2022-23, the state estimates to receive Rs 17,121 crore in the form of share in central taxes, an increase of 2% over the revised estimates of 2021-22.
  ▪ **Devolution:** In 2022-23, the state estimates to receive Rs 17,121 crore in the form of share in central taxes, an increase of 2% over the revised estimates of 2021-22.

- **State's own tax revenue:** In 2022-23, total own tax revenue of the state is estimated to be Rs 74,098 crore,an increase of 26% over the revised estimate of 2021-22. State's own tax revenue as a percentage of GSDP is estimated to rise from 6% of GSDP in 2020-21 (as per actuals) to 7.4% of GSDP in 2022-23 (as per budget estimate)
- **State's own tax revenue:** In 2022-23, total own tax revenue of the state is estimated to be Rs 74,098 crore,an increase of 26% over the revised estimate of 2021-22. State's own tax revenue as a percentage of GSDP is estimated to rise from 6% of GSDP in 2020-21 (as per actuals) to 7.4% of GSDP in 2022-23 (as per budget estimate
- In 2022-23, SGST is estimated to be the largest source of own tax revenue (50%). SGST revenue in 2022-23 is estimated at Rs 36,818 crore, which is a 51% increase over the revised estimates of 2021-22
- In 2022-23, revenue from Sales Tax/VAT is expected to increase by 9% over revised estimates of 2021-22. Sales Tax/VAT is the second largest source of own tax revenue after SGST in 2022-23 (34% of own tax revenue). State excise is estimated to increase by 14% in 2022-23

<u>Deficits and Debt Targets for 2022-23</u>

Revenue Balance: It is the difference of revenue expenditure and revenue receipts. A revenue deficit implies that the government needs to borrow to finance its expenses which do not increase its assets or reduces its liabilities.

Fiscal deficit: It is the excess of total expenditure over total receipts. This gap is filled by borrowings by the government and leads to an increase in total liabilities of the state government. In 2022-23, the fiscal deficit is estimated to be Rs 39,117 crore (3.91% of GSDP). It is within the limit of 4% of GSDP permitted by the central government in 2022-23 as per the Union Budget (of which, 0.5% of GSDP will be made available upon undertaking power sector reforms.

Outstanding liabilities: Outstanding liabilities is the accumulation of total borrowings at the end of a financial year, it also includes any liabilities on public account. Outstanding liabilities are set to rise from 31.58% of GSDP in 2019-20 to 37.18% of GSDP in 2022-23.

Outstanding Government Guarantees: Outstanding liabilities of states do not include a few other liabilities that are contingent in nature, which states may have to honour in certain cases. State governments guarantee the borrowings of State Public Sector Enterprises (SPSEs) from financial institutions.

Kerala Economic Survey

- The Gross State Domestic Product (GSDP) of Kerala for 2023-24 (at current prices) is estimated at Rs 11.3 lakh crore it accounts to growth of 11.2 per cent.
- . • Receipts (excluding borrowings) for 2023-24 are estimated to be Rs 1,36,427 crore, which accounts to a 5 per cent increase in them.
- Revenue deficit in 2023-24 is estimated to be 2.1% of GSDP, higher than the initial one of 2 per cent. In 2022-23, the revenue deficit is expected to be lower than the budget estimate of 2.3 per cent.
- Fiscal deficit for 2023-24 is targeted at 3.5% of GSDP (Rs 39,662 crore. The fiscal deficit is estimated to be 3.6 per cent.
- Revenue augmentation: Stamp duties, electricity duty, and taxes on vehicles will be increased. Property tax and royalty on minor minerals will be revised for revenue augmentation.
- The Make in Kerala project accounts to 100 crores for resource development.
- Energy: A new energy park will be set up for harnessing renewable sources. Support will be provided for setting up green hydrogen hubs in Kochi and Thiruvananthapuram. An EV industrial park will be set up
- . • Nava Kerala Nagara Nayam: A commission will be set up to formulate a new policy for urbanisation. The programme basically tries to uplift the weaker sections of the society.

Kerala Economic Survey

- The Gross State Domestic Product (GSDP) of Kerala for 2023-24 (at current prices) is estimated at Rs 11.3 lakh crore it accounts to growth of 11.2 per cent.

. ▪ Receipts (excluding borrowings) for 2023-24 are estimated to be Rs 1,36,427 crore, which accounts to a 5 per cent increase in them.

▪ Revenue deficit in 2023-24 is estimated to be 2.1% of GSDP, higher than the initial one of 2 per cent. In 2022-23, the revenue deficit is expected to be lower than the budget estimate of 2.3 per cent.

▪ Fiscal deficit for 2023-24 is targeted at 3.5% of GSDP (Rs 39,662 crore. The fiscal deficit is estimated to be 3.6 per cent.

▪ Revenue augmentation: Stamp duties, electricity duty, and taxes on vehicles will be increased. Property tax and royalty on minor minerals will be revised for revenue augmentation.

▪ The Make in Kerala project accounts to 100 crores for resource development.

▪ Energy: A new energy park will be set up for harnessing renewable sources. Support will be provided for setting up green hydrogen hubs in Kochi and Thiruvananthapuram. An EV industrial park will be set up

. ▪ Nava Kerala Nagara Nayam: A commission will be set up to formulate a new policy for urbanisation. The programme basically tries to uplift the weaker sections of the society.

CHAPTER TEN

Development Finance and Crisis in Kerala

Consumer behaviour in Kerala

Mohamed Naseef K

Consumer behaviour among individuals is said to exist based on decision making. This type of decision making will differ in rural and urban areas. Decision-making among individuals differs from decision making among families, but so does the decisions they make together. Sometimes, there is similarity between the products purchased by some consumers and we can see that such consumers feel a similar decision making. The products that make decisions with families are more likely to be big budget products. Interests, emotions, attitude and preferences are the factors that influence consumer behavior more.

Every consumer's choice will be varied. Because,Each consumer's needs will be different, their interests will be different and so will their choice. Collective decision refers to the decisions made by a group of people.A decision is made for the first time. There will be reasons for reaching it. Several alternative scenarios are identified and the correct alternative is found by collecting data from it. A person reaches a correct decision by finding the correct decision and thinking about its consequences.When it comes to collective decision making, the group members hold a discussion and concentrate on an idea. Similarly, collective decision making involves face-to-face interaction with individual members. In case of any disagreements in collective decision making, voting systems can be used and the decision with the highest number of votes will be the final decision.

The modeling of consumer behaviour is greatly aided by what is called the consumer decision making process. Through this, the consumer reaches decision making. Online marketing, digital marketing, influencer marketing, broker marketing and blogger marketing come as influences on the decision making process. Brands, bloggers and celebrities are influencing the fashion industry.

The extent to which each consumer factor affects the product depends on the product the consumer buys, as well as the consumer's behaviour. Various consumer behavior patterns are used in the sale of various products in each district of Kerala.For example:- Even if the interest of women in Kerala cosmetics sector is interpreted positively, the demand of women to buy more of it is increasing. Women are naturally fond of various fashion designs in Kerala.If we look at the social and economic factors of the cosmetic sector in Kerala, we can understand that more money is being spent on this.

In consumer goods items, there are products of various brands that cater to the needs of various consumers.Consumer goods items are classified into two categories namely essential goods and luxury goods items.Examples of essential goods include food items.Examples of luxury goods include Tv,refrigerator, washing machine, laptop, jewellery , four wheeler items etc.

Good and service tax (GST)

GST first came into effect from July 2017 in Kerala. Kerala's service tax is 18 percent. In Kerala's GST of 12%, sugared food, Sewing machines, Flint buttons , Cooking utensils,glasses,Corrective spectacles, Dairy products, Packaged products,Dry fruits and nuts like almonds are all included. The 28 percent GST includes beverages, tobacco and cigarettes.Some say net price is adding GST to the original amount.GST amounts calculated are the original amount multiply GST amounts divided by hundred.

In 2023, Kerala received GST revenue of 26 percent. This is overtaking the record of 2022. 3010 crores as GST revenue received from Kerala in the month of April 2023. In the month of 2022, only 2689 crore GST revenue was received from Kerala.That means, there was an increase in the GST revenue received by Kerala in 2023.

Table 10.1 GST revenue in 2022 and 2023

Month and year	GST Revenue (crore)	Month and year	GST Revenue(crore)
April 2022	2689	April 2023	3010
May 2022	2064	May 2023	2297
June2022	2160.89	June 2023	2725.08

Source:-The hindu newspaper July 2,2023

The table 10.1 shows that Kerala has received much more GST revenue in 2023 than the GST revenue received in 2022.

13 products sold through SupplyCo have been exempted from GST in Kerala. It was presented in the 47th meeting of the GST Council. Specified food items like pulses, cereals, flour and other dairy products are exempted from GST.

Various Factors about Financial Development and Fiscal deficit in Kerala

HARSHA V K

Gold and Diamond

As far as Kerala is concerned, there are many chains for selling gold and diamonds. Kerala Government GST tax of 5 percent is levied on gold.The Kerala and central government have levied GST tax of 3% on gold bar,coin and Jewellery, 5% on making charge jewelery,5% on goldsmith or silversmith service and 15% (including customs duty of 7.5% and 3% GST) on import gold.

The people of Kerala have made investments in this sector (jewellery, gold coins, gold ETFs, SGB, digital gold, gold derivatives) but the people of Kerala mostly buy gold and diamonds which are gold derivatives in the commodities market. GST is charged on all types of gold investments in India.

Gold mutual funds are taxed up to 20 percent. Tax exemptions exist for sovereign gold bonds that are withdrawn after eight years. But 10% tax is payable on withdrawal before five years. Similarly, 20% tax is payable on withdrawals between five and eight years.

Digital gold investments are often done through mobile wallets like Google Pay, Paytm, etc. 20% tax is to be paid on digital gold investments above three years. Non Resident Indians (NRIs) have to pay TDS redemption of 20% for long-term mutual funds and 30% for short-term mutual funds in Kerala.

Reports indicate that the consumption of diamonds has increased in Kerala as well as the consumption of gold. Many diamond showrooms have opened in Kerala. Kerala is going through a period of increasing consumption of diamond jewellery.Diamond Jewellery in Kerala is subject to five percent VAT and 10 percent import duty. In 2005, 15 percent of the sales of Diamond in Kerala was achieved. About 400 crores worth of sales took place.

Share Market

Kerala State Industrial Corporation has 12 stocks worth ₹508.8 crore on 30 June 2023.Porinju V Veliyath publicly has 18 stocks ₹201.9 crore on June 2023.The main reason for the loss of Indian stocks is the plagued that exists between the global markets. Among the investors in Kerala, 2022 have lost money due to this type of plagued.

When it comes to share markets, it is only natural that money comes and goes. It takes good planning, self study and research on how to share markets online. One must know how to use the online share trading apps correctly, decide the correct stock orders and know the costs behind the spread. A long-term view should be taken on long-term investments.Short term goals, value traps and short selling should be avoided.48% of the investors held shares within 12 months in Kerala. However, 39 percent of investors held the shares for less than 12 months in 2020. Investors below the age of 30 hold shares for less than 1 year in Kerala.

Real estate

If we look at the last three months of 2022, more than 50 percent of the growth rate of the real estate sector has been acquired in Kerala. Flats have come up for sale at an offer price in Kochi, the metro city of Kerala. Investing in real estates is a safe bet these days in Kerala.

Owning a house is every symbol and builders turn it into a valuable investment in Kerala. Demand for houses is also increasing among consumers in Kerala. The growth in the real estate sector is due to the advancement of industrial, education and infrastructure in many cities of Kerala. A house buying a plot is possible after various document checks.

More profit is obtained from the sale of commercial real estates for retail, office and parking purposes. 2023 is a likely price hike year in Kerala real estate sector. Kochi, the industrial hub of Kerala, is at the forefront of the real estate price hike.More builders are attracted to Kerala due to good availability of land, low price, resale value and construction cost is less.

The infrastructural developments and potential in the real estate sector of the nearby areas such as Technopark in Thiruvananthapuram, Infopark in Kochi and Cyber Park in Kozhikode are significant. Known as the Golden City of India, Thrissur also has the potential to make leaps and bounds in the real estate sector. Sharing the border with Kochi is another reason for real estate growth in Thrissur. A water-friendly real estate is taking advantage of the opportunities in Kochi.In Kochi and Thiruvananthapuram, about 70% real estate-related share stocks have been sold. In Thrissur district, 75.8% share stocks of estates in residential areas have been sold through unorganized developers.

Excise

The Excise Department of Kerala has its headquarters in Thiruvananthapuram. Excise Department of Kerala was formed in November 30,1998. The laws related to liquor, narcotic drugs and psychotropic substances, medicinal preparations containing alcohol and narcotics are handled by the Excise Department of Kerala.The slab of excise duty in Kerala ranges from 21.5% to 23.5% nominal proof litre. Liquor is the second largest revenue earner of Kerala.

The Kerala State Beverages Corporation Limited (BEVCO) started in 1984, under the Kerala Government. Now a days,There are 23 Warehouses (FL-9 Shops) and 270 Retail Outlets (FL-1 Shops) under Beverage Corporations in Kerala. During 2021-22, the revenue of Kerala was ₹14576.21 crore from beverages. Kerala Beverage Corporation has a total of 5263 workers. Beverages Corporation made a profit of more than 100 crores on the occasion of the new year of 2023.Beverages Corporation had a turnover of 215 crores on Christmas 2021.Beverage corporations have been closed many times during the covid era of 2020.

Social and economic problems arise in many families in Kerala due to excessive alcohol consumption. Drugs have hit society like an epidemic. Attacks on women are often caused by individuals with excessive drinking habits. Likewise, drug and alcohol abuse comes into play as a factor when checking criminal backgrounds.

Fiscal deficit

Target figures record the fiscal deficit in Kerala as ₹ 39,117 crore for the period 2022-23.The revenue deficit of Kerala during the period 2022-23 was ₹ 22,968 crore. The revenue deficit of Kerala during the period 2021-22 was ₹ 16,910 crore. If we check the figures of Kerala since 2021, we can see that the revenue deficit is increasing.

During 2016-17 Kerala's debt was ₹ 1,86,453.86 crore. By 2021-22, ₹ 3,35,641.15 crore had increased.The most fiscal crisis occurred in Kerala during the period 1998-2001. As far as the state government is concerned, the central government may have borrowed more than the stated limit in the situation where there is no source of income to overcome the day-to-day expenditure. The most fiscal crisis occurs in Kerala where GSDP stands at from 4.8% to 6.6%.In 2016, the state government had to produce a white paper. The fiscal deficit was aggravated in Kerala due to the failure of the plan spender and the inability to find sources in the budget in 2016.

The main reason for the Fiscal deficit is the government's inability to control its expenditure. A big question is whether it is possible to reduce the spending of the government in such a way? The government will never be able to escape from these expenses for those welfare pensioners as well as service pensioners and salaried government employees. In a way it is true that such expenditure is necessary for a government.One way to avoid fiscal deficit is to make more use of existing resources and make them profitable.

CHAPTER ELEVEN

Others

Composition of service sectors in India

Dr.SHEELA M C

In India, the national income classification given by Central Statistical Organisation is followed. In the National Income Accounting in India, service sector includes the following:

1) Trade, Hotels and Restaurants (THR)

1.1 Trade

1.2 Hotels and Restaurants

2) Transport, Storage and Communication

2.1 Railways

2.2 Transport by other Means

2.3 Storage

2.4 Communication

3) Financing, Insurance, Real Estate and Business Services

3.1 Banking and Insurance

3.2 Real Estate, Ownership of Dwellings and Business Services

4) Community, Social and Personal Services

4.1 Public Administration and Defense (PA & D)

4.2 Other Services

From a low level of 27.5 per cent of GDP in 1950-51, the share of services increased to about 60.0 per cent in 2011-12. Between 1950-51 and 1990-91, the share of Services Sector in GDP rose by only 13.1 percentage points, which is an increase of about 0.3 percentage points per annum. However, between 1990-91 and 1999-2000, the share had increased by 7.3 percentage points, which is an increase of 0.8 percentage points per annum. Clearly, the rate of growth was significantly higher in the 1990s. As we will see below, the sector maintained rapid growth in subsequent decade also.

Key service industries

- Information Technology and Business Process Outsourcing (IT-BPO) Services Over the past decade, IT-BPO services have emerged as key contributors to India's export earnings, investment, employment and overall economic and social development. Competitive labour costs, English language skills, technical expertise, political stability, favourable tax rates and a reputation for high-quality services have driven the sector's rapid growth.
- **Factors Affecting Demand**

Factors affecting demand for India's IT-BPO services include economic and financial conditions in key export markets, the relative attractiveness of competing providers, and changes in the domestic market for outsourced IT-BPO services.

- **Factors Affecting Supply**

Workforce challenges and government incentives affect the industry's supply of services. Among the former, attrition, wage inflation, and skill levels pose particular challenges. High attrition tends to undermine the quality of services and to boost costs for recruitment and training

- **Telecommunication Services**

Leading Indian telecommunication service companies are Aircel, Maxis, Apollo Group, Bharat Sanchar Nigam Ltd. (BSNL), Bharti Airtel Bharti Telecom Group, Pastel Ltd, Indian Continent Investment Ltd , HFCL Infotel, Himachal Futuristic Communications Ltd, Idea Cellular Birla TMT Holdings, AT Birla Nuvo, Hindalco Industries, Grasim Industries, Loop Mobile BPL Communications, Capital Global, Gypsy Rover, Mahanagar Telephone Nigam Ltd. (MTNL) Government, Reliance Communications Anil Dhirubhai Ambani Group, Sistema Shyam TeleServices Sistema, Spice Communications Modi Wellvest, Telecom Malaysia, Tata Teleservices Tata Group, NTT DoCoMo, Tata Communications (VSNL) Tata Group, Vodafone Essar Vodafone Group.

- **Internet Services**

In general, the proliferation of Internet services in India is hampered by high levels of poverty, particularly in rural areas, and associated low levels of personal computer ownership. Internet subscriber growth over the past decade has been driven almost entirely by the adoption of residential broadband Internet services, which grew at a CAGR of 153 per cent from 135,000 subscribers in 2004 to 8.1 million at the beginning of 2012. In India, broadband Internet services are predominantly delivered over fixed-line networks (i.e., DSL service), as opposed to delivery via cable television networks

- **Energy Services**

India is the fifth largest electricity producer in the world, behind the United States, China, Japan and Russia. During the last decade, India has increased the quantity of electricity it produced by more than any other country in the world, aside from China. Demand, however, has increased at an even faster rate, resulting in a shortage of electricity and frequent power outages during peak hours. In addition to a shortage of generation capacity, India faces significant challenges in electricity transmission and distribution. Due to the lack of an integrated national transmission system, India sometimes experiences simultaneous electricity surpluses in some areas and deficits in others. . Electrical equipment is damaged and burns out more quickly as a result of outages and fluctuating voltage, workers are idled during blackouts, and businesses need to invest in costly diesel generators.

- **Air Transport Services**

India's air passenger transport market is relatively small, accounting for only 2 per cent of airline traffic worldwide. Indian airlines transport approximately 61 million passengers per year, more than 80 per cent of whom are domestic travellers. Operating revenue for India's air transport industry is roughly $9.0 billion, and the number of workers employed in the sector is nearly 60,000. Although India's air transport industry has experienced substantial growth over the past one decade, such growth has been slowed by the recent financial crisis. Despite the current downturn, growth potential remains as the young and increasingly affluent Indian population selects air transport over other modes of domestic travel. Major airlines in India are Indian Airlines, Alliance Air, Go Airways, Indigo Airlines, Jet Airways, Kingfisher Airlines, Paramount Airways and Spice Jet Airlines.

- **Education Services**

A small portion of India's higher education institutions is renowned for producing graduates who are adequately prepared for advanced degree programmes, research or employment in scientific, technological or commercial fields in India and abroad. However, most of India's universities and colleges lack the financial resources, authority and flexibility to equip graduates with the skills demanded by India's expanding business and technology sectors. Many students from India, therefore, pursue higher education opportunities abroad.

Despite India's progress in recent years in making elementary education more available – especially to historically underrepresented segments such as girls and children in eastern India, and culturally disadvantaged groups – substantial numbers of students continue to exit the education system at every level. As a result, only about 13 per cent of 18- to 24- year-olds in India had enough prior education to advance to higher education in 2011. The 12th five-year plan (2012–17) has elevated the policy and fiscal priorities of higher education relative to other levels of education.

Despite India's progress in recent years in making elementary education more available – especially to historically underrepresented segments such as girls and children in eastern India, and culturally disadvantaged groups – substantial numbers of students continue to exit the education system at every level. As a result, only about 13 per cent of 18- to 24- year-olds in India had enough prior education to advance to higher education in 2011. The 12th five-year plan (2012–17) has elevated the policy and fiscal priorities of higher education relative to other levels of education.

Performance of service sector in india

This pattern of structural change in Indian economy has deviated from the development pattern of Western and South East Asian economies. Those economies experienced first a shift from primary to secondary sector and only in their advanced stage did they experience a significant shift in favour of tertiary sector. That pattern of development enabled them to transfer growing labour force from primary to secondary sector. In India, this has not been possible because secondary sector has not expanded fast enough to absorb growing labour force.

The unskilled and uneducated rural masses have continued to struggle in the primary sector and those who have been forced out by economic, social and political factors have joined the urban slum sector. Moreover, the sharp increase in the share of tertiary sector in GDP in India has occurred at a much lower level of per capita income than that in the developed countries when they experienced a similar expansion.

- ### Employment Contribution of the Service Sector

The sectoral distribution of workforce in India during the period 1983 to 2009- 10 reveals that the structural changes in terms of employment have been slow in India as the primary sector continued to absorb 54.9 per cent of the total workforce even in 2009-10, followed by tertiary and industrial sectors (25.5 per cent and 19.6 per cent) respectively. There has been disproportionate growth of tertiary sector, as its share in employment has been far less when compared to its contribution to GDP. It is important to understand that, within the services sector employment growth rate is highest in finance, insurance, and business services, followed by trade, hotels and restaurants, and transport etc. The community, social and personal services occupy the last rank in growth rates of employment.

The process of acceleration in growth started in 1980s rather than in 1990s. Of the 2.4 percentage point increase in the rate of economic growth that took place in the post-1980 period, about 40 per cent is accounted for by a faster growth in TFP in services. The three sectors viz. agriculture, industry and services have witnessed acceleration in the growth rates of output, output per worker and total factor productivity (TFP) in the post-1980 period. However, the increase is more marked in case of services. Partially, the spurt in growth rate is attributable to productivity growth in certain sub-sectors of services sector. It has been noticed that growth rate in output per man is highest in case of PA &D and other community social and personal services (4.2 per cent p.a), followed by transport, storage, communication (3.3 per cent pa), trade , hotels, restaurants (2.9 per centpa) and banking, insurance, real estate and business services.

Export in India

- **Prospects and opportunities**

Both domestic and international factors augur well for the growth of services sector in India. 10.8.1 Domestic Factors Some of the important factors can be briefly stated as follows:

i. As real per capita GDP grows, demand for services increases more than proportionately and this, in turn, reinforces GDP growth itself.
ii. Within the services sector, demand for producer and government services, which constitute mainly intermediate consumption, have strong multipliers effects on real GDP
iii. The growth of such dynamic service activities, which are intensive users of communication and information technology, will generate employment opportunities on a rising scale.
iv. IV. The process of economic growth has itself led to the emergence and expansion of new series such as advertising, publicity, marketing, etc. These sub-sectors provide essential service inputs to other sectors in the economy, thereby developing strong linkages with the rest of the economy.
v. V. Efficient delivery of services increases the productivity of both labour and capital in the economy as a whole. In general, services sector appears to be highly growth inducing with positive externalities for other services making service a catalytic agent of growth.
vi. Recent Policy Initiatives in Services Sector
vii. Various initiatives have been taken by the Government to help the services sector. Some recent measures include the increase in SEIS (Service Export from India Scheme) incentives by 2% for notified services such as Business, Legal, Accounting, Architectural, Engineering, Educational, Hospital, Hotels and Restaurants; increasing the validity period of the Duty Credit Scrips from 18 months to 24 months to enhance their utility in the GST framework; reducing the GST rate for transfer/sale of scrips to zero from the earlier rate of 12%; and creating a new Logistics Division in the Department of Commerce to develop and coordinate implementation of an Action Plan for the integrated development of the logistics sector.

Industrial growth and structure

KRISHNA R

A study of the evolution of Indian industrial structure and its growth should imperatively begin with examining the pattern of Indian planning process immediately after independence. At the time of independence, the debate on planning was never on whether there should be planning, but about what sort of planning there should be? The broad agreement on the need for planning was in tune with the intellectual ambience of the period which reflected the state of the international economy. The Great Depression of the inter-war period had destroyed any faith in the virtue of the free market, and Keynesianism, a product of the Depression, advocated not just State intervention in demand management but the necessity of socialising investment decision.

In terms of the strategy lab orated at that time, the State would not merely ensure a sharp increase in the rate of savings in the system, but also ensure an enhanced allocation of that savings to the heavy industrial sector in general and machine tools in particular, so as to reduce the economy's dependence on international capital and commodity markets.

The First Five Year-Year Plan, was essentially a collection of several projects. The plan sought to fix the growth rates in GDP to be achieved and specify the required savings rate to achieve the targeted GDP growth. This approach was based on the framework provided by Harrod –Domar Model which, in nut shell, specified the following: given the capital output ratio and given the growth target, what is the required savings rate?

In terms of the strategy lab orated at that time, the State would not merely ensure a sharp increase in the rate of savings in the system, but also ensure an enhanced allocation of that savings to the heavy industrial sector in general and machine tools in particular, so as to reduce the economy's dependence on international capital and commodity markets.

The H-D model thus, in effect, gave ample scope for targeting the economic growth using three macro parameters: viz. capital-output ratio, savings rate and growth rate of GDP. The Second Five Year Plan marked a distinct shift in favour of heavy capital goods industries. The approach to the Second Five-Year Plan was slightly different in that it also incorporated the essentials of the Feldman-Mahalanobis structural model which emphasised on the physical aspects of investment needs. This approach, in essence, accorded importance to physical targets to be achieved subject to restrictive assumptions about transformation possibilities in terms of the three macro parameters as held forth by the H-D approach.

The underlying causes which pushed for such a developmental strategy were the following. Firstly, the basic constraint on development was seen as being an acute deficiency of material capital which prevented the introduction of more productive technologies. Secondly, the limitation on the rate or pace of capital accumulation was seen to lie in the low capacity to save. Thirdly, it was assumed that even if the domestic capacity to save is raised by means of suitable fiscal and monetary policies, there were structural limitations preventing conversion of savings into productive investment.

Fourthly, it was assumed that whereas agriculture was subject to diminishing returns, industrialisation would allow surplus labour currently underemployed in agriculture to be more productively employed in industries which operated according to increasing returns to scale. A fifth assumption was that if market mechanism were accorded primacy, this would result in excessive consumption by the upper income groups, along with relative underinvestment in sectors essential to the accelerated development of the economy.

The direction of industrial development in India is traced to several industrial promotion policies viz. the statement of Industrial Policy of 1945; the Industrial Policy Resolution of 1948, the enactment of the Industries (Development and Regulation) Act, 1951, the First and the Second Five-Year Plan documents and the Industrial Policy Resolution of 1956. The 1945 statement of Industrial Policy is remarkable as a originator of all the thinking on the other key industrial policy resolutions after independence.

The statement also mentioned the concept of industrial licensing. Special importance was given to the development of steel, heavy engineering, machine tools and heavy chemical industries. The idea of licensing was mainly thought to be an instrument for the dispersal of industries preventing the establishment of excess capacity in only some industries and regions.

The First Five-Year Plan stated the objective of industrial planning as making good the deficiencies in production of key industrial items and initiate a developmental process which would enable the cumulative expansion of such basic production. The scope and need for development of India's industries was felt to be so great that it was necessary for public sector to develop those industries in which private enterprise would either be unable or unwilling to invest the resources required taking the risks involved. The industrial Policy Resolution of 1948 had identified certain industries to be reserved for production by the central/ state governments.

The system of Indian industrial licensing has its origins in experiences of situations like: the post-war situation, nationalistic aspirations, socialistic leanings of the founding fathers of the country, etc. The planners and policy makers in India therefore felt the need for using a wide variety of instruments and controls to steer the course of Indian industrial development in a desired direction

Around 1960s, it was realised that the system of approvals and licenses was unsuited for directing investments. The government appointed several committees to examine the industrial licensing system. Most of them identified that the licensing mechanism was not serving its purpose of channelising investments in the desired directions. For instance, the Hazari Committee (1967) observed that:

the extent up to which the industrial licensing has served to channelise investment in the desired directions appears extremely doubtful;

1 the gains in terms of balanced regional development and wider distribution of entrepreneurship are at best moderate;

2 there is very little follow-up of licensing system to verify whether the approved projects fructified in time; and

in attempting to cover almost the whole range of large-scale industrial development, licensing and other such legislative provisions have lost sight of the relative importance of different projects /products. This is to say that all applications have been treated by a similar processing process without any regard to the criticality of the projects to the economy.

a. The first is the P. C. Alexander Committee on Import-Export Policies and Procedures set up in 1977. The main recommendations of this committee included:

(i) import licensing should be gradually liberalised;

(ii) the scope of open general licensing (OGL) for import and sale should be expanded; (iii) actual user condition should be gradually relaxed by substituting, in the first instance, licensing with equivalent tariffs and later by focusing on reducing the 'equivalent tariffs' more and more ;

(iv) the developmental role of imports should be recognised and imports should not be regarded only as a negative element in the BOP accounts and always controlled;

(v) the name of Chief Controller of Imports and Exports be changed to Director General of Foreign Trade (DGFT) whose role should be one of promoting exports and managing imports so as to serve the developmental needs of the economy;

(vi) the DGTD (Director General of Technical Development) and other bodies connected with licensing and control should be revamped;

(vii) export subsidies should be phased out to the minimum level so that exports become competitive on their own after the initial hurdles of new markets and products are overcome; and

(viii) commercial representatives (CRs) in the Indian embassies abroad should be made more professional by drawing the personnel from the business world. The liberalisation of the import policies began with this Alexander Committee Report submitted in 1978.

Growth and structural composition of indian industry

The industrial sector consists of three broad subsectors viz.

  i. manufacturing,
 ii. mining and quarrying and
iii. electricity, gas and water supply.

One is the Factory Sector (referred to as the Registered Sector registered under the Indian Factories Act, 1948 also called as the Organised Manufacturing Sector; also called as the Unorganised Manufacturing Sector) consisting of all manufacturing enterprises. The other is the Non-Factory Sector (or the Unregistered Manufacturing Sector; also called as the Unorganised Manufacturing Sector) consisting of all manufacturing enterprises which are not registered under the Indian Factories Act.

Phases of industrial growth

It is necessary to understand the ups and downs of India's industrial performance by looking into the factors responsible for it. We can analyse this in four phases: the first phase of rapid growth from 1951 to 1966, the second phase of low growth (and deceleration) from 1966- 80, the third phase of recovery and revival of growth in the1980s and the fourth phase of growth with a renewed vigour during the period of New Economic Policy (or economic reforms) in the1990s and beyond. An analysis of the underlying causes will enable us to understand the measures that can help promote industrial growth in a faster, efficient and equitable manner.

The First Phase of Rapid Growth (1950-51 to 1965-66)

There were several factors that influenced the industrial growth during this period. These factors emerged in the changed political context after the country's independence. The anti-industry attitude of the British Government before 1947 was replaced by the strongly pro-industry aims of the Indian Government

Government's key role: During this phase the government played the most important role in which a number of industries were set up in the public sector. Most of these were basic and capital goods industries (see Key Words) like electricity, steel, machinery, etc. These were the industries in which the gestation period was long and required investment levels were very high, and therefore the fruits could be realised over a long term time frame. The government simultaneously undertook measures to ensure that these (and other) industries in the private sector also developed.

The Second Phase of Deceleration (1965-66 to 1979-80)

The industrial growth experienced during the Second and the Third Five Year Plan periods could not be sustained. In fact, there was discernible reduction in the growth rates. There are several reasons put forward for this downturn which can be broadly classified into two broad categories, namely, the supply side constraints and the demand side constraints. Supply Side Constraints In the first place there were some major disturbances caused by wars (with China in 1962 and with Pakistan in 1965 & 1971), the draughts in 1965 & 1966 and the steep rise in oil prices in 1973 (first 'oil' shock).

- Second was the reduced availability of critical inputs for production like power, infrastructure and raw material. Imports became costlier and fluctuations in agricultural production adversely affected the agro based industries.
- Third was the organisational weakness due to which many industries fell sick. Many industries were functioning at sub-optimal capacity owing to poor inventory control and financial management. There were losses due to work stoppage which adversely affected the production.
- A fourth factor was the controls and regulatory measures. In the earlier years, these controls and regulatory measures were essential when saving/ investments were low. With improvement in the saving/investment ratio the controls and regulatory measures had become restrictive in character acting as impediments to industrial growth.
- Demand Side Constraints Among the demand side factors inhibiting industrial growth, the principal ones are the following.
- One was the declining demand due to policies of import substitution. For instance, till about the mid-1960s, industries were setup to replace imported goods.
- This affected the capital goods industries as it was the import of these goods which were replaced under the policy of import substitution initiated in the Second Plan.
- Two, there was a decline in the growth of public sector investment resulting in a corresponding decline in the private sector investment. Since the public sector acted as the leader, there was a general slackening of investment level in the economy. Associated with this trend, there was a rise in the incremental capital output ratio for the industrial output.

The Third Phase of Recovery and Revival (1980- 81 to 1989-90)

The factors behind the resurgence of growth in the 1980s were exactly similar to those that contributed for its deceleration in the mid-sixties. Empirical evidence which pointed out to favourable trends included:

i. improvement in the rate of growth (and pattern) of gross domestic capital formation in general and public investment in particular;
ii. step-up in infrastructure investment and more efficient management of the infrastructure facilities;
iii. iii) trends in the inter-sectoral terms of trade favouring the agricultural sector;
iv. iv) increase in the use of manufactured inputs in crop production; v) growth in per capita agriculture incomes and
v. vi) reforms in industrial and trade policies contributing to revival of growth in industrial output.

The Phase of Industrial Growth Under New Economic Policy (1991-2007)

- During this phase, industry and trade policy reforms were accelerated. Public investment contracted sharply to reign in the fiscal imbalance. Financing of industrial development changed considerably as part of the financial sector reform which cut into directed lending. Although formal changes in industrial labour laws were avoided due to lack of political consensus, there were adequate signals to employers that the government would not come in the way of restructuring the industrial relations .

In the words of an yet another leading economist, Jagdish Bhagwati's views, the three main elements of India's policy framework that stifled growth and efficiency were:

i. Extensive bureaucratic controls over production, investment and trade;
ii. inward looking trade and foreign investment policies, and
iii. a substantial public sector going well beyond the conventional confines of public utilities and infrastructure.
iv. The long-term constraint in a developing economy is one of low savings for investment. Thus, from a variety of analytical perspectives, autonomous public investment has the potential to generate demand for industrial goods as well as improve the infrastructural inadequacies. Macro-econometric evidence also unambiguously supports the view that public investment 'crowds-in' private investment. Combining all the arguments, it can be asserted that industrial growth in India is largely dependent on the twin engines of agriculture productivity and public investment.

Linkage between economic and structure reforms and economic outcomes

- The long-term constraint in a developing economy is one of low savings for investment. Thus, from a variety of analytical perspectives, autonomous public investment has the potential to generate demand for industrial goods as well as improve the infrastructural inadequacies. Macro-econometric evidence also unambiguously supports the view that public investment 'crowds-in' private investment. Combining all the arguments, it can be asserted that industrial growth in India is largely dependent on the twin engines of agriculture productivity and public investment.
- Neither of these was functioning well in the 1990s which explains the swings experienced in the industrial performance during the decade of 1990s.
- Agricultural Performance: When we compare the performance of agricultural production between 1980s and 1990s, we observe that except wheat, the rate of growth of production of all other crops viz. foodgrains, non-food grains, cereals, as well as rice went down. The poor agricultural performance in the 1990s was associated with the much commented slowdown in public investment in this sector.
- Public Investment: In the initial years of economic reforms, public investment – over one-half of which is in infrastructure – was deliberately reduced. The decline in infrastructure's share which had started in the second half of the 1980s particularly became sharp in the mid-1990s. Its impact was seen in the manufacturing sector's share in gross fixed capital formation (GFCF). If we take a longer time-period, we see that the share of public investment in the late 1990s, at about 30 per cent of total GFCF, had fallen close to the level at which it was in the early 1950s. A basic reason behind the disappointing performance is the adverse impact of import liberalisation and the decline in the role of the government in demand generation.
- Poor export growth in the mid-1990s made it worse. If import liberalisation results in higher efficiency through higher exports, higher production and higher employment the rationale for import liberalisation gets vindicated. But if import liberalisation (and other policies) result in inefficient production leading to lower demand with the consequent lower production and employment, then the policy needs to be seriously re-examined. If export demand is not high enough, then there is need to generate demand through other means by more government expenditure.

Indian agriculture

- India ranked second worldwide in farm output
- Agriculture and allied sectors like forestry, logging and fishing

  accounted for 17% of the GDP.

- The sector employed 49% of its total workforce in 2014.
- Crop-yield-per-unit-area of all crops has grown since 1950, due to the special emphasis placed on agriculture in the five-year plans and steady improvements in irrigation, technology, application the Green Revolution in India.

- However, international comparisons reveal the average yield in India is

  generally 30% to 50% of the highest average yield in the world

- The statesofUttarPradesh,Punjab,Haryana, Madhya

  Pradesh,AndhraPradesh,Telangana,Bihar, West Bengal,GujaratandMaharashtraarekeycontributors to Indian agriculture.

- India is the largest producer of milk, jute and pulses, and has the

  world's second-largest cattle population with 170 million animals.
Green Revolution in India

- Green Revolution in India was introduced in 1966. M.S. Swaminathan is known as the father of Green Revolution in India Within India, this started in the early 1960s and led to an increase in foodgrainproduction,especiallyinPunjab,Haryana,andUttar Pradeshduringtheearly phase.
- The main development was higher-yielding varieties of wheat and rice production.
- High Yielding Varieties (HYV) of seeds.
- Irrigation (a) surface and (b) ground.
- Use of fertilizers (chemical).
- Use of Insecticides and Pesticides.
- Command Area Development (CAD)- Command Area Development Programme is a centrally sponsored scheme which was launched in January 1975.
- Consolidation of holdings.
- Land reforms.
- Supply of agricultural credit.
- Rural electrification.
- Rural Roads and Marketing.
- Farm Mechanisation.
- Agricultural Universities.

Second Green Revolution in India

Second Green Revolution in India was introduced in 2004 with an initial fund of Rupees 50,000 crores.Second Green Revolution in India Second Green Revolution, also known as Evergreen Revolution or Sustainable Agriculture,It is also known as the "Rainbow Revolution".

It includes the following practices:

1. Replacing chemical fertilisers with bio-fertilisers.

2. Bio-pesticides were to be used instead of chemical pesticides.
3. Conservation of water, balanced cropping pattern and proper crop combinations were the major objectives.
4. Doubling the rate of growth of irrigated areas.
5. Improving water management, watershed development and rain water harvesting.
6. Focus on soil quality.
7. Promoting animal husbandry and fishery.
8. Providing easy access to credit at affordable rates.
9. Focus on land reforms issues.

Land Reforms in India

Intermediaries like Zamindars, Talukdars, Jagirs and Inams had dominated the agricultural sector in India by the time the country attained independence.After independence, measures for the abolition of the Zamindari system were adopted in different states.The first Act to abolish intermediaries was passed in Madras in 1948. Since then, state after state passed legislation abolishing Zamindari rights.

Rural India witnesses three types of tenants.

a. permanent or occupancy tenants,
b. temporary or non-occupancy tenants, and
c. sub-tenants. -Sub-tenants are the tenants who cultivate the land of the big land owners.
d. Ceiling on land holdings implies the fixing of the maximum amount of
e. land that an individual or family can possess.
f. For example, in Andhra Pradesh, the limit of ceiling varied from 27 to
g. 216 acres. In Rajasthan it varied from 22 to 366 acres.

Consolidation of Holdings means bringing together the various small plots of land of a farmer scattered all over the village as one compact block, either through purchase or exchange of land with others.In Orissa, the Consolidation Act was passed in 1972.It has been advocated to solve the problems of sub-division andfragmentation of holdings.In this system, farmers pool their small holdings for the purpose of cultivation and reap benefits of large scale farming.The Bhoodan Movement was spearheaded by Acharya Vinoba Bhabe.He collected land from the rich landlords and distributed that to the landless.About 4.2 million acres of land were received under Bhoodan, but sofar only about 1.3 million acres have been distributed.

1.Zamindari System

Zamindari System was introduced by Cornwallis in 1793 through Permanent Settlement Act.It was introduced in provinces of Bengal, Bihar, Orissa and Varanasi. Also known as Permanent Settlement System.Zamindars were recognized as owner of the lands.Under this Raja's , Talukdars and Zamindars were given the rights to collect the rent from the peasants.The realized amount would be divided into 11 parts. 1/11 of the share belongs to Zamindars and 10/11 of the share belongs to East India Company.This fix amount not to be increase in future.

2.Ryotwari System

Ryotwari System was introduced by Thomas Munro in 1820.Major areas of introduction include Madras, Bombay, parts of Assam and Coorgh provinces of British India.In Ryotwari System the ownership rights were handed over to the peasants.Under this system land may be held in single independent holding.British Government collected taxes directly from the peasants. The revenue rates of Ryotwari System were 50% where the lands were dry and 60% in irrigated land.The individual holder responsible for payment to land revenue.First Ryotwari system made in Madras in 1972.This system is product of Hindu tradition.Ryots have fully enjoy the power of permanent right of tenancy.

3.Mahalwari System

Mahalwari system was introduced in 1833 during the period of William Bentick.It was introduced in Central Province, North-West Frontier, Agra, Punjab, Gangetic Valley, etc of British India.The Mahalwari system had many provisions of both the Zamindari System and Ryotwari System.In this system, the land was divided into Mahals. Each

Mahal comprises one or more villages.In this system village land held jointly by the village community. They all are responsible for the payment of land revenue.

Agriculture price policy in India

In India, the price policy was first introduced in 1947 with the formation of Food grains Policy Committeethe foodgrains Price Committee was appointed in 1964.In 1965, the Food Corporation of India (FCI) was set up for making necessary procurement, storage and distribution of foodgrains.The policy of minimum support prices was accepted by the Fourth Plan but its effectiveness depends on the efficacy of the purchasing machinery like FCI and State Trading Corporation (STC).In 1965, the Agricultural Price Commission was set up which announced the minimum support prices and procurement prices NAFED is also an important agency which appoints state agencies for undertaking Price Support Scheme (PSS) operations.

Objectives of Agriculture Price Policy in India are:

1. Providing incentives for increasing production or marketable surplus or bringing about the change in agriculture output mix.

1. Stability of prices of agriculture goods.
2. Determine the minimum price of a crop for farmers in case of a glut or to fix a maximum price for consumers in case of scarcity or shortages.
3. Provision of food grains at prices below the market prices to the weaker sections of the society.
4. Maintaining the stability of income of farming sector.
5. Increase earnings of foreign exchange.
6. It would encourage investments in agriculture to help increase production of agriculture sector.
7. Ensure regular flow of raw material.

Features of Agricultural Price Policy in India:

1. The Agricultural Price Commission was set up in 1965 which announced the minimum support prices and procurement prices for the agricultural products.In 1985, the name of this institution was changed into Agricultural Cost and Prices Commission.Moreover, the foodgrains Policy Committee was appointed by the Government in 1966 which also recommended various measures of price support.

2. The Food Corporation of India FCI:

The Food Corporation of India was set up in 1965 for making necessary procurement, storage and distribution of food grains.

(ii) Minimum Support Price:

The government fixes the minimum support prices of agricultural products like wheat, rice, maize, cotton, sugarcane, pulses etc., regularly for safeguarding the interest of farmers.MSP cover 25 agricultural product.14 crops of the kharif season viz. paddy, jowar, bajra, maize, ragi, arhar, moong, urad, groundnut-in-shell, soyabean, sunflower, sesamum, nigerseed and cotton; 6 rabi crops viz. wheat, barley, gram, masur

3.other commercial crops.

(iii)Protecting the Consumers: In order to safeguard the interest of the consumers, the agricultural price policy has made provision for buffer stock of foodgrains for its distribution among the consumers through public distribution system.

Economic survey

KAVEYA P

The Union Minister for Finance & Corporate Affairs, Smt. Nirmala Sitharaman presented the Economic Survey 2021-22 in Parliament on January 31, 2022. Read to know about the Economic Survey 2021-22 highlights.

Economic Survey is the flagship annual document of the Ministry of finance – released usually a day before the Budget for the next year is presented in the Indian Parliament.

Economic Survey gives a detailed account of the various sectors of the economy and overall economic scenario of the country in the past years and provides an outline for the year ahead.

The central theme of this year's Economic Survey is the "Agile approach", implemented through India's economic response to the COVID-19 Pandemic shock.

Another theme highlighted in this Economic Survey relates to the art and science of policy-making under conditions of extreme uncertainty.

Agile approach mentioned in the Economic Survey 2021

As per the Agile approach, short-term policy responses can be tailored to an evolving situation rather than what a model may have predicted.

The short-term policy response is possible because of the explosion of real-time data that allows for constant monitoring. Such information includes GST collections, digital payments, satellite photographs, electricity production, cargo movements, internal/external trade, infrastructure roll-out, delivery of various schemes, mobility indicators etc.

The "Agile approach" is based on feedback loops, real-time monitoring of actual outcomes, flexible responses, safety-net buffers and so on. The "Agile approach" is based on feedback loops, real-time monitoring of actual outcomes, flexible responses, safety-net buffers and so on. Planning is not done in the Agile approach as a deterministic prediction of the flow of events. Still, planning is relevant in the framework – mostly for scenario analysis, identifying vulnerable sections, and understanding policy options.

- Economic Survey 2021-22 estimates that the Indian economy (GDP) may grow by 9.2 per cent in real terms in 2021-22 (as per first advanced estimates) subsequent to a contraction of 7.3 per cent in 2020-21.

- GDP is projected to grow by 8- 8.5 per cent in real terms in 2022-23.
- The year ahead is poised for a pickup in private sector investment with the financial system in a good posit.ion to provide support for the economy's revival.
- Projection is comparable with World Bank and Asian Development Bank's latest forecasts of real GDP growth of 8.7 per cent and 7.5 per cent respectively for 2022-23.
- As per IMF's latest World Economic Outlook projections, India's real GDP is projected to grow at 9 per cent in 2021-22 and 2022-23 and at 7.1 per cent in 2023-2024, which would make India the fastest-growing major economy in the world for all 3years.
- Agriculture and allied sectors are expected to grow by 3.9 per cent; industry by 11.8 per cent and services sector by 8.2 per cent in 2021-22.
- On the demand side, consumption is estimated to grow by 7.0 per cent, Gross Fixed Capital Formation (GFCF) by 15 per cent, exports by 16.5 per cent and imports by 29.4 per cent in 2021-22.
- Macroeconomic stability indicators suggest that the Indian Economy is well placed to take on the challenges of 2022-23.
- A combination of high foreign exchange reserves, sustained foreign direct investment, and rising export earnings will provide an adequate buffer against possible global liquidity tapering in 2022- 23.
- The economic impact of the "second wave" was much smaller than that during the full lockdown phase in 2020-21, though the health impact was more severe.
- Government of India's unique response comprised of safety-nets to cushion the impact on vulnerable sections of society and the business sector, significant increase in capital expenditure to spur growth and supply-side reforms for a sustained long- term expansion.
- The government's flexible and multi-layered response is partly based on an "Agile" framework that uses feedback-loops, and the use of eighty High- Frequency Indicators (HFIs) in an environment of extreme uncertainty.
- Economic Survey 2021-22 observes that the revenue receipts from the Central Government (April to November 2021) have gone up by 67.2 per cent (YoY) as against the expected growth of 9.6 per cent in the 2021-22 Budget Estimates (over 2020- 21 Provisional Actuals).

- Gross Tax Revenue registers a growth of over 50 per cent from April to November 2021 in YoY terms. This performance is strong compared to pre- pandemic levels of 2019-2020 also.
- During April-November 2021, Capex has grown by

13.5 per cent (YoY) with a focus on infrastructure- intensive sectors.

- Sustained revenue collection and a targeted expenditure policy have contained the fiscal deficit for April to November 2021 at 46.2 per cent of BE.
- With the enhanced borrowings on account of COVID-19, the Central Government debt has gone up from 49.1 per cent of GDP in 2019-20 to 59.3 per cent of GDP in 2020-21 but is expected to follow a declining trajectory with the recovery of the economy
- India's merchandise exports and imports rebounded strongly and surpassed pre-COVID levels during the current financial year.
- There was a significant pickup in net services with both receipts and payments crossing the pre-pandemic levels, despite weak tourism revenues.
- Net capital flows were higher at US$ 65.6 billion in the first half of 2021-22, on account of continued inflow of foreign investment, revival in net external commercial borrowings, higher banking capital and additional special drawing rights (SDR) allocation.
- India's external debt rose to US $ 593.1 billion at the end- September 2021, from US $ 556.8 billion a year earlier, reflecting additional SDR allocation by IMF, coupled with higher commercial borrowings

- Foreign Exchange Reserves crossed US$ 600 billion in the first half of 2021-22 and touched US $ 633.6 billion as of December 31, 2021.
- As of end-November 2021, India was the fourth-largest forex reserves holder in the world after China, Japan and Switzerland.

Monetary Management and Financial Intermediation

- Economic Survey 2021-22 notes that the liquidity in the system remained in surplus.
- Repo rate was maintained at 4 per cent in 2021- 22.
- RBI undertook various measures such as G-Sec Acquisition Programme and Special Long-Term Repo Operations to provide further liquidity.
- The economic shock of the pandemic has been weathered well by the commercial banking system:
- YoY Bank credit growth accelerated gradually in 2021-22 from 5.3 per cent in April 2021 to 9.2 per cent as of 31st December 2021.
- The Gross Non-Performing Advances ratio of Scheduled Commercial Banks (SCBs) declined from 11.2 per cent at the end of 2017-18 to 6.9 per cent at the end of September 2021.
- Net Non-Performing Advances ratio declined from 6 per cent to 2.2 per cent during the same period.
- The capital to risk-weighted asset ratio of SCBs continued to increase from 13 per cent in 2013-14 to 16.54 per cent at the end of September 2021.
- The Return on Assets and Return on Equity for Public Sector Banks continued to be positive for the period ending September 2021.
- Exceptional year for the capital markets:
- Rs. 89,066 crores were raised via 75 Initial Public Offering (IPO) issues in April-November 2021, which is much higher than in any year in the last decade.
- Sensex and Nifty scaled up to a touching peak at 61,766 and 18,477 on October 18, 2021
- Among major emerging market economies, Indian markets outperformed peers in April-December 2021.

- The average headline CPI-Combined inflation moderated to 5.2 per cent in 2021-22 (April- December) from 6.6 per cent in the corresponding period of 2020-21.
- The decline in retail inflation was led by the easing of food inflation.
- Food inflation averaged at a low of 2.9 per cent in 2021- 22 (April to December) as against 9.1 per cent in the corresponding period last year
- Effective supply-side management kept prices of most essential commodities under control during the year.
- Proactive measures were taken to contain the price rise in pulses and edible oils.
- Reduction in central excise and subsequent cuts in Value Added Tax by most States helped ease petrol and diesel prices.
- Wholesale inflation based on the Wholesale Price Index (WPI) rose to 12.5 per cent during 2021-22 (April to December).This has been attributed to:
- Low base in the previous year,
- Pick-up in economic activity,
- A sharp increase in international prices of crude oil and other imported inputs, andHigh freight costsThe divergence between CPI-C and WPI Inflation:
- The divergence peaked at 9.6 percentage points in May 2020.
- However, this year there was a reversal in divergence with retail inflation falling below wholesale inflation by 8.0 percentage points in December 2021.
- This divergence can be explained by factors such as
- Variations due to base effect,
- The difference in scope and coverage of the two indices,
- Price collections,
- Items covered,
- With the gradual waning of the base effect in WPI, the divergence in CPI-C and WPI is also expected to narrow down.olesale

Sustainable Development and Climate Change

- India's overall score on the NITI Aayog SDG India Index and Dashboard improved to 66 in 2020-21 from 60 in 2019-20 and 57 in 2018-19.
- The number of Front Runners (scoring 65-99) increased to 22 States and UTs in 2020-21 from 10 in 2019-20.
- In North-East India, 64 districts were Front Runners and 39 districts were Performers in the NITI Aayog North-Eastern Region District SDG Index 2021-22.
- In 2020, the forests covered 24% of India's total geographical, accounting for 2% of the world's total forest area.
- In August 2021, the Plastic Waste Management Amendment Rules, 2021, was notified which is aimed at phasing out single- use plastic by 2022
- Draft regulation on Extended Producer Responsibility for plastic packaging was notified.
- The Compliance status of Grossly Polluting Industries (GPIs) located in the Ganga main stem and its tributaries improved from 39% in 2017 to 81% in 2020.

- The consequent reduction in effluent discharge has been from 349.13 million litres per day (MLD) in 2017 to 280.20 MLD in 2020.
- The Prime Minister, as a part of the national statement delivered at the 26th Conference of Parties (COP 26) in Glasgow in November 2021, announced ambitious targets to be achieved by 2030 to enable further reduction in emissions.
- The need to start the one-word movement 'LIFE' (Lifestyle for Environment) urging mindful and deliberate utilization instead of mindless and destructive consumption was underlined.

- The Agriculture sector experienced buoyant growth in the past two years, accounting for a sizeable 18.8% (2021-22) in Gross Value Added (GVA) of the country registering a growth of 3.6% in 2020-21 and 3.9% in 2021-22.
- Minimum Support Price (MSP) policy is being used to promote crop diversification.
- Net receipts from crop production have increased by 22.6% in the latest Situation Assessment Survey (SAS) compared to the SAS Report of 2014.
- Allied sectors including animal husbandry, dairying and fisheries are steadily emerging to be high growth sectors and major drivers of overall growth in the agriculture sector.
- The Livestock sector has grown at a CAGR of 8.15% over the last five years ending 2019-20. It has been a stable source of income across groups of agricultural households accounting for about 15% of their average monthly income.
- Government facilitates food processing through various measures of infrastructure development, subsidized transportation and support for the formalization of micro food enterprises.
- India runs one of the largest food management programmes in the world.
- The government has further extended the coverage of food security networks through schemes like PM Gareeb Kalyan Yojana (PMGKY).
- ***Industry and Infrastructure***

  - Index of Industrial Production (IIP) grew at 17.4 per cent (YoY) during April-November 2021 as compared to (-)15.3 per cent in April-November 2020.
  - The extent of road construction per day increased substantially in 2020-21 to 36.5 Kms per day from 28 Kms per day in 2019-20 – a rise of 30.4 per cent.

- Capital expenditure for the Indian railways has increased to Rs. 155,181 crores in 2020-21 from an average annual of Rs. 45,980 crores during 2009-14 and it has been budgeted to further increase to Rs. 215,058 crores in 2021-22 – a five times increase in comparison to the 2014 level.
- Net profit to sales ratio of large corporates reached an all- time high of 10.6 per cent in the July-September quarter of 2021-22 despite the pandemic (RBI Study).
- Introduction of Production Linked Incentive (PLI) scheme, the major boost provided to infrastructure- both physical as well as digital, along with measures to reduce transaction costs and improve ease of doing business, would support the pace of recovery.
- GVA of services crossed pre-pandemic level in July- September quarter of 2021-22; however, GVA of contact intensive sectors like trade, transport, etc. still remain below pre-pandemic level.
- Overall service Sector GVA is expected to grow by
- 8.2 per cent in 2021-22.
- During April-December 2021, rail freight crossed its pre-pandemic level while air freight and port traffic almost reached their pre-pandemic levels, domestic air and rail passenger traffic are increasing gradually – shows the impact of the second wave was much more muted as compared to during the first wave.
- During the first half of 2021-22, the service sector received over US$ 16.7 billion FDI – accounting for almost 54 per cent of total FDI inflows into India.
- IT-BPM services revenue reached US$ 194 billion in 2020-21, adding 1.38 lakh employees during the same period.
- Major government reforms include removing telecom regulations in the IT-BPO sector and opening up of space sector to private players.
- Services exports surpassed the pre-pandemic level in the January-March quarter of 2020-21 and grew by 21.6 per cent in the first half of 2021-22 – strengthened by global demand for software and IT services exports.
- India has become 3rd largest start-up ecosystem in the world after US and China. The number of new recognized start-ups increased to over 14000 in 2021-22 from 733 in 2016-17.

- 44 Indian start-ups have achieved unicorn status in 2021 taking the overall tally of unicorns to 83, most of which are in the services sector.
- 157.94 crore doses of COVID-19 vaccines administered as of 16th January 2022; 91.39 crores first dose and 66.05 crores second dose.
- With the revival of the economy, employment indicators bounced back to pre-pandemic levels during the last quarter of 2020-21
- As per the quarterly Periodic Labour Force Survey (PFLS) data up to March 2021, employment in the urban sector affected by pandemic has recovered almost to the pre-pandemic level.
- According to Employees Provident Fund Organisation (EPFO) data, formalization of jobs continued during the second COVID wave; the adverse impact of COVID on the formalization of jobs was much lower than during the first COVID wave.
- Expenditure on social services (health, education and others) by Centre and States as a proportion of GDP increased from 6.2 % in 2014-15 to 8.6% in 2021-22 (BE)
- As per the National Family Health Survey-5: Total Fertility Rate (TFR) came down to 2 in 2019-21 from 2.2 in 2015-16; Infant Mortality Rate (IMR), under-five mortality rate and institutional births have improved in 2019-21 over the year 2015-16.
- Under Jal Jeevan Mission (JJM), 83 districts have become 'Har Ghar Jal' districts.
- Increased allotment of funds to Mahatma Gandhi National Rural Employment Guarantee Scheme (MNREGS) to provide a buffer for unorganized labour in rural areas during the pandemic.

Trends in India's Labour Market: Male and Female Employment

FASLA RAHMAN K

Macroeconomic, demographic, environmental, and technological changes, whose dynamics are often complicated, have an indirect and direct impact on employment patterns. Additionally, nations plagued by ongoing hostilities and political instability have uprooted millions of people both internally and externally, creating a record-breaking influx of migrants and refugees. With a focus on the labour force and work force and an emphasis on gender differences, the study analyses the gender aspects of India's employment patterns using the NSSO PLFS data. On the future scenario of employment quantity and quality, these elements will have gender-specific effects. The study also examines how gender equality in policy could affect how people will work in the future.

Keywords: Employment, Labour force participation rate, Work force participation rate and Unemployment rate

The employment growth in India is not comparable to the faster population growth. Despite five-year goals, the jobless rate has been steadily rising since independence. One of the important economic and social variables for the growth of the economy is the changing employment pattern in India. In India, employment has always been a part of the country's development strategy.Rates of growth and shifts in the structural makeup of output and the workforce are the two key markers of structural transformation in any economy. Particularly since the 1991 reforms, India has seen reasonably regular changes in the first indicator; nevertheless, the trend in employment has not shown any clear or consistent pattern. Even if the Periodic Labour Force Survey (PLFS) shows a rise in the worker-to-population ratio and a reduction in the gender wage gap in recent years, India's unemployment situation is still dismal.

There has been an odd tendency in India. It was anticipated that India's young population would significantly benefit the nation as it developed. The evidence, however, indicates a different picture. The percentage of the population who are working age and either employed or looking for work, or the labour force participation rate, has decreased from 55.5 percent in 2011–12 to 49.8 percent in 2017–18, according to data recently released by the National Sample Survey Organization (NSSO) in its Periodic Labour Force Survey.This suggests that the majority of people in the country who are of working age are not employed.

Women's work participation rates (WPR) in India have been declining over the past few decades. According to the 38th and 68th rounds of the National Sample Survey, it has decreased from 29.6% in 1983 to 21.9% in 2011-2012, and further, to 16.5%, according to the recently released Periodic Labour Force Survey (PLFS 2017–2018). Women's employment rates have been falling, and the total number of women working has likewise been decreasing. From 148.59 million in 2004–2005 to 104.1 million in 2017–2018, it has decreased. The economy is seriously affected by the declining trend in women's labour market involvement because India's demographics appear to be favourable at the moment. India is currently regarded as the youngest nation in the world and has the highest proportion of young adults (15–34) who are employed. If women don't find jobs, the demographic dividend's advantages could be hindered. In this context, it's crucial to remember that a woman's economic well-being does not necessarily follow from her mere participation in the labour force.

Using data from the NSSO PLFS, this research compares employment trends for men and women in India with an emphasis on the labour force and a focus on gender inequalities. These issues will have differing effects on women and men in terms of employment quantity and quality in the future.

- **Labour force participation rate**

The term "labour force," sometimes known as the "economically active population," refers to the group of people who provide or aspire to provide labour for production. This group comprises both "employed" and "unemployed" people.

The percentage of people in the labour force among all people in the population is known as the labour force participation rate (LFPR). The LFPRs for people of all ages at the all-India level are provided in the below figure along with the corresponding rates from the NSSO's quinquennial employment and unemployment surveys conducted during NSS, 61st (2004-2005), 66th (2009-10) and 68th (2011-12) rounds.

Labour force participation rate is significantly lower for females than for males. During 2018-19, according to usual status (ps+ss), about 55.6 per cent of males and 18.6 per cent of females were in the labour force.. Between 2004-05 and 2011-12 as well as between 2011-12 and 2018-19, LFPR in usual status (ps+ss) for males remained almost at the same level. Between 2004-05 and 2011-12, for female, LFPR decreased by nearly 7 percentage points and between 2011-12 and 2018-19 it further decreased by around 4 percentage points.

LFPR in usual status (ps+ss) for persons of age 15 years and above is also presented. It is seen that during 2017-18 , LFPR of age 15-29 was nearly 58.8 percent for male and 16.4 percent for female . and LFPR of age 15 years above was nearly 75.8 percent for male and 23.3 percent for female .From these it is cleared that labour force participation across gender has been falling over time in India, the downward trend is particularly sharp for the females.

- **<u>Work force participation rate</u>**

Worker Population Ratio (WPR) is the percentage of persons employed among the persons in the population.

Between 1972-73 and 2017-18, WPR in usual status (ps+ss) in India decreased by nearly 7 percentage points: from around 42.3 per cent in 1977-78 to 34.7 per cent in 2017- 18. Between 2004-05 and 2011-12, WPR in usual status (ps+ss) for males remained at the same level, while it decreased by about 7 percentage point for females. Between 2011-12 and 2018-19, WPR in usual status (ps+ss) for males decreased by nearly 2 percentage points ,while it decreased by about 4 percentage point for females .

<u>Worker Population Ratio (WPR) for persons of age groups 15 to 29 years and 15 years and above</u>

It is seen that during 2017-18 WPR for age 15 years and above was nearly 71.2 percent for male and 22.0 percent for female and WPR for age 15-29 was nearly 48.3 percent for male and 13.5 percent for female.

Worker population Ratio for male age group 15-29 years decreased by 11.9 percentage point between 2004-05 and 2011-12which further decreased by 8 percentage point between 2011-12 and 2017-18.

Unemployment trends

the quinquennial rounds, in 2017-18 the unemployment rates in both usual status (ps+ss) and CWS were higher for both males and females. Among different quinquennial rounds, unemployment rate in usual status (ps+ss) was around 1.2 to 1.8 per cent among rural males and 0.5 to 2.4 per cent among rural females while it was around 2.8 per cent to 5.4 per cent among urban males and 4.9 per cent to 12.4 per cent among urban females. Among different quinquennial rounds, unemployment rates in CWS was around 3 to 4.2 per cent among rural males and 2.9 to 5.5 per cent among rural females while it was around 3.8 per cent to 7.1 per cent among urban males and 6.7 per cent to 10.9 per cent among urban females

Conclusion

Employment is a crucial component of economic growth. Because they do not follow the typical U-shaped curve seen in economies, the trends in female participation rates are unexpected. Women who were previously labouring to make ends meet leave the labour force as income rises, causing a fall in female labour force participation at first along with economic expansion. Then, due to structural changes, it climbs. Despite these structural adjustments, including declining fertility rates and increased access to education for women, India's FLFPR is on the decline.

In India, the labour force participation rate has been declining over time for both sexes, but the tendency is more severe for women. For the population of 15 years old, the percentage of women who are in the labour force has virtually halved between 2004–05 and 2017–18, going from 42.7% to 23.3%. It also demonstrates how the gender participation gap in the labour force has grown over time. In 2004–05, there were twice as many men as women in the labour force; by 2017–18, this difference had increased to three times. All types of unemployment have decreased over the past ten years, but rural women have been quitting the workforce and are still doing so. These data are alarming from an economic perspective as well as from the perspective of women's independence and autonomy. According to studies, increasing female economic engagement benefits women as well as the overall economy. Women can play a key part in shaping the Indian economy's future growth story at this point, when the COVID pandemic has severely damaged the country's economy. Investigating the barriers preventing women from participating in the labour market is therefore vital.

Taking into account these findings, policymakers in India and the rest of the region should adopt a comprehensive strategy to improve the labour market outcomes for women by enhancing access to and the relevance of education and training programmes, developing skills, gaining access to child care, protecting pregnant women, and providing safe and accessible transportation, in addition to promoting a growth pattern that generates job opportunities. Policymakers should be more concerned about whether women can access better employment or establish their own businesses, and take advantage of new labour market opportunities as a country grows, in addition to traditional labour force participation rates. In order to create a policy framework that encourages and facilitates women's participation, it is important to be aware of the "gender-specific" challenges that most women confront. Gender responsive policies need to be contextually developed.

Psychology in Everyday Life

KRISHNA PRIYA

In the realm of psychology, little attention is given to the topic of daily life as a specific subject of enquiry. In recent times, everyday life has been analysed largely in psychological studies that examine the reasons individuals conduct themselves and think when they act in situations mentioned as mundane and ordinary. These studies primarily focus on two subfields of social psychology, known as social cognition and social representation theory, respectively. The purpose of this essay is to examine how these disciplines approach some characteristics that are frequently associated with human life. To pinpoint where these two domains converge, the discussion is focused on familiarity, consistency and stability through time and automaticity.

Numerous research psychologists are working to make our lives better in the modern environment. In the sentences that follow. I'll go over some of the ways that psychologists are attempting to make our lives better. I'll provide the studies and examples from the video. You can better comprehend the subject of psychology in daily life after reading this summary.

The investigation of sleep is one crucial area of psychology. The 1950s saw the start of sleep research, which is still going strong today. Rosalind Cartwright was a pioneer herself. She invented a lot of the methods that we still apply in sleep studies today. She concluded that dreams control our emotions. This still forms the cornerstone of sleep studies today. James Moss is another outstanding researcher in this field. Mr. Moss devotes a significant portion of his waking hours to educating others about sleep deprivation and its numerous negative repercussions. He claims that daytime fatigue is an unusual state of being. Additionally, he discovered that 56% of research participants who worked shifts doze off once a week. Accuracy and productivity suffer from fatigue. Adults who are working require eight hours of sleep every night, he claimed. Students in high school and college need nine hours or more, and adults who are working while going to school need even more. These individuals often manage 6 hours or fewer per night. He realised that getting enough sleep is crucial for learning. He claims that memories are formed and ingrained in the most accessible region of our minds between the first and last two hours of an eight-hour sleep cycle. You literally become foolish if you sleep for fewer than 8 hours a day, such as when you pull a "all-nighter" and only get 2-3 hours of sleep. Similar to sleep deprivation, sleep apnea has negative repercussions. You wake up in the night 600 times on average if you have sleep apnea. It drains all of your energy. Lack of sleep and memory loss are the results. These might trigger other health issues.

Mal Cohen is another researcher who is looking towards how microgravity tends to affect how people interact. This improves our comprehension of how we interact under ordinary gravitation. He found in his research that the flow of blood changes under microgravity. Swelling of the face and limbs is one of the problems it causes. This makes lip reading necessary because it makes it difficult to read facial expressions during microgravity. In contrast to microgravity, we face each other with our heads raised and our chins lowered. This makes it simpler to interpret posture and facial expressions. We encounter one other in new dimensions in microgravity, which makes it challenging to communicate and comprehend one another. In a spacecraft or pod, it is also incredibly noisy. We must therefore develop our ability to read lips and practise showing one another more tolerance. With regard to these three aspects of microgravity, communication is significantly more challenging due to facial swelling, a loud environment, and numerous facial postures. By applying various ways in our gravity, we may better comprehend ourselves thanks to this research. University of California, San Francisco psychiatrist Nick Kanas had unheard-of access to the MiR space station to investigate gender, cultural differences, and relationships. He looked at 58 ground workers and 13 astronauts or cosmonauts. He examined conflict, unity, and leadership in both mission control and space, as part of his research. The connections between them are similar. "Displacement"—a phenomenon—appeared. When you feel isolated, you may not get along with your supervisor or be able to communicate your feelings to him or her. You leave work, go home, and rant at or dispute with someone about what irritated you at work over something absolutely unrelated. He discovered that this ground control and MiR relationship happens exactly as it does in real life.

In our legal system, psychology plays a crucial role in educating lawyers about ethics and the right ways to interrogate witnesses in order to obtain the truth. Psychologists are occasionally requested to assess the testimony and the significance of the data it contains. Judges are also taught how to recognise the telltale symptoms of inadvertently lying using this method. Additionally, it instructs attorneys to refrain from asking questions repeatedly that can alter how witnesses perceive the facts.

We look for new and more effective ways to settle disputes because violent conflict resolution still accounts for majority of conflict resolution. MIT's Sloan School of Management's Jared Curran created a programme for aspiring negotiators. Several countries throughout the world employ this programme and its methods. It focuses on educating teenagers about nonviolent techniques to diffuse conflict. Teaches practical methods for resolving disputes. He occasionally gives examples like how something awful can happen if you don't apply these strategies effectively and how something positive can happen if you do. It aims to show the variety of directions that any choice can go in. This is taught through role-playing and the use of different approaches to problem-solving. One of the most successful tactics he has discovered is empathy. His curriculum aims to instruct students in peaceful conflict resolution through negotiation. He learned that there are different levels of negotiation and that modifying what we want—and what we actually want—is the goal of negotiation. In our legal system, psychology plays a crucial role in educating lawyers about ethics and the right ways to interrogate witnesses in order to obtain the truth. Psychologists are occasionally requested to assess the testimony and the significance of the data it contains. Judges are also taught how to recognise the telltale symptoms of inadvertently lying using this method.

We look for new and more effective ways to settle disputes because violent conflict resolution still accounts for the majority of conflict resolution. MIT's Sloan School of Management's Jared Curran created a programme for aspiring negotiators. There are several countries throughout the world that employ this programme and its methods. It focuses on educating teenagers about nonviolent techniques to diffuse conflict. teaches practical methods for resolving disputes. He occasionally gives examples like how something awful can happen if you don't apply these strategies effectively and how something positive can happen if you do. It aims to demonstrate the variety of directions that any choice might go. This is taught through role-playing and the use of different approaches to problem-solving. One of the most successful tactics he has discovered is empathy. His curriculum aims to instruct students in peaceful conflict resolution through negotiation. He learned that there are different levels of negotiation and that modifying what we want—and what we want—is the goal of negotiation. The most significant of all the potential uses that we have examined and researched would be the promotion of peace and understanding of human nature.

We must first understand what psychology is before we discuss about how important it is to our daily lives. Psychology is defined as the scientific study of behaviour and the mind, yet it has many additional applications in daily life. Every action we take in life has a psychological component. In its simplest form, psychology is the study of who we are, why we are the way we are, and what we can become.

The research that has been done on numerous deadly diseases is one illustration of why psychology is vital in so many different ways. Parkinson's disease, Alzheimer's disease, and numerous other neurological disorders have all been researched by psychologists utilising psychological techniques. We now know a lot more about these diseases than we did in the past, and scientists have even been able to develop medications that could aid those who are afflicted with them. The study of psychology is crucial in the educational process. Students can be assessed and provided the right amount of assistance in school by employing IQ test schools. For instance, IQ testing are used to place kids in "gifted programmes," guaranteeing that the students in those programmes would get the greatest education possible at the ideal pace for them. On the other side, these assessments also enable academics and teachers identify which kids might want additional support in particular academic areas.

The knowledge that earlier study has provided us with is another factor in the significance of psychology. For instance, we can learn about the functioning of the body and mind by studying psychology. The ability to handle stress, schedule our time efficiently, and study more effectively is only one example of how vital it is to understand how the mind and body function. Another illustration would be the study of mental diseases. Doctors have now created medication and even disease cures using psychological studies. I value psychology because it aids in my self-understanding and explains why I make some of the decisions I do in life. Psychology is really essential to me right now since I want to work as a marriage and family counsellor later in life. I use what I've learned to benefit those around me, but I also use it to simplify my own life. I improved my time management, my ability to handle my stress, and my overall well-being by understanding the concepts psychology teaches. In our daily lives, psychology is all around us. It affects our social lives, careers, and educational institutions. In the absence of psychology, we wouldn't have the level of education we do now.

How useful psychology is in everyday life

Psychology is not a single subject of enterprise as in fact it can be pinned down to quite a lot of collated specialties for example developmental psychology, clinical psychology, cognitive psychology, physiological psychology which all have different focus points.

The focus of developmental psychology is on understanding the age-related changes that take place in all living things over the course of a lifetime. Conversely, clinical psychology focuses more on identifying the root causes of psychological diseases and coping issues like depression and phobias and treating them. Physiological psychology, on the other hand, focuses primarily on the investigation of the relationship between the brain and behaviour. The focus of cognitive psychology is on investigating the most fundamental questions surrounding mental functions like perception, thinking, memory, and language.

The following sections of this article will use the aforementioned examples to highlight one or more of these psychological topics in order to clarify the idea of "how psychology is beneficial in everyday life."

Clinical psychology will be the main topic of discussion because it is an important aspect of daily life, especially for individuals who deal with disorders and other issues.

Clinical psychology is the term most often used to refer to the diagnosis, treatment, and prevention of mental diseases and disabilities in relation to psychology.

A range of issues are treated and resolved through therapeutic psychology. Psychological issues like: anxiety, phobias, learning disabilities, relationship issues, mania, depression, and other major mental diseases.

Clinical psychologists typically work in hospitals, community health teams, child and adolescent mental health services and social services, health centres, nursing homes, and other health and social care environments. Clinical psychologists typically collaborate with a group of other professionals in these settings, such as social workers and medical professionals, as most of these persons are constrained by the National Health Service.

As the question for this essay is 'How useful is psychology in everyday life.?' and clinical psychology is pretty much linked to abnormal psychology which is the nature and development of abnormal behavior, thoughts, feelings associated with distress or 'impaired functioning that is not a culturally expected response to an event. '

Psychological study helps us to understand that the most obvious types of stress are traumatic events, which are situations of extreme danger that are beyond the reach of any human experience. Many people go through a specific series of psychological reactions following traumatic events (Horowitz, 1986).

With this in mind, psychology can be helpful in daily life since it can identify the root of the stress, its symptoms, and whether or not the person has been given a diagnosis for any other diseases.

Psychologists have also conducted various research that highlight the effects of specific occurrences. Some of these studies suggest that in the first six months following being traumatised by rape or other assaults, both men and women exhibit high levels of anxiety, despair, terror, and many other signs of mental distress. (Duncan et al., 1996; Kessler et al., 1997).

Psychology is therefore highly helpful in helping to arrange therapy strategies for such persons as a result of studies like the ones mentioned above.

According to the diathesis-stress model of mental illness, some people have a long-term susceptibility factor combined with a proximal stressor that causes them to develop a mental condition. This indicates that occasionally neither the disease nor the stressor are necessary to produce symptoms. (Hewstone, Fincham, and Foster, p. 319).

Psychology is helpful in this case since it helps to understand the problems, how they appear, how they progress, and their causes before drawing conclusions about some possible biological and psychological causes of the disorders.

Psychology generally aims to comprehend the relationship between the brain, environment, situation, etc., and human behaviour. This gives people a better knowledge of why people behave the way they do and deals with theories like the social learning theory, which holds that people pick up behaviour through observation and straightforward imitation of what they see. Psychology clarifies our understanding of the mind's capabilities and limitations. It enables people to immediately assess their circumstances and devise strategies to handle them. Take care of your mental health and get to know yourself, advised Socrates, because doing so will help you understand how to care for others.

Because psychology aids in the comprehension of particular behaviour patterns, such as aggressive behaviour, it is immensely helpful in daily life. Psychology offers the door to understanding these situations by researching the brain, hormones, genetic features, social interaction with parents and other people, and triggers that encourage violent conduct. People who exhibit aggressive conduct have benefited from psychology because of its understanding of the relationship between compulsive violence and tumours and damage to the temporal lobe, a specific area of the brain. (Elliot, 1988).

Psychology contends that a significant aspect of interpersonal connections in daily life is the ability to manage one's emotions and comprehend those of others around one. According to Daniel Goleman (1995), having a high EIQ is actually more significant in life than having an IQ.

In a broader sense, how might psychology be applied to daily tasks to better your situation? Here is a list of some of the best methods to use psychological knowledge in practical situations.

Examples: -

• Visualize Your Goals and Dreams

Nearly all elite athletes who are asked how they do it will likely respond that it all comes down to visualisation and working hard to reach a goal.

• Dare Yourself to Achieve More

Psychology is at work when you dare to do something outside of your comfort zone. You need to persuade yourself to take a risk that could pay off handsomely but also put you in a humiliating and depressing position if you fail. However, you consider the dangers and give yourself the motivation to continue despite them.

• Remain Motivated

One of the most difficult psychological techniques to learn is maintaining motivation, especially if you are working on a task you are not very passionate about..

• Seek assistance and receive It

Most individuals believe that asking for assistance shows weakness. Even if it's true that some people would rather live off of handouts than put their all into something, asking for assistance isn't always a sign of weakness.

• Be and Stay Unique

In the world we live in, mass production is celebrated. This frequently results in a uniform appearance among many of us. Recognizing your individuality is the best approach to stand out and be someone you can be proud of.

Too many people adopt a conformist worldview out of laziness. Recognize this as a possibility and make an intentional effort to handle situations your way.

A personal skills audit might be the best course of action, for instance, if you wish to identify the greatest vocation for you moving forward. Think about the traits and qualities that best describe you. Your personal analysis may spark ideas for different professional possibilities.

Benefits from Studying Psychology

1. People Skills
2. Success Strategies
3. Personal Therapy
4. Problem-Solving Skills
5. Conceptual Reasoning
6. Communication Skills
7. Behavioural Training Skills
8. Memorisation Techniques

1. People skills

When it comes to interactions with friends, family, coworkers, employers, and even in love relationships, studying psychology, especially in its online form, gives you a competitive advantage. You have a greater chance of achieving harmony and shared satisfaction.

Important concepts and technologies are introduced in academic courses. You'll soon discover that you can handle your own interpersonal connections more effectively by putting the puzzle pieces together. The secret to happiness, harmony, and a higher standard of living is having healthy relationships.

2. Success Strategies

You create plans for success and personal progress, which is another benefit. These should be the outcomes of your study if you were paying attention and connecting your coursework to your personal life.

You can create a foundation for your own personal growth and development by mastering psychology. You get more conscious of your own thoughts, beliefs, and self-perception as well as how these cognitions affect your daily life. As a result, you are more prepared to create the habits and techniques that will help you succeed in life.

3. Personal Therapy

You are introduced to CBT, a crucial therapy method, in psychology courses. You can get proficient at using CBA by yourself with sufficient practise. Although psychology courses at the bachelor's level do not extensively cover the treatment of problems, you will understand the foundations of CBT and how it is applied.

Everybody occasionally has unpleasant thoughts. The main goal of CBT is to replace negative ideas and behaviours with more constructive ones. According to cognitive behavioural therapy (CBT), our thoughts influence how we feel, act, and even how we relate to others.

4. Problem-Solving Skills

Studying psychology teaches you to look at issues from several angles, which is essential for coming up with the best and most advantageous solutions. Psychology helps you to reflect on your own thought processes. When facing obstacles and making decisions in life, this is really advantageous.

5. Conceptual Reasoning

Studying psychology is an excellent way to improve your thinking if you desire to do so. Learning about scientific concepts in psychology enables you to reason, think critically, and ask questions like a scientist. Your ability to think critically and logically will improve.

6. Communication Skills

Graduates in psychology have effective communication abilities that are useful in a variety of contexts. You might, for instance, have a better understanding of how to introduce oneself to a new group of people or create a compelling job application.

There are two key factors that improve communication skills. One is that the training gives you the chance to improve your writing and presentation abilities. Second, by approaching your conversations with a psychological mindset, you can shape them to elicit the reactions you desire. Graduates are frequently hired for marketing positions due to their aptitude for influencing and interacting with audiences.

7. Behavioural Training Skills

No matter if you want to train your dog, child, spouse, or even yourself, learning psychology gives you an advantage as a behavioural trainer. When you study psychology, you can better understand why certain individuals are terrified of flying or heights, why our hearts beat faster when we hear a loud noise, and why people flee when they see an insect. You'll probably take at least one or two courses at a university or college that introduce you to classical and operant conditioning. These are the two major mechanisms via which learning occurs.

8. Memorisation Techniques

Knowing memorisation strategies is another benefit of psychology that may be useful while preparing for an exam or professional presentation.Students learn how to acquire and use memory in psychology classes, as well as strategies for improving memory. You'll probably take at least one course in a degree programme where you understand the neurological underpinnings of memory as well as strategies for memory consolidation and retrieval.

Conclusion

In conclusion, psychology plays a significant role in daily life and has been involved in the majority of research studies on serious disorders. These investigations have helped psychologists learn more about conditions including Parkinson's disease, Alzheimer's disease, and other neurological disorders. Doctors have been able to create medications and even treat some diseases by using psychology. Psychology is helpful in terms of lifestyle and daily living since it provides ways for individuals to become motivated. For instance, the majority of athletes have psychologists who suggest various strategies to energise them before competitions. Through techniques like research methods and memory training, among other things, psychology can be a useful tool in assisting people to develop their leadership skills, communication, personal memory, and decision-making abilities. The study of psychology is significant and helpful in daily life.

References

Pre-Post Economy

Kerala Economy in pre – Independence and Post – Independence Period

1)B A Prakash, Jerry Alwin (Ed) (2018), Kerala's Economic Development: Emerging Issues and Challenges, Sage, New Delhi

2)B A Prakash, (June 9, 2021), Sixty Years of Kerala's Economy: Economic Policies, Development strategy and Development, Available in www.keralaeconomy.com

3)B A Prakash (September 2020), The Impact of COVID – 19 on Kerala's Economy: A Preliminary Assessment

4)Issac Thomas and Tharakan Michael (1986), An Enquiry into the Historical Roots of Industrial Backwardness of Kerala – A Case Study of Travancore Region, Working

5)K K George (2011), Kerala economy: Growth, Structure, Strength and Weakness, Working paper No: 25, Kochi, Centre for Socio- Economic and Environmental Studies (CSES),

6)Mahadevan Ramanan (1991), 'Industrial Entrepreneurship in Princely Travancore: 1930 – 1947' South Indian Economy: Agrarian change, Industrial structures and State Policy, 1914 – 1947, PP 189 – 197, New Delhi, Oxford University Press.

7)Muranjan S K (1952), Modern Banking in India, Bombay, Kamala Publishing House

8)National Council of Applied Economic Research, 1967, Estimates of State Income, New Delhi.

9)Oomman M A (1976) 'Rise and Growth of Banking in Kerala', Social Scientist, Vol 5, No 3, PP 24 – 26

10)paper No: 215, Thiruvananthapuram, Centre for Development Studies (CDS)

11)Panikar P G K, Krishnan T N and Raj Krishna N (1978), Population Growth and Agricultural Development – A case study of Kerala, Rome, Food and Agriculture Organisation.

12)Panikar P G K and Soman C R (1985) Health status of Kerala, Thiruvananthapuram, Centre for Development Studies (CDS).

13)Ramachandran V K (2010), 'On Kerala's Development Achievements' in Jean Dreze and Amartya Sen (Eds), Indian Development: Selected Regional Perspectives, PP 205 – 356, New Delhi, Oxford University Press.

14)Raghaviah Jaiprakash (1990), Basel Mission Industries in Malabar and South Canara 1834 – 1914: A study of its Economic and Social impact, New Delhi, GIAN Publishing House

15)Rene veron, The new Kerala Model: Lessons for sustainable development, World development Vol.29, PP 601 – 617, 2001

17)Saradamoni K (1994) 'Women, Kerala and some Development Issues', Economic and Political Weekly, Vol 9, PP 501 – 509

18)Singh Bright (1944) 'Financial Development in Travancore: 1900 – 1940', Unpublished PhD Thesis, Thiruvananthapuram, University of Travancore.

19)Tharakan Michael (2005), 'Evolution of Economy and Society in Kerala: A long term perspective', Kerala Economy: Trajectories, challenges and Implications, PP 11 – 24, Cochin, Directorate of Publication and Public relations, Cochin University of Science and Technology.

20)Vineesh O K (2019), Impact Assessment of Kerala Flood 2018 and 2019, A Journal of Composition Theory, Vol 12, Issue 11, PP 168 – 174.

Goblin or Ghosts :are Tulu Brahmins a Unique Specimen?An Economic Approach

21)Census of India, 1971

22)Dr. U Upadhyaya (E.d) Coastal Karnataka, Studies on Folk tourist and Linguistics, Traditions of Dakshina Karnataka region of the Western coat of India, Rashtrakavi Govind Pai Samshodhana Kendra, Udupi, 1966, p. viii

23)Ganapayya Bhat.P, Pre-history of Coastal Karnataka, JMS; Vol LXX, No. 1-12, 1979

Kekunaya Padmanabha, A Comparitive Study of Tulu dialects, Rashtrakavi Govind Pai Research Centre, Udupi,1994, p.5

24)Karnataka State Gazetteer, Part II, 1983, p. 973

25)Mohan Krishna Rai.K.Tulunadu, Kannada nadu, Tulu Karnataka Nadu, Nadi Chinthana Harapi, 2012, pp. 255-267, pp. 46.

26)Naduvattom Gopalakrishnan, Kannada and Tulu Elements in Malayalam, International school of Dravidian Linguistics, Thiruvananthapuram, 2015

27)Personal Interview wtith Prof.Rama, International School of Dravidian Linguistics,Thiruvananthapuram on 4/5/2016.

28)Robert Caldwell, A Comparitive Grammar of the Dravidan or South Indian Family of Languages University of Madras, p.32.

29)Robert caldwell, ibid, p.33.

30)Sturrock.J, Madras District Manuals, South Canara, Vol I, Madras, 1894, pp.1

31)Sturrock, South Canara District Manual, VAI, p.57

32)Virakkal T. Balakrishnan Nair, Theranjedutha Prabhandangal(mal), Kerala Sahitya Academy, 1981, p.233

Future Economy

Old age economy

33)Andrew mason, sang-hyop lee, And donghyun park,Demographic Change, Economic Growth,and Old-Age Economic Security:Asia and the World, Asian development Bank

34)H.S. Borji,Robert C. Kelly, Pete Rathburn,Global Economic Issues of an Aging Population,August 09, 2021

35)How will an ageing population affect the economy? Behavioral science,World Economic forum, Apr 9, 2015

36)Kerala Economic Review 2021: State's elderly population to touch 21% by 2031, The Indian Express,March 12, 2022

37)Ronald Lee and Andrew Mason,Cost of Aging,FINANCE & DEVELOPMENT, March 2017, Vol. 54, No. 1

38)Sarah Harper,The positive impacts of an ageing population,Director of the Oxford Institute of Population Ageing, 2022

39)Wolfgang Fengler,The silver economy is coming of age: A look at the growing spending power of seniors, Brookings,Thursday, January 14, 2021

Work from home: issues and challenges faced by working women in the it sector (during covid-19 pandemic)

40)Basuroy, T. (2022, 15 March). Number of Facebook users across India as of January 2018, by age and gender Statista Retrieved 22 April,2022,

41)Bonney, N., & Reinach, E. (1993). Housework Reconsidered: The Oakley Thesis Twenty Years Later. Work, Employment & Society, 7(4), 615–627

42)Borah, P. R. (2021). Work from (at) home: Female educators during Covid-19 pandemic (M.A. dissertation

43)Chauhan, P. (2021). Gendering COVID-19: Impact of the Pandemic on Women's Burden of Unpaid Work in India. Gender Issues, **38**, 395–419 (2021).

44)Castaño, C., & Webster, J. (2011). Understanding Women's Presence in ICT: the Life Course Perspective. International Journal Of Gender, Science And Technology, 3(2),364 -386.

45)Choudary, P. (2020). Our Work-From-Anywhere Future. Harvard Business Review (November-December, 2020).

46)Darouei, M., & Pluut, H. (2021). Work from home today for a better tomorrow! How working from home influences work-family conflict and employees' start of the next workday. Stress and health : journal of the International Society for the Investigation of Stress, 37(5), 986–999. 47)Gamburd, M. R. (2012). Breadwinners No More: Masculinity in Flux. In J. Goodman (Eds), Global Perspective on Gender and Work: Reading and Interpretation (pp. 355- 366). Rowman & Littlefield Publisher

48)Giddens, A., & Sutton, P. W. (2017). Work and the Economy. Sociology (pp. 244-293). Wiley.

49)Hall, D., & Richter, J. (1988). Balancing Work Life and Home Life: What Can Organizations Do to Help? The Academy of Management Executive (1987-1989), 2(3), 213-223.

50)Herman, C., & Webster, J. (2010). Taking a Lifecycle Approach: Redefining Women Returners to Science, Engineering and Technology. International Journal Of Gender, Science And Technology,2(2).

51)Hondagneu-Sotelo, P. (2012). Families on the Frontier: From Braceros in the Field to Braceras in the Home. In J. Goodman (Eds), Global Perspective on Gender and Work: Reading and Interpretation (pp. 471-479). Rowman & Littlefield Publishers.

52)Hutchinson, F., & Ilavarasan, P. V. (2008). The IT/ITES Sector and Economic Policy at the Sub-National Level in India. Economic and Political Weekly, 43(46), 64–70.

53)Jain, P. (2021). WORK FROM HOME: A Study of High School Women Teachers of Chandigarh during the Pandemic(M.A.dissertation).

54)Lindsey, L. L. (2011). Gender Roles: A Sociological Perspective. Person Prentice Hall.

55)Marimuthu, P., & Vasudevan, H. (2020). The Psychological impact of working from home during coronavirus (Covid 19) pandemic: A case study. CnR's International Journal of Social & Scientific Research, 6(1) 18-29.

56)Micha, A. Digital security concerns and threats facing women entrepreneurs. J Innov Entrep **2**, 7 (2013).

57)Musungwimi, S., Zhou, T., & Musungwimi, L. (2020). Challenges facing women in ICT from a women perspective: A case study of the Zimbabwean Banking Sector and Telecommunications Industry. Journal of System Integration 11, 1 (2020), 21-33.

58)Neetha, N. (2004). Making of Female Breadwinners: Migration and Social Networking of Women Domestics in Delhi. Economic and Political Weekly, 39(17), 1681–1688.

59)Oswald, A. J., Proto, E., & Sgroi, D. (2015). Happiness and Productivity. Journal of Labor Economics, 33(4), 789–822. https://doi.org/10.1086/681096

60)Roy, E (2020, April 3). Domestic violence, abuse complaints rise in coronavirus lockdown: NCW.The Indian Express.

61)Salinger, L. (2012). Trope Chasing: Making a Local Labor Market. In J. Goodman (Eds), Global Perspective on Gender and Work: Reading and Interpretation (pp. 325- 338). Rowman & Littlefield Publishers.

62)Shamir, B., & Salomon, I. (1985). Work-at-Home and the Quality of Working Life. The Academy of Management Review, 10(3), 455-464.

63)Sharma, U. (2021). Women's perception of household work: A qualitative study of housewives in Guwahati,Assam(M.A.dissertation).

64)Stuart, M., Grugulis, I., Tomlinson, J., Forde, C., & MacKenzie, R. (2013). Introduction: Reflections on work and employment into the 21st century: between equal rights, force decides. Work, Employment & Society, 27(3), 379–395

65)Rey A. L. Taganas, & Vijay Kumar Kaul. (2006). Innovation Systems in India's I.T. Industry: An Empirical Investigation. Economic and Political Weekly, 41(39), 4178–4186. http://www.jstor.org/stable/4418760

66)Van Ruysseveldt, J., Proost, K., & Verboon, P. (2011). The Role of Work-home Interference and Workplace Learning in the Energy-depletion Process. Management Revue, 22(2), 151-168.

Growth and Development

Growth Rate

67)Neelambaran (2023), Kerala clocks strong industrial growth focus on divers MSME's to sustain growth,News click, February 23

68)IT boom that Kerala can cash in on (2022), The Indian express

69)Onmanorama (2023),Kerala's growth rate improved to 12.1% in 2021-22: Economic Review, February 2, Thiruvananthapuram

Infrastructural development

70)John Spacey (2018), what is infrastructural development?,Simplicable, January 16

71)State level bankers committee (2020), infrastructure in Kerala, Thiruvananthapuram

72)Indo-American chamber of commerce, Kerala infrastructural development (2023)

73)Aneesh Jacob (2023), Kerala development

74)Kerala to prioritise 10 development projects in annual plan worth Rs 38,629 cr, Mathrubhumi,January 28,Thiruvananthapuram

Tribal Poverty and Women

Tribal Poverty and Livelihood in Kerala

75)Centre for Development Studies (CDS) Study on Tribal Poverty in Kerala

76)Centre for Development Studies. (2015). Kerala Human Development Report. Thiruvananthapuram: Government of Kerala

77)Government of India. (2011). Census of India 2011: Kerala. New Delhi: Ministry of Home Affairs

78)International Institute for Population Sciences (IIPS) and ICF. (2021). National Family Health Survey (NFHS-5), India, 2019-20: Kerala. Mumbai: IIPS

79)Kerala State Planning Board. (2021). Statistical Handbook of Kerala 2021

80)Menon, M. (2016). Land Alienation and the Decline of Tribal Communities in Kerala. Economic and Political Weekly, 51(43), 34-40

81)Tribal Development in Kerala" by Tribal Welfare Department, Government of Kerala, 2016. Government of Kerala Report, 2008

82)Socio Economic and Caste Census (SECC) 2011:

83)Sunitha, A,S.(2014).Intra- tribal disparities in human development indicators: Inference from the tribes of Kerala. International Journal of Social Sciences and Humanites.1,2 , January- June ,Centre for Study of Social Exclusive and Inclusive Policy, Cochin University of Science and Technology, Cochin

Socio-Cultural amplitudes of Women's discriminations in rural societies

84)Ali, W., Fani M.I., Afzal S., and Yasin G. (2010), Cultural barriers in women empowerment: A sociological analysis of Multan, Pakistan, European Journal of Social Sciences, 18(1): 147-155.

85)Annie Marie Golla, Anju Malhotra, Understanding and measuring Women's Economic Empowerment, ICRW 2011, www.icrw.org.

86)Avasthi, Abha and Srivastava A.K. (ed.) (2001), Modernity, Feminism and Women Empowerment, Jaipur and New Delhi: Rawat Publications.

87)Ayevbuomwan, O.S., Popoola, O.A and Adeoti, A.I (2016) Analysis of Women Empowerment in Rural Nigeria: A Multidimensional Approach: Global Journal of Human-Social Science: Sociology & Culture Volume 16 Issue 6 Version 1.0 Year 2016.

88)Berta – Esteve – Volast, (2004), "Gender discrimination and Growth: Theory and Evidence from India," London, London School of Economics and Political Sciences.

89)Boender, Carol, Malhorta A. and Schuler R. S., (2002), Measuring Women's Empowerment as a Variable in International Development, Background Paper Prepared for the World Bank Workshop on Poverty and Gender: New Perspectives,

90)Hossain Md, A. (2011) Socio-Economic Obstacles of Women Empowerment in Rural Bangladesh: A Study on Puthia Upazila of Rajshahi District Research on Humanities and Social Sciences Vol.1, No.4http://www.oecd.org/cfe/smes/31919215.pdf Accessed 7 July 2018).

91)Jehan Q.(2000), "Role of women in economic development of Pakistan", PhD diss., University of Balochistan, Quetta.

92)Kabeer, N. (2001), "Conflict over Credit: Re-evaluating the Empowerment Potential of Loans to Women in Rural Bangladesh", World Development, Vol. 29, No. 1, pp. 63-84.

93)Maherukh Khan, Dr. Shabana Mazhar (2017) Socio–Cultural Impediments & Women Empowerment, ISSN – 2455-0620 Volume - 3, Issue - 7, July – 2017, www.ijirmf.com.

94)Malhotra A. and Schuler R. S.(2005), "Women's empowerment as a variable in international development" Measuring empowerment: Crossdisciplinary perspectives (2005): 71-88.

95)Mason, Oppenheim K., and Smith L.H.. (2003), "Women's empowerment and social context: Results from five Asian countries", Gender and Development Group, World Bank, Washington, DC.

96)Md. Aminur Rahman (2013). Women's. Empowerment: Concept and Beyond by Global Journal of Human Social Science Volume XIII Issue VI 2013.

97)Obi, Anulika Virginia (2017), Over coming Socio- Cultural barriers on economic empowerment of rural women through entrepreneurship in agriculture in south-east State, Nigeria, Vol 6, Pg 199-224, www.researchgate.net.

98)Smith, RH (2008), Understanding Career decisions: Women Teachers and Head teachers Perceptions of Secondary headship, London, Leicester University Press.

99)Yusuf, L. (2013). Influence of Gender and Cultural Beliefs on Women Entrepreneurs in Developing Economy, Scholarly Journal of Business Administration 3(5), 117–119

Educated unemployment and underemployment

An analysis of kottayam district to determine why people are unemployed despite all have degrees

100)Andrew. (2014). Unemployment and attitudes to work. employment and Society, pp68(a)

101)Easwararasad (1979). Education and Unemployment of Professional Manpower in India. Economic and Political Weekly

102)Indrajith, Bairagya. (2018). Why is unemployment higher among the educated. Economic and Political Weekly, 31-65.

103)Juha, ketturn. (1997). Education and Unemployment duration. Economics of education review.

104)Lekshmi Devi. (2002). Education, Employment and Job preference of women in Kerala: A micro-level case study. CDS

105)Mehandra , dev. (2011) Youth employment and unemployment in India, IGIDR.

106)Mithra. (2006). Human capital attainment and female labor force participation- The Kerala Puzzle. Journal of Economic Issues.

107)Neilsen, Jacob, Arendt. (2005).The Importance of Literacy for Employment and Unemployment Duration. Department of Business and Economics

108)Satya, Paul. (1988). Unemployment and underemployment in rural India" by Satya Paul, Economic and Political Weekly

109)Zernike, K. (2015, October 25) Trends in rural unemployment in India. Economic and Political Weekly

Underemployment

110) Unacademy(2023), Kerala psc

Service sector

A study on consumer perception towards high-priced drugs and pricing by pharmaceutical companies

Books:

111)Koçkaya G & Wertheimer A.(Eds) (2016). Pharmaceutical Market Access in Developed Markets. SEEd.

112)Koçkaya G & Wertheimer A.(Eds) (2018), Pharmaceutical Market Access in Emerging Markets. SEEd.

Magazines:

113)Wapner, J. (2017, April). How Prescription Drugs Get Their Prices, Explained; the High Price of Prescription Drugs Is an Ever-Increasing Cause of Concern in the United States. Here, an Insider Shares Her Knowledge of How the Drug-Pricing Sausage Gets Made.Newsweek,168(13).

Journals articles, research papers, thesis:

114)Ahire, K., Shukla, M., Gattani, M., Singh, V., & Singh, M. (2013). A survey based study in current scenario of generic and branded medicines. Int J Pharm Pharm Sci, 5(3), 705-11.

115)Khanna, M. (2013). A study on consumers' perception towards ayurvedic drugs vis-à-vis allopathic drugs. University of Lucknow, Lucknow

116)Khoso, I., Ahmed, R. R., & Ahmed, J. (2014). Pricing strategies in pharmaceutical marketing. The Pharma Innovation Journal, 3(7), 13-17.

117)Shekhar, S. K., Jose, T. P., & Rehin, K. R. (2019). Consumer buying behavior and attitude towards pharmaceuticals. International Journal of Research in Pharmaceutical Sciences, 10(4), 3392-3397.

118)Saxena, S. K. (2010). A Review of Marketing Strategies Work by Different Pharmaceutical Companies. Department of Management, Rakshpal Bahadur

119)Yadav, P. (2010). Differential pricing for pharmaceuticals. DFID: London.

Upshots of Reverse Migration during Pandemic

120)Kumar, N. A. (November, 2011). Vulnerability of Migrants and Responsiveness of the State:The Case of Unskilled Workers in Kerala, India. Kochi: Centre for Socio Economic Studies (CSES)

121)Joy Puthuma(2016):Impact of migrant workers in the Kerala Economy", International Journal of informative and futuristic research, Volume 3 Issue 8 .April 2016 p-2943- 2948.

122)Raj Kumar Sangappa Sali(2015): Causes and consequences of migration in India: a sociological perspective" Golden Research Thoughts Volume-4 Issue-7 Jan-2015

123)Rukmini Thapa, Satyam Kumar Yadav(2015): Rural Labour Migration in India: Magnitude and Characteristics" International Journal of Applied Research; 1(2): 114-118

124)Santhosh Mehrotra and Baikunth Roy (2020): Will Bihar's economy rise to the Reverse Migration Challenge", The Hindu News Paper.

125)Sen Sunanda ,(2020):"Rethinking of Migration and Informal Indian Economy in the Time of a Pandemic", The Hindu News Paper.

126)Swaminathan Madhura(2020): Reset Rural Job Policies, Recognize Women's Work". The Hindu News Paper.

127)Udaya S Misra and Irudaya Rajan(2018): "Internal Migration", Draft Thematic Paper 2, ILO

Health and Tourism

Declining Child Sex Ratio in India and Kerala – An Examination

128)Annual Report. (2019-20). Department of Health and Family WElfare, Ministry of Health and Family Welfare, Government of India.

129)Census of India. (2011). Registrar General and Census commissioner of India, Ministry of Home Affairs, Government of India.

130)Provisional Population Totals, Paper 2 of 2001, Series 33. Kerala: Director of Census Operations.

131)National Family Health Survey (NFHS-4). (2015-16). Ministry of Health and Family Welfare, Government of India.

132)National Family Health Survey (NFHS-5). (2019-21). Ministry of Health and Family WElfare, Government of India.

133)Patel, V. (2002). Adverse Juvenile Sex Ratio in Kerala. Economic and Political Weekly, 2124-2125.

134)Rajesh Kumar Rai, Prashant Kumar Singh, Sulabha Parasuraman. (2013). Declining Sex Ratio of the Child Population in India: A Decomposition Analysis. XXVII IUSSP Inernational Conference. Busan, Republic of Korea.

135)Sex Ratio in India. (2015). Reference Note, No.32/RN/Ref./October/2015 (pp. 1-14). Parliament Library and Reference, Research,Documentation and Information Service (LARRDIS), Lok Sabha Secretariate.

136)Waldron, I. (1998). Sex Differences in Infant and Early Childhood Mortality : Major Causes of Death and Possible Biological Causes. In Too Young to Die: Genes or Gender (pp. 64-83). New York: United Nations Publications.

137)Women and Men in India.(2022) Social Statistical Division,National Statistical Office, Ministry of Statistics & Programme Implemention, Government of India.

138)World Population Prospects .(2019) United Nations

Development and Growth of Kerala Tourism

139)Economic Review, 2015, 2016, 2019, 2020, 2021, 2022, State Planning Board, Government of Kerala.

140)India Tourism Statistics, 2015, Ministry of Tourism, Government of India.

141)Kerala Tourism Statistics, 2015, 2016, 2019, 2020, 2021, Department of Tourism, Kerala.

142)Kerala Tourism Policy", 2012, Department of Tourism, Government of Kerala.

Official Site of Kerala Tourism Department,

143)Kerala Tourism Executive Summary- Tata Economic Consultancy Services, Bangalore, (2012).

144)Thirteenth Five-Year Plan (2017-2022) Working Group on Tourism Report, Kerala State Planning Board, Government of Kerala

Financial development and crisis in Kerala

Consumer behaviour in Kerala

145)Dr. Edakkotte Shaji, Consumer Behaviour,Associate Professor & Head (Vice Principal) Department of Commerce ,Government Arts & Science College,Meenchanda,Kozhikode,Kerala, India

146)Sangeeta sahney,behaviour of female consumers towards cosmetic products,Associate Professor,Vinod Gupta School of Management,Indian Institute of Technology (IIT), Kharagpur, Oxford University press

147)Sreekanth i.s* & sreenath i.s,consumer behavior towards two-wheelers A Comparative Study of Rural and Urban Consumers of Kollam District Kerala,Research Schololar,Rajagiri Dawood Batcha College of Arts and Science, Papanasam,Thanthai Hans Roever college, Perambalur

Gold and Dimond

148)Nevin John (2013), Diamond sales in Kerala up 15 per cent, Business standard, February 25, Thiruvananthapuram

149)Sakshi Shah(2023),Income Tax on Gold - Investment Types, Rates, Exemptions,UICKO

Share Market

150)FINCASH(2023), Share Market

151)Muhammed Zameel K M (2020), study on investment strategy of people in Kerala, Research Nebula,volume 9, issue 3

152)Trendlyne(2023),Kerala state industrial corporation's portfolio and holdings

Real estate

153)Real estate industry (2022) The real estate sector sees a boost in sales in Kerala,home capital,March 4

154)Unravelling Kerala (2023),JLL

Excise

155)Business standard (2023),All-time liquor sale in Kerala on a high during New Year eve: BevCo, Kochi

156)Kerala State Excise department

157)The Kerala State Beverages Corporation Limited (BEVCO)(2023)

Fiscal deficit

158)B A Prakash (2019), Kerala's alarming fiscal crisis,Former Chairman,Kerala Public Expenditure Review Committee

159)IASP Conference, December 13

160)Kerala budget analysis 2022-23

Good and service tax (GST)

161)Goods and services tax council, government of India

162)Hindustan Times (2022), Kerala to avoid implementation of GST on 13 food products: Minister, July 31

163)The hindu newspaper(2023),Kerala's GST revenues up in first quarter,July 2,

164)The hindu newspaper(2023),Revamp of Kerala State GST department completed, January 19

165)State goods and services tax, Kerala

Others

Trends in India's Labour Market: Male and Female Employment

166)Himanshu (2011): "Employment Trend in India: A Re-examination", Economic & Political Weekly, 46 (37), pp 43-59

167)National Sample Survey Organization Employment and Unemployment Survey Report 2011-2012

168)Nation Sample Survey Organisation Periodic Labour Survey Report 2017-18,2018-19.

Psychology in Everyday Life

169)Atkinson, R, L. Atkinson, R, C. Smith E, E. Bem, D, J. Hoeksema S, N. (2000). Hilgard's Introduction to Psychology. 13th edn. Orlando. Harcourt college publishers

170)Duncan, R. D., & Saunders, B, E., Kilpatrick, D. G., Hanson, R. F., & Resnick, H. S. (1996). Childhood physical assault as a risk factor for PTSD, depression, and substance abuse: Findings from a national survey. American journal of Orthopsychiatry, 66, 437-448

171)Elliot, F. A 1988, 'Neurological factors' in V.B. van Hasselt, R.L. Morrison, A.S. Bellack, & M. Hersen (eds), Handbook of family Violence, Plenum Press, New York.

172)Hewstone, M. Finchman, F D. Foster, J. (2005). Psychology. Oxford UK. The British Psychological Society and Blackwell Publishing Ltd.

173)Hogg, A, M. Vaughan, M, G. (2008). Social psychology. 5th edn. London. Pearson: Prentice Hall

173)Horowitz, M. (1986). Stress- response syndromes: A review of posttraumatic and adjustment disorders. Hospital & Community psychiatry, 37, 241-249.

174)Kessler, R. C., Davis, C. G., & Kendler, K. S. (1997). Childhood adversity and adult psychiatric disorder in the US National comorbidity survey. Psychological medicine, 27, 1101-1119

Note: - Never underestimate the role psychology has in our daily lives. Utilizing psychology to achieve your higher goals will contribute to the depth of your life's journey.

Websites:

Pre-Post Economy

Kerala Economy in pre – Independence and Post – Independence Period

An Overview

www.keralaeconomy.com

https://keralaeconomy.com/details.aspx?mid=006&sid=006a

https://www.thehindu.com/news/national/kerala-defeating-nipah-is-payoff-of-social-spending/article24584934.ece

https://m.economictimes.com/nri/invest/remittances-from-gulf-countries-dropped-sharply-in-fy21-due-to-covid-19/articleshow/92937846.cms

https://www.newindianexpress.com/opinions/2013/apr/13/what-nitaqat-means-for-kerala-467454.html

https://www.mathrubhumi.com/education/features/migration-of-kerala-students-1.8106948

https://m.economictimes.com/news/economy/indicators/covid-lockdown-impact-kerala-estimates-q1-loss-of-rs-80000-crore-to-gva/articleshow/75601314.cms

https://www.thehindubusinessline.com/opinion/keralas-growth-prospects-a-long-term-view/article37057643.ece

Work from home: issues and challenges faced by working women in the it sector (during covid-19 pandemic)

https://www.statista.com/statistics/717615/india-number-of-facebook-users-by-age- and-gender/

http://www.jstor.org/stable/23746023

https://doi.org/10.1007/s12147-020-09269-http://genderandset.open.ac.uk/index.php/genderandset/article/view/168/333

https://doi.org/10.1002/smi.3053

http://genderandset.open.ac.uk/index.php/genderandset/article/view/59/191

http://www.jstor.org/stable/40278183

http://localhost:8080/xmlui/handle/123456789/14313

https://doi.org/10.1186/2192-5372-

http://www.jstor.org/stable/4414927

https://doi.org/10.1086/681096

https://indianexpress.com/article/india/domestic-violence-abuse-complaints-rise-in-   coronavirus-lockdown-ncw-6344641/

http://localhost:8080/xmlui/handle/123456789/14497

http://www.jstor.org/stable/24442299

http://www.jstor.org/stable/4418760

https://www.lawinsider.com/dictionary/it-sector

Agriculture and Industrial sector

Industrial sector

https://byjus.com/free-ias-prep/public-sector-india/

https://www.slideshare.net/ridhiima/the-role-and-growth-of-public-sector-in-india/8

https://www.yourarticlelibrary.com/economics/indian-economy/roles-played-by-public-sector-in-indian-economy/62893

https://www.businesstoday.in/opinion/columns/story/five-ways-indias-public-sector-enterprises-pses-can-further-its-climate-agenda-low-carbon-economy-271170-2020-08-26

Service sector

A study on consumer perception towards high-priced drugs and pricing by pharmaceutical companies

https://www.slideshare.net/rvmfinishingschool/pharma-industry-17272482

https://www.ibef.org/industry/pharmaceutical-india.aspx

https://www.nhp.gov.in/drugs-and-pharmaceuticals_pg

https://www.expresspharma.in/cover-story/evolution-of-the-indian-pharma-industry/

https://www.sciencedirect.com/topics/nursing-and-health-professions/drug-development

https://www.sciencedaily.com/terms/drug_discovery.htm

https://www.news-medical.net/health/Drug-Patents-and-Generics.aspx

https://en.wikipedia.org/wiki/Over-the-counter_drug

https://journals.sagepub.com/doi/abs/10.1057/palgrave.jmm.5040220?journalCode=mmja

https://clootrack.com/knowledge_base/what-is-customer-perception/https://bizfluent.com/info-8406791-importance-consumer-perception.html

https://www.emerald.com/insight/content/doi/10.1108/00346659910277650/full/html

https://snowberrymedia.com/how-consumer-perception-influences-buying-decisions/

https://blog.hubspot.com/service/improve-customer-perception

https://blog.blackcurve.com/what-is-strategic-pricing-and-why-is-it-important

Lottery

https://www.statelottery.kerala.gov.in/index.php/revenue-collection

http://keralalotteries.com/

https://www.lottoland.asia/magazine/kerala-state-lotteries.html

https://www.keralalotteries.net/p/kerala-state-lottery-draw-system.html?m=1

https://livekerala.com/blog/kerala-lotteries/

https://youtu.be/ER5mxghVGYs

https://en.m.wikipedia.org/wiki/Kerala_State_Lotteries

https://www.quora.com/Which-type-of-lottery-runs-in-Kerala

Agriculture and industrial sector

Kerala agriculture

https://unacademy.com/content/kerala-psc/study-material/kerala/the-economy-of-kerala-state-major-agriculture/

https://vikaspedia.in/schemesall/schemes-for-farmers

https://en.wikipedia.org/wiki/Kerala

Kerala budget

https://budget.kerala.gov.in/portal/home

https://prsindia.org/budgets/states/kerala-budget-analysis-2023-24

https://www.livemint.com/news/india/kerala-budget-2023-24-govt-to-allocate-rs-1-000-crore-for-make-in-kerala-11675464370772.html

Kerala economic survey

https://prsindia.org/files/budget/budget_state/kerala/2023/KL_State_Budget_Analysis_2023-24.pdf

https://www.indiabudget.gov.in/economicsurvey/doc/echapter.pdf

https://static.pib.gov.in/WriteReadData/userfiles/file/EconomicSurvey2023Q44O.pdf

Growth and Development

KIIFB (Kerala Infrastructure Investment Fund Board)

https://kiifb.org/

https://en.m.wikipedia.org/wiki/Kerala_Infrastructure_Investment_Fund_Board

https://www.google.com/amp/s/www.thehindu.com/news/national/kerala/kiifb-nod-for-64-more-projects-worth-568198-cr/article66560883.ece/amp/

http://kiidc.kerala.gov.in/kiifb-funding-projects/

https://www.google.com/amp/s/www.livelaw.in/amp/tags/kiifb

https://www.google.com/amp/s/www.deccanherald.com/amp/national/south/kerala-finance-minister-thomas-isaac-hits-out-at-cag-for-faulting-kiifb-915592.html

Kerala bank

https://keralacobank.com/

https://en.m.wikipedia.org/wiki/Kerala_Bank

https://unacademy.com/content/upsc/study-material/economy/kerala-bank/

https://www.thehindu.com/news/national/kerala/kerala-bank-sets-new-benchmark-in-loan-disbursement/article65663324.ece

https://www.iasparliament.com/current-affairs/kerala-bank

https://abhipedia.abhimanu.com/Article/IAS/MTMyMjQx/Kerala-Bank-Economic-Affairs-IAS

Health and Tourism

Declining Child Sex Ratio in India and Kerala – An Examination

https://englisharchives.mathrubhumi.com/features/web-exclusive/at-birth-gender-disparity-1.625439

https://www.keralawomen.gov.in/sites/default/files/2020-02/Schemes-for-Kerala-Women%281%29.pdf

https://www.centreforpublicimpact.org/case-study/reducing-child-mortality-india

https://www.pmindia.gov.in/en/government_tr_rec/beti-bachao-beti-padhao-caring-for-the-girl-child/

Development and Growth of Kerala Tourism

https://en.wikipedia.org/wiki/Tourism_in_Kerala

https://irisholidays.com/keralatourism/best-places-to-visit-in-kerala/

https://www.keralatourism.org/

Tribal Poverty and Women

Tribal Poverty and Livelihood in Kerala

http://spb.kerala.gov.in/wp-content/uploads/2021/06/Statistical-Hand-Book-2021.pdf

https://secc.gov.in/statewiseHouseholdReport-print.php?statecode=32&lbname=KERALA

https://www.cds.edu/wp-content/uploads/2016/08/343.pdf

Future Economy

Old-age economy

https://www.google.com/amp/s/indianexpress.com/article/cities/thiruvananthapuram/kerala-economic-review-2021-states-elderly-population-to-touch-21-by-2031-7816407/lite/

https://www.oecd.org/economy/ageing-inclusive-growth/

https://www.investopedia.com/articles/investing/011216/4-global-economic-issues-aging-population.asp#:~:text=A%20rapidly%20aging%20population%20means,to%20fill%20in%2Ddemand%20roles.

https://www.imf.org/external/pubs/ft/fandd/2017/03/lee.htm

https://www.google.com/amp/s/www.brookings.edu/blog/future-development/2021/01/14/the-silver-economy-is-coming-of-age-a-look-at-the-growing-spending-power-of-seniors/amp/

https://www.weforum.org/agenda/2015/04/how-will-an-ageing-population-affect-the-economy/

https://www.ageinternational.org.uk/policy-research/expert-voices/the-positive-impacts-of-an-ageing-population/

https://www.google.com/amp/s/indianexpress.com/article/cities/thiruvananthapuram/kerala-economic-review-2021-states-elderly-population-to-touch-21-by-2031-7816407/lite/

https://www.google.com/amp/s/m.timesofindia.com/india/kerala-has-highest-share-of-elderly-in-population-bihar-lowest/amp_articleshow/85088230.cms https://www.google.com/amp/s/www.thehindu.com/news/national/kerala/kerala-witnessing-a-demographic-transition/article35525769.ece/amp/

Trade,Export,Budget and Survey

Trade sector

https://en.m.wikipedia.org/wiki/Tradable_sector#:~:text=The%20tradable%20sector%20of%20a,plausible%20variation%20in%20relative%20prices.

https://spb.kerala.gov.in/economic-review/ER2016/chapter06_02.php

https://www.thomascook.in/blog/complete-guide-on-kerala-shopping

Educated unemployment and underemployment

Educated unemployment

https://www.cppr.in/archives/the-problem-of-educated-unemployment-in-kerala

https://www.malayalamnewsdaily.com/node/636961/kerala/special-story

https://www.manoramaonline.com/news/business/2022/07/06/unemployment-in-kerala.html

https://www.deshabhimani.com/editorial/nsso-report-on-employment/780361

https://keralakaumudi.com/news/mobile/news.php?id=102137

Underemployment

https://www.google.com/amp/s/www.onmanorama.com/news/business/2023/02/25/unemployment-rate-dips-kerala-labour-force-india.html

https://keralakaumudi.com/en/news/mobile/news.php?id=811540&u=kerala-has-the-highest-unemployment-rate-in-country-after-jammu--kashmir-only-4%-in-gujarat